PENGUIN  CLASSICS

CONFESSIONS

ADVISORY EDITOR: BETTY RADICE

St Augustine of Hippo, the great Doctor of the Latin Church, was born at Thagaste in North Africa, in AD 354. The son of a pagan father and a Christian mother, he was brought up as a Christian, and at the age of sixteen went to Carthage to finish his education for the law. In 375 on reading Cicero's *Hortensius* he became deeply interested in philosophy. He was converted to the Manichean religion, some of whose tenets he continued to hold after he had founded his own school of rhetoric at Rome, in 383. At Milan he was offered a professorship and came under the influence both of Neoplatonism and of the preaching of St Ambrose. After agonizing inward conflict he renounced all his unorthodox beliefs and was baptized in 387. He then returned to Africa and formed his own community; but in 391 he was ordained priest against his wishes, and five years later he was chosen bishop of Hippo.

For thirty-four years St Augustine lived in community with his cathedral clergy. His written output was vast; there survive 113 books and treatises, over 200 letters, and more than 500 sermons. Two of his longest works, his *Confessions* and *City of God*, have made an abiding mark not only on Christian theology but on the psychology and political philosophy of the West since the Dark Ages. He died in 430 as invading Vandals were besieging Hippo.

R. S. Pine-Coffin, a Roman Catholic, was born in 1917. He was educated at Ampleforth and Peterhouse, Cambridge. He died in 1992.

SAINT AUGUSTINE
CONFESSIONS

Translated with an Introduction by

R. S. PINE-COFFIN

PENGUIN BOOKS

PENGUIN BOOKS

Published by the Penguin Group
Penguin Books Ltd, 80 Strand, London WC2R 0RL, England
Penguin Putnam Inc., 375 Hudson Street, New York, New York 10014, USA
Penguin Books Australia Ltd, 250 Camberwell Road, Camberwell, Victoria 3124, Australia
Penguin Books Canada Ltd, 10 Alcorn Avenue, Toronto, Ontario, Canada M4V 3B2
Penguin Books India (P) Ltd, 11 Community Centre, Panchsheel Park, New Delhi – 110 017, India
Penguin Books (NZ) Ltd, Cnr Rosedale and Airborne Roads, Albany, Auckland, New Zealand
Penguin Books (South Africa) (Pty) Ltd, 24 Sturdee Avenue, Rosebank 2196, South Africa

Penguin Books Ltd, Registered Offices: 80 Strand, London WC2R 0RL, England

www.penguin.com

First published 1961
48

Copyright © R. S. Pine-Coffin, 1961
All rights reserved

Printed in England by Clays Ltd, St Ives plc
Set in Monotype Bembo

Contents

our earth is the firmament which God created on the second day – On the third day he made the earth and the sea by giving form to the formless matter which he had created before the first day – How the Heaven of Heavens differs from the material creation – A discussion of other interpretations of the verse: 'In the Beginning God made heaven and earth'

BOOK XIII

An allegorical interpretation of the first chapter of Genesis

The light which God created on the first day is the spiritual creation, which became light by the reflection of God's glory – The darkness, which God divided from the light, represents the soul still without God's light

The firmament which separates the waters above from the waters below is a figure of the Scriptures, which are like a shield held above us for our protection – Above it are the angels, safe in the presence of God

On the third day the waters of earth were gathered together to form the sea, and God commanded the dry land to appear – The 'sea' means the human race, embittered by estrangement from God, and the 'dry land' which stands out from the sea represents the good soul – The dry land produces plants and trees which bear fruit in works of mercy and charity

The lights which God set to shine in the firmament on the fourth day are wisdom and knowledge given to men so that those who possess them also shine like lights in the world

On the fifth day God commanded the waters to bring forth moving creatures, that is, signs and sacraments by which men are convinced of the truth and are helped to overcome the temptations of the world – The winged things, which the waters were also commanded to produce, are the teachers who bring God's message to man

On the sixth day the earth was told to produce the living soul, that is, the soul which lives because it has

faith and keeps itself intact from the love of the world –
Man was made in the likeness of God in that he was
given the gift of reason by which he might understand
God's truth – His rule over the animals is a symbol of
this and of the power of spiritual judgement given to the
Church – The plants given to man for his food represent
works of charity which nourish the soul

On the seventh day God rested, as we too shall rest
in eternity when our work in the world is done

Introduction

THE life of Saint Augustine has a special appeal because he was a great sinner who became a great saint, and greatness is all the more admirable if it is achieved against odds. From his own account we know that he lived a life of sin until the age of thirty-two, and even after he was intellectually convinced of Christian truth he was prevented from accepting the faith by weakness in dealing with sexual temptation. In the *Confessions* he paints so black a picture of his past that the reader may easily lose sight of the good qualities which he certainly possessed as a young man. Whether he was a greater sinner than others living in the notorious city of Carthage we cannot tell, but whatever his vices, they were not without compensating virtues. Some of the most striking passages in the book are those in which he writes of his mother, and it is clear that he was always a good and affectionate son, although he may not have appreciated Saint Monica's true worth until after his own conversion. On her deathbed she told him that she had never heard him speak a harsh word against her, and this is not hard to believe, for whatever other sins he felt himself bound to confess, unkindness to others was not one of them. He showed unusual loyalty, too, to the mistress whom he kept for so many years, and he was truly fond of Adeodatus, the son whom she bore him. Outside his own family he also had a remarkable gift for making friends. This was in itself a danger, for as a boy it was his love of their company that led him to rob an orchard. Later, in adolescence, simply to win their admiration, he used to boast of sins which he had not committed, and it was most probably by their influence and example that he became a regular spectator at the theatre and learned to enjoy the cruel sport of the arena.[1] Yet he did not always allow his friends to lead him into adventures which he would not have undertaken by himself, and it is a point in his favour that he refused to take

---

[1] Saint Augustine's insistence upon the wickedness of the theatre needs some explanation. The morality of plays drawn from mythology was often repugnant to Christians. Even worse were the obscene performances given during the pagan festivals, at which the loves of the gods were realistically mimed before audiences of both sexes.

part in the activities of the rowdies who made it their business to scandalize newcomers to the schools at Carthage. Add to this the obvious fact that he was a serious and studious youth and it becomes difficult to avoid the conclusion that the terms in which he writes of his sinful past are unnecessarily harsh. Perhaps his training as a teacher of rhetoric accounts for this. He was, after all, trying to make out a case against himself before an audience which was predisposed to believe him a saintly man. When he wrote the *Confessions* he already had a considerable reputation for sanctity, and one of the reasons why he wrote was to persuade his admirers that any good qualities he had were his by the grace of God, who had saved him so often from himself.

Of all the sins which he wished to confess there was one which was at the root of all the others. It was not an isolated act or a repeated habit, but a condition of mind which was part of his life and provided him with a ready excuse for doing what his conscience told him to be wrong. For when, as a young man, he became curious about the world and its origin and started his search for the truth, instead of turning to God in simple faith he accepted the theories by which the Manichees explained away these problems. As a catechumen he had received some instruction, but he had no clear idea of what Christians believed. As literature, the Scriptures compared poorly with the polished prose of Cicero and he thought them fit only for the simple-minded. He was too conceited to study them and his reason could not accept the discrepancies and contradictions which he thought they contained. He could not account for the presence of evil in a world created by a God who was good, nor could he understand that God is a spiritual Being. In his perplexity he turned to the Manichees, whose specious reasoning seemed to supply the answers to these problems as well as a system of morals which permitted the blame for sin to be cast elsewhere than on the sinner. The dangers of these beliefs were still very present to Saint Augustine when he wrote the *Confessions*, for it was only ten or twelve years since he had escaped from them himself. In the meantime he had written at least five books against the Manichees and no man was better qualified to do so than himself. The *Confessions*, of course, cannot be considered as simply another work of controversy. They are far too personal for that. But as he wrote them Saint Augustine was conscious above all else that the Manichees were wrong and that only the mercy of God had saved him from this evil.

He was only eighteen when he first allied himself with the Manichees. Their founder Manes, or Mani, a fanatic who regarded himself as the Paraclete, had been crucified in Persia in 277. His religion spread rapidly both during and after his lifetime, and when Saint Augustine came under its influence a century later, there were groups of Manichees throughout the Roman world, especially in North Africa. By this time they were a proscribed sect and were obliged to practise their religion in secret, but numerically they were strong and their doctrines, with various modifications, survived into the Middle Ages. Manes did not entirely reject Christianity, but since he held that its teaching was only partially true, he supplemented it by borrowing from other religions and adding his own theories. He alleged that there were inconsistencies in the Scriptures and that the text was corrupt and therefore untrustworthy. In particular he denied the virgin birth and Christ's crucifixion, since the flesh was tainted with evil and any association with it was unworthy of God.

This belief was derived from the fundamental doctrine of Manicheism, which was that in the beginning there were two independent principles described as Good and Evil or Light and Darkness. The evil power invaded the kingdom of the good power and in part captured it, so that the two became mixed. Matter was therefore composed partly of good and partly of evil, both being present in a given substance in a greater or smaller degree. Good and evil were permanently in conflict because the captive particles of good or light were always struggling to escape from the evil or darkness which enveloped them. In flesh of all sorts very few traces of the light-element were present, and for this reason meat was not to be eaten by a good Manichee. Light was present in greater quantities in vegetable matter, which could therefore be eaten. The light-particles were freed from imprisonment when the elect, or higher order of Manichees, ate these foods, but it was wrong for a member of the sect to cut down a tree or even pluck fruit, or to commit any other act of violence harmful to the good elements in plants. These operations were to be performed by the wicked on behalf of the Manichees, that is, by those who were considered as lost souls and belonged to neither the higher nor the lower order of the sect. The elect were supposed to be particularly scrupulous and to avoid either doing violence to the good elements or taking any action which might assist the powers of darkness. They were forbidden to marry, because the act of procreation was construed as collusion with these powers. For the lower order of the sect, called 'hearers' or 'aspirants', the rules were less strict, but they were expected to serve the elect and to give food to no one but them, since to do so would be to deliver the good elements into the hands of the devil.

It seems incredible that a man of Saint Augustine's intellectual calibre could have been taken in by these fantastic theories, but the Manichees' plausible explanation of the problem of evil and his own inability to think of God except as a material being combined to win him over. At first he was convinced by these arguments and even influenced others to accept them. Although he never rose to a higher degree than that of aspirant, he remained with the sect for nearly ten years, during which he carried out the duties expected of its junior members. But before the end of this period serious doubts had begun to trouble him. He was assured that Faustus, a leading figure among the Manichees, would be able to settle all his problems, but when this Solomon proved incompetent, he at length determined to remain a Manichee in name only, while he waited for something better to turn up.

Once he had made this decision his mind was open to other influences. He was introduced to the philosophy of the Neo-Platonists and their books helped him towards a conception of the spiritual nature of God. At the same time he began to understand that evil results from man's misuse of free will. This was the beginning of conversion. He listened with greater attention to the sermons of Saint Ambrose, to which he had first been attracted only by professional interest in the preacher's reputation as a fine speaker. He learned how to approach the Scriptures and how to look for the spiritual meaning behind the literal sense. He went on to read Saint Paul's Epistles, where for the first time he heard of God's mercy and grace and learned to think of Christ as the Redeemer and no longer simply as a specially gifted teacher. Finally there came the decisive moment when the truth became so clear to him that he could no longer reject it.

Saint Augustine's decision to accept the faith is of course the central point of the *Confessions*. After it he continues the narrative in order to include his baptism and the beginning of the return journey to Africa, during which his mother died. This takes us to the end of Book IX, but at this point the biographical part of the book comes to an end. In Book X Saint Augustine examines his ability, at the time of writing, to deal with temptation in its various forms, and Books XI – XIII are an exposition of the first chapter of Genesis. This apparent lack of cohesion between the two parts of the work has been the subject of much debate. Though it is generally agreed that Book X was a later interpolation, inserted to satisfy readers who were naturally curious to know how the faith had changed Saint Augustine's life, there is less agreement about the purpose of Books XI – XIII. The traditional explanation is that they are no more than an appendix, but this avoids the issue, since appendixes are normally added for a definite purpose.

Some commentators are content to point out that the first nine books describe Saint Augustine's search for the truth, while the last three contain his thoughts upon its meaning after he has found it. Others see a connexion between the pattern of the *Confessions* and Saint Augustine's method for the instruction of catechumens. In his work *De catechizandis rudibus*, written only four or five years after the *Confessions*, he suggests that the catechist should first point out to the convert that God has always taken good care of him and then proceed to instruct him in the Scriptures, starting with the story of the creation. This plan of instruction clearly corresponds with the arrangement of the *Confessions*, and the suggestion is that Saint Augustine is applying the method to his own case in retrospect. Another view, more recently put forward,[1] is that Saint Augustine's original plan was to write a complete exposition of the faith as it is derived from Scripture, but found it too lengthy a task and abandoned it after he had dealt with the first chapter of Genesis. The story of his own early life and errors was intended merely as a preamble. The evidence in support of this theory is taken chiefly from certain passages[2] in the text where the author implies that he is hastening to complete the narrative part of his work in order to devote himself to other more important matters.

[1] Courcelle, Pierre. *Recherches sur les Confessions de Saint Augustin.* Paris (Boccard), 1950.
[2] e.g. in Book IX, chapter 4, and Book XI, chapter 2.

Probably there is some truth in all these explanations, although it is hard to believe that the *Confessions* as we have received them are only the beginning of a longer work, projected but never finished. Whatever his precise plan may have been, it is unlikely that Saint Augustine would have been content merely to repudiate his early errors. His logical mind would require, not only that falsehood should be demolished, but also that the truth should be made apparent. If he was to confess his errors, he must also confess the true beliefs for which he had renounced them, and the foundation of these was to be found in the book of Genesis. What better answer could be made to the Manichean theory of the twin powers of good and evil than God's own statement that he made heaven and earth and that he saw what he had made and found it very good? Saint Augustine was satisfied that this was all that was needed to reduce the fundamental principle of Manicheism to absurdity.[1]

If this was how the work was planned, the pattern of the *Confessions* becomes clear. In the first place it is a confession of the writer's sin and error, in the second a recognition of God's goodness and truth. These two purposes are complementary and the title of the book covers both. In the third place, because he has been saved from error and the truth has been made clear to him, Saint Augustine offers praise to God and thanks him for his mercy. He is led from confession of sin to confession of faith and finally to confession of God's glory. The first words in the book, '*Magnus es, Domine, et laudabilis valde*', are the key to the whole.

There has been no lack of English translators of the *Confessions*. The first to attempt the task was Sir Tobie Matthew, the courtier and diplomat, whose version was published anonymously and without imprint at Saint-Omer in 1620. It contained a long and controversial introduction to which the next translator, William Watts, Rector of St Alban's, Wood Street, took objection on the ground that it was 'so arrantly, partially Popish'. He began his own translation, which was published in London in 1631, as a Lenten devotion, but, he tells us, 'I quickly found it to exercise more than my devotion: it exercised my skill (all I had): it exercised my patience, it exercised my friends too, for 'tis incomparably the hardest taske that ever I yet undertooke.'

[1] See Book XIII, chapter 30.

Watts was followed by Abraham Woodhead, the Catholic writer, who published a translation of the first ten books in 1660. An anonymous version, now recognized as the work of Bishop Challoner, appeared in 1739; this also contained only Books I–X. Next came E. B. Pusey's revision of Watts, published in 1838, which became the standard translation. Entirely new versions were produced in 1878 by W. H. Hutchings (Books I–X) and in 1897 by C. Bigg (Books I–IX), and in the last quarter of a century, to my knowledge, there have been at least five new translations, some of them published in the United States and not easily available in this country. Translators in other languages have also produced their quota. These facts alone are ample evidence of the continued and widespread interest in Saint Augustine, for few books have been translated so often into so many languages.

In preparing this translation I decided at the outset to use 'you' rather than 'thou'. Although the *Confessions*, as might be expected, are written in the form of prayer, it seemed to me that in a work of this length it would merely be tiresome to retain the conventional usage. For the sake of consistency I have also taken the liberty of changing 'thou' to 'you' in the quotations from Scripture. These are from the Knox version and are printed in italics.[1] I have also modified the English text of Knox, within strict limits, wherever Saint Augustine modifies the Latin text, that is, wherever he omits a phrase or adds words of his own. Some transposition of words in the English text has also been necessary for grammatical reasons, because Saint Augustine frequently combines passages from Scripture, not only with one another, but also with sentences of his own. In a small number of cases it has been impossible to quote the Knox version and I have had to content myself with giving the appropriate reference. The reasons for this are several. Too much stress need not be laid upon the first of them, which is that the text from which the saint quotes – presumably from memory – is earlier than the Latin version of Saint Jerome; this accounts for some variations in wording. In the second place, while it may be grammatically possible to combine two or more sentences as they are written in one language, it does not necessarily follow that they can be combined in the same way once

---

[1] I have used both Knox versions of the Psalms indiscriminately. The reference is to the Vulgate numeration.

they have been translated independently into another idiom; here again the number of cases is small. Thirdly, in a few passages the meaning which Saint Augustine elicits from the sacred text does not correspond with that given in Knox. The most obvious example is his interpretation of Genesis 1: 1, 2 (see Books XI and XII). He may sometimes have been misled by an ambiguous Latin version, for whereas Knox translated from the Vulgate 'in the light of the Hebrew and Greek originals', Saint Augustine is known to have had a profound distaste for Greek and it is very doubtful whether he had any knowledge of Hebrew.

R.S.P.-C.

Dates of Events Recorded in the Confessions

A.D.

354 13 November: birth of Augustine at Thagaste (now Souk-Ahras, south of Bône, in Algeria). He has at least one brother, Navigius, and two sisters, whose names are not recorded. His father, Patricius, a small landowner and official of the local government, is still a pagan, but Monica, his mother, is a devout Christian.

365–9 At school at Madaura (now Mdaurouch) about twenty miles from Thagaste.

369–70 He spends a year at home while his father saves money to send him to Carthage.

370 Conversion of Patricius.

371–4 Augustine studies at Carthage.

371 Death of Patricius.

372 Birth of Augustine's son Adeodatus.

375 Augustine teaches rhetoric at Thagaste.

376–83 Teaching in Carthage.

383 The voyage to Rome.

384 Augustine goes to Milan as professor of rhetoric and meets Ambrose.

385 Monica arrives in Milan.

386 February: the persecution of Justina.

   June: discovery of the bodies of the martyrs Gervasius and Protasius.

   July: Augustine's talks with Simplicianus.

   August: the episode in the garden and Augustine's conversion. He goes to Cassiciacum (now Cassago in Brianza, near Como).

387 March: he returns to Milan.

   24 April, Holy Saturday: baptism of Augustine, Alypius, and Adeodatus.

   Autumn: the journey to Ostia. Death of Monica.

At this point the narrative part of the *Confessions* ends. After his mother's death Augustine spent some months in Rome, returning to Thagaste in August 388. In the following year Adeodatus died. By now Augustine was living a monastic life, devoting himself to study and writing. In 391 he visited Hippo (now Bône) and was persuaded by the bishop, Valerius, to offer himself for ordination. This meant that he had to leave the community at Thagaste, but he was permitted to found a new monastery near Hippo. In 396 he was consecrated assistant bishop of Hippo to aid the aged Valerius who died a year later. The care of the diocese now fell upon Augustine and was to occupy him fully for the rest of his life.

Besides his pastoral work Augustine was a powerful adversary of all heretics and enemies of the Church. Much of his prodigious literary output was devoted to this cause, but the importance of the *Confessions* (*Confessiones*), written in 397–8, is as a personal document and statement of faith. In 410 came the sack of Rome by Alaric and the Goths. This was the occasion which inspired Augustine to write *City of God* (*De civitate Dei*), his great work in twenty-two books, begun in 413 and completed in 426. The fall of the city after a thousand years, during which no foreign invader had penetrated its walls, was attributed by many to loss of faith in the pagan gods, whose cult had recently been largely suppressed by the joint emperors Gratian and Theodosius. The disaster was hailed as a direct consequence of the spread of Christianity, and this was a challenge which Augustine could not ignore. After disproving the claim that the prosperity of man depended upon the propitiation of a miscellaneous array of gods, he went on to define the Christian answer to the religious, philosophical, and political problems of the world and its government.

The *Confessions* and the *City of God* rightly belong to the great literature of the world. Augustine's numerous other works are read chiefly by theologians and scholars. In addition to a great many letters and sermons, of which about five hundred have been preserved, he wrote books on theology and philosophy, controversial works against the Manichees, Donatists, and Pelagians, and works of biblical exegesis.

In 428 the Vandals invaded North Africa and Hippo was under siege from May 430 to July 431. In the fourth month of the siege, on 28 August 430, Augustine died. In 497, when the Arian king of the Vandals, Thrasamund, forced the bishops to leave Numidia, they carried Augustine's remains with them to Sardinia. The island was repeatedly raided by the Saracens in the eighth century and during the incursion of 721–2, to save the body from desecration, Liutprand, king of the Lombards, sent envoys to ransom it. They brought it to Pavia in northern Italy, where it was re-interred in the monastery of San Pietro in Ciel d'Oro.

BOOK I

I

CAN *any praise be worthy of the Lord's majesty?*[1] *How magnificent his strength! How inscrutable his wisdom!*[2] Man is one of your creatures, Lord, and his instinct is to praise you. He bears about him the mark of death, the sign of his own sin, to remind him that you *thwart the proud.*[3] But still, since he is a part of your creation, he wishes to praise you. The thought of you stirs him so deeply that he cannot be content unless he praises you, because you made us for yourself and our hearts find no peace until they rest in you.

Grant me, Lord, to know and understand whether a man is first to pray to you for help or to praise you, and whether he must know you before he can call you to his aid. If he does not know you, how can he pray to you? For he may call for some other help, mistaking it for yours.

Or are men to pray to you and learn to know you through their prayers? Only, *how are they to call upon the Lord until they have learned to believe in him? And how are they to believe in him without a preacher to listen to?*[4]

Those who look for the Lord will cry out in praise of him,[5] because all who look for him shall find him, and when they find him they will praise him. I shall look for you, Lord, by praying to you and as I pray I shall believe in you, because we have had preachers to tell us about you. It is my faith that calls to you, Lord, the faith which you gave me and made to live in me through the merits of your Son, who became man, and through the ministry of your preacher.

---

[1] Ps. 144: 3 (145: 3). In references to the Psalms the number according to the Vulgate is given first. This is followed by the Authorized Version number in brackets.   [2] Ps. 146: 5 (147: 5).   [3] 1 Pet., v. 5.   [4] Rom. 10: 14.
[5] Ps. 21: 27 (22: 26).

2

How shall I call upon my God for aid, when the call I make is for my Lord and my God to come into myself? What place is there in me to which my God can come, what place that can receive the God who made heaven and earth? Does this then mean, O Lord my God, that there is in me something fit to contain you? Can even heaven and earth, which you made and in which you made me, contain you? Or, since nothing that exists could exist without you, does this mean that whatever exists does, in this sense, contain you? If this is so, since I too exist, why do I ask you to come into me? For I should not be there at all unless, in this way, you were already present within me. I am not in hell, and yet you are there too, for *if I sink down to the world beneath, you are present still.*[1] So, then, I should be null and void and could not exist at all, if you, my God, were not in me.

Or is it rather that I should not exist, unless I existed in you? For *all things find in you their origin, their impulse, the centre of their being.*[2] This, Lord, is the true answer to my question. But if I exist in you, how can I call upon you to come to me? And where would you come from? For you, my God, have said that you *fill heaven and earth,*[3] but I cannot go beyond the bounds of heaven and earth so that you may leave them to come to me.

3

Do heaven and earth, then, contain the whole of you, since you fill them? Or, when once you have filled them, is some part of you left over because they are too small to hold you? If this is so, when you have filled heaven and earth, does that part of you which remains flow over into some other place? Or is it that you have no need to be contained in anything, because you contain all things in yourself and fill them by reason of the very fact that you contain them? For the things which you fill by containing them do not sustain and support you as a water-vessel supports the liquid which fills it. Even if they were broken to pieces, you would not flow out of them and away. And when you pour yourself out over us, you are not drawn down to us but draw us up to yourself: you are not scattered away, but you gather us together.

[1] Ps. 138: 8 (139: 8).   [2] Rom. 11: 36.   [3] Jer. 23: 24.

You fill all things, but do you fill them with your whole self? Or is it that the whole of creation is too small to hold you and therefore holds only a part of you? And is this same part of you present in all things at once, or do different things contain different parts of you, greater or smaller according to their size? Does this mean that one part of you is greater and another smaller? Or are you present entirely everywhere at once, and no single thing contains the whole of you?

4

What, then, is the God I worship? He can be none but the Lord God himself, for *who but the Lord is God? What other refuge can there be, except our God?*[1] You, my God, are supreme, utmost in goodness, mightiest and all-powerful, most merciful and most just. You are the most hidden from us and yet the most present amongst us, the most beautiful and yet the most strong, ever enduring and yet we cannot comprehend you. You are unchangeable and yet you change all things. You are never new, never old, and yet all things have new life from you. You are the unseen power that brings decline upon the proud. You are ever active, yet always at rest. You gather all things to yourself, though you suffer no need. You support, you fill, and you protect all things. You create them, nourish them, and bring them to perfection. You seek to make them your own, though you lack for nothing. You love your creatures, but with a gentle love. You treasure them, but without apprehension. You grieve for wrong, but suffer no pain. You can be angry and yet serene. Your works are varied, but your purpose is one and the same. You welcome all who come to you, though you never lost them. You are never in need yet are glad to gain, never covetous yet you exact a return for your gifts. We give abundantly to you so that we may deserve a reward; yet which of us has anything that does not come from you? You repay us what we deserve, and yet you owe nothing to any. You release us from our debts, but you lose nothing thereby. You are my God, my Life, my holy Delight, but is this enough to say of you? Can any man say enough when he speaks of you? Yet woe betide those who are silent about you! For even those who are most gifted with speech cannot find words to describe you.

[1] Ps. 17: 32 (18: 31).

5

Who will grant me to rest content in you? To whom shall I turn for the gift of your coming into my heart and filling it to the brim, so that I may forget all the wrong I have done and embrace you alone, my only source of good?

Why do you mean so much to me? Help me to find words to explain. Why do I mean so much to you, that you should command me to love you? And if I fail to love you, you are angry and threaten me with great sorrow, as if not to love you were not sorrow enough in itself. Have pity on me and help me, O Lord my God. Tell me why you mean so much to me. *Whisper in my heart, I am here to save you.*[1] Speak so that I may hear your words. My heart has ears ready to listen to you, Lord. Open them wide and *whisper in my heart, I am here to save you.* I shall hear your voice and make haste to clasp you to myself. Do not hide your face away from me, for I would gladly meet my death to see it, since not to see it would be death indeed.

My soul is like a house, small for you to enter, but I pray you to enlarge it. It is in ruins, but I ask you to remake it. It contains much that you will not be pleased to see: this I know and do not hide. But who is to rid it of these things? There is no one but you to whom I can say: *if I have sinned unwittingly, do you absolve me. Keep me ever your own servant, far from pride.*[2] *I trust, and trusting I find words to utter.*[3] Lord, you know that this is true. For have I not *made my transgression known to you? Did you not remit the guilt of my sin?*[4] I do not wrangle with you for judgement,[5] for you are Truth itself, and I have no wish to delude myself, for fear that my malice should be self-betrayed.[6] No, I do not wrangle with you, for, *if you, Lord, will keep record of our iniquities, Master, who has strength to bear it?*[7]

6

But, dust and ashes though I am, let me appeal to your pity, since it is to you in your mercy that I speak, not to a man, who would simply laugh at me. Perhaps you too may laugh at me, but you will

---

[1] Ps. 34: 3 (35: 3).   [2] Ps. 18: 13, 14 (19: 12, 13).   [3] Ps. 115: 10 (116: 10).
[4] Ps. 31: 5 (32: 5).   [5] See Jer. 2: 29.   [6] See Ps. 26: 12 (27: 12).
[7] Ps. 129: 3 (130: 3).

relent and have pity on me.[1] For all I want to tell you, Lord, is that I do not know where I came from when I was born into this life which leads to death – or should I say, this death which leads to life? This much is hidden from me. But, although I do not remember it all myself, I know that when I came into the world all the comforts which your mercy provides were there ready for me. This I was told by my parents, the father who begat me and the mother who conceived me, the two from whose bodies you formed me in the limits of time. So it was that I was given the comfort of woman's milk.

But neither my mother nor my nurses filled their breasts of their own accord, for it was you who used them, as your law prescribes, to give me infant's food and a share of the riches which you distribute even among the very humblest of all created things. It was also by your gift that I did not wish for more than you gave, and that my nurses gladly passed on to me what you gave to them. They did this because they loved me in the way that you had ordained, and their love made them anxious to give to me what they had received in plenty from you. For it was to their own good that what was good for me should come to me from them; though, of course, it did not come to me from them but, through them, from you, because you, my God, are the source of all good and *everywhere you preserve me*.[2] All this I have learned since then, because all the gifts you have given to me, both spiritual and material, proclaim the truth of it. But in those days all I knew was how to suck, and how to lie still when my body sensed comfort or cry when it felt pain.

Later on I began to smile as well, first in my sleep, and then when I was awake. Others told me this about myself, and I believe what they said, because we see other babies do the same. But I cannot remember it myself. Little by little I began to realize where I was and to want to make my wishes known to others, who might satisfy them. But this I could not do, because my wishes were inside me, while other people were outside, and they had no faculty which could penetrate my mind. So I would toss my arms and legs about and make noises, hoping that such few signs as I could make would show my meaning, though they were quite unlike what they were meant to mime. And if my wishes were not carried out, either because they had not been understood or because what I wanted would have harmed me, I

[1] See Jer. 12: 15.   [2] II Kings (2 Sam.) 23: 5.

would get cross with my elders, who were not at my beck and call, and with people who were not my servants, simply because they did not attend to my wishes; and I would take my revenge by bursting into tears. By watching babies I have learnt that this is how they behave, and they, quite unconsciously, have done more than those who brought me up and knew all about it to convince me that I behaved in just the same way myself.

My infancy is long since dead, yet I am still alive. But you, Lord, live for ever and nothing in you dies, because you have existed from before the very beginning of the ages, before anything that could be said to go before, and you are God and Lord of all you have created. In you are the first causes of all things not eternal, the unchangeable origins of all things that suffer change, the everlasting reason of all things that are subject to the passage of time and have no reason in themselves. Have pity, then, on me, O God, for it is pity that I need. Answer my prayer and tell me whether my infancy followed upon some other stage of life that died before it. Was it the stage of life that I spent in my mother's womb? For I have learnt a little about that too, and I have myself seen women who were pregnant. But what came before that, O God my Delight? Was I anywhere? Was I any-body? These are questions I must put to you, for I have no one else to answer them. Neither my father nor my mother could tell me, nor could I find out from the experience of other people or from my own memory. Do my questions provoke you to smile at me and bid me simply to acknowledge you and praise you for what I do know?

I do acknowledge you, Lord of heaven and earth, and I praise you for my first beginnings, although I cannot remember them. But you have allowed men to discover these things about themselves by watching other babies, and also to learn much from what women have to tell. I know that I was a living person even at that age, and as I came towards the end of infancy I tried to find signs to convey my feelings to others. Where could such a living creature come from if not from you, O Lord? Can it be that any man has skill to fabricate himself? Or can there be some channel by which we derive our life and our very existence from some other source than you? Surely we can only derive them from our Maker, from you, Lord, to whom living and being are not different things, since infinite life and infinite being are one and the same. For you are infinite and never change. In you 'today' never comes to an end: and yet our 'today' does come to an end in you, because time, as well as everything else, exists in you. If it did not, it would have no means of passing. And since your years never come to an end, for you they are simply 'today'. The countless days of our lives and of our forefathers' lives have passed by within your 'today'. From it they have received their due measure of duration and their very existence. And so it will be with all the other days which are still to come. But you yourself are eternally the same. In your 'today' you will make all that is to exist tomorrow and thereafter, and in your 'today' you have made all that existed yesterday and for ever before.

Need it concern me if some people cannot understand this? Let them ask what it means, and be glad to ask: but they may content themselves with the question alone. For it is better for them to find you and leave the question unanswered than to find the answer without finding you.

7

Hear me, O God! How wicked are the sins of men! Men say this and you pity them, because you made man, but you did not make sin in him.

Who can recall to me the sins I committed as a baby? For in your sight no man is free from sin, not even a child who has lived only one day on earth. Who can show me what my sins were? Some small baby in whom I can see all that I do not remember about myself? What sins, then, did I commit when I was a baby myself? Was it a sin to cry when I wanted to feed at the breast? I am too old now to feed on mother's milk, but if I were to cry for the kind of food suited to my age, others would rightly laugh me to scorn and remonstrate with me. So then too I deserved a scolding for what I did; but since I could not have understood the scolding, it would have been unreasonable, and most unusual, to rebuke me. We root out these faults and discard them as we grow up, and this is proof enough that they are faults, because I have never seen a man purposely throw out the good when he clears away the bad. It can hardly be right for a child, even at that age, to cry for everything, including things which would harm him; to work himself into a tantrum against people older than himself and not required to obey him; and to try his best to strike and hurt others who know better than he does, including his own parents, when they do not give in to him and refuse to pander to whims which would only do him harm. This shows that, if babies are innocent, it is not for lack of will to do harm, but for lack of strength.

I have myself seen jealousy in a baby and know what it means. He was not old enough to talk, but whenever he saw his foster-brother at the breast, he would grow pale with envy. This much is common knowledge. Mothers and nurses say that they can work such things out of the system by one means or another, but surely it cannot be called innocence, when the milk flows in such abundance from its source, to object to a rival desperately in need and depending for his life on this one form of nourishment? Such faults are not small or unimportant, but we are tender-hearted and bear with them because we know that the child will grow out of them. It is clear that they are not mere peccadilloes, because the same faults are intolerable in older persons.

You, O Lord my God, gave me my life and my body when I was born. You gave my body its five senses; you furnished it with limbs and gave it its proper proportions; and you implanted in it all the instincts necessary for the welfare and safety of a living creature. For these gifts you command me to acknowledge you and *praise you and sing in honour of your name,*[1] because you are Almighty God, because you are good, and because I owe you praise for these things, even if you had done nothing else. No one but you can do these things, because you are the one and only mould in which all things are cast and the perfect form which shapes all things, and everything takes its place according to your law.

I do not remember that early part of my life, O Lord, but I believe what other people have told me about it and from watching other babies I can conclude that I also lived as they do. But, true though my conclusions may be, I do not like to think of that period as part of the same life I now lead, because it is dim and forgotten and, in this sense, it is no different from the time I spent in my mother's womb. But if *I was born in sin and guilt was with me already when my mother conceived me,*[2] where, I ask you, Lord, where or when was I, your servant, ever innocent? But I will say no more about that time, for since no trace of it remains in my memory, it need no longer concern me.

[1] Ps. 91: 2 (92: 1).   [2] Ps. 50: 7 (51: 5).

8

The next stage in my life, as I grew up, was boyhood. Or would it be truer to say that boyhood overtook me and followed upon my infancy – not that my infancy left me, for, if it did, where did it go? All the same, it was no longer there, because I ceased to be a baby unable to talk, and was now a boy with the power of speech. I can remember that time, and later on I realized how I had learnt to speak. It was not my elders who showed me the words by some set system of instruction, in the way that they taught me to read not long afterwards; but, instead, I taught myself by using the intelligence which you, my God, gave to me. For when I tried to express my meaning by crying out and making various sounds and movements, so that my wishes should be obeyed, I found that I could not convey all that I meant or make myself understood by everyone whom I wished to understand me. So my memory prompted me. I noticed that people would name some object and then turn towards whatever it was that they had named. I watched them and understood that the sound they made when they wanted to indicate that particular thing was the name which they gave to it, and their actions clearly showed what they meant, for there is a kind of universal language, consisting of expressions of the face and eyes, gestures and tones of voice, which can show whether a person means to ask for something and get it, or refuse it and have nothing to do with it. So, by hearing words arranged in various phrases and constantly repeated, I gradually pieced together what they stood for, and when my tongue had mastered the pronunciation, I began to express my wishes by means of them. In this way I made my wants known to my family and they made theirs known to me, and I took a further step into the stormy life of human society, although I was still subject to the authority of my parents and the will of my elders.

9

But, O God my God, I now went through a period of suffering and humiliation. I was told that it was right and proper for me as a boy to pay attention to my teachers, so that I should do well at my study of grammar and get on in the world. This was the way to gain the respect of others and win for myself what passes for wealth in this world. So I was sent to school to learn to read. I was too small to understand what purpose it might serve and yet, if I was idle at my studies, I was beaten for it, because beating was favoured by tradition. Countless boys long since forgotten had built up this stony path for us to tread and we were made to pass along it, adding to the toil and sorrow of the sons of Adam.

But we found that some men prayed to you, Lord, and we learned from them to do the same, thinking of you in the only way that we could understand, as some great person who could listen to us and help us, even though we could not see you or hear you or touch you. I was still a boy when I first began to pray to you, my Help and Refuge. I used to prattle away to you, and though I was small, my devotion was great when I begged you not to let me be beaten at school. Sometimes, for my own good, you did not grant my prayer, and then my elders and even my parents, who certainly wished me no harm, would laugh at the beating I got – and in those days beatings were my one great bugbear.

O Lord, throughout the world men beseech you to preserve them from the rack and the hook and various similar tortures which terrify them. Some people are merely callous, but if a man clings to you with great devotion, how can his piety inspire him to find it in his heart to make light of these tortures, when he loves those who dread them so fearfully? And yet this was how our parents scoffed at the torments which we boys suffered at the hands of our masters. For we feared the whip just as much as others fear the rack, and we, no less than they, begged you to preserve us from it. But we sinned by reading and writing and studying less than was expected of us. We lacked neither memory nor intelligence, because by your will, O Lord, we had as much of both as was sufficient for our years. But we enjoyed playing games and were punished for them by men who played games themselves. However, grown-up games are known as 'business', and even though boys' games are much the same, they are punished for them by their elders. No one pities either the boys or the men, though surely we deserved pity, for I cannot believe that a good judge would approve of the beatings I received as a boy on the ground that my games delayed my progress in studying subjects which would enable me to play a less creditable game later in life.

Was the master who beat me himself very different from me? If he were worsted by a colleague in some petty argument, he would be convulsed with anger and envy, much more so than I was when a playmate beat me at a game of ball.

10

And yet I sinned, O Lord my God, creator and arbiter of all natural things, but arbiter only, not creator, of sin. I sinned, O Lord, by disobeying my parents and the masters of whom I have spoken. For, whatever purpose they had in mind, later on I might have put to good use all the things which they wanted me to learn. I was disobedient, not because I chose something better than they proposed to me, but simply from the love of games. For I liked to score a fine win at sport or to have my ears tickled by the make-believe of the stage, which only made them itch the more. As time went on my eyes shone more and more with the same eager curiosity, because I wanted to see the shows and sports which grown-ups enjoyed. The patrons who pay for the production of these shows are held in esteem such as most parents would wish for their children. Yet the same parents willingly allow their children to be flogged if they are distracted by these displays from the studies which are supposed to fit them to grow rich and give the same sort of shows themselves. Look on these things with pity, O Lord, and free us who now call upon you from such delusions. Set free also those who have not yet called upon you, so that they may pray to you and you may free them from this folly.

11

While still a boy I had been told of the eternal life promised to us by Our Lord, who humbled himself and came down amongst us proud sinners. As a catechumen, I was blessed regularly from birth with the sign of the Cross and was seasoned with God's salt, for, O Lord, my mother placed great hope in you. Once as a child I was taken suddenly ill with a disorder of the stomach and was on the point of death. You, my God, were my guardian even then, and you saw the fervour and strength of my faith as I appealled to the piety of my own mother and to the mother of us all, your Church, to give me the baptism of

Christ your Son, who is my God and my Master. My earthly mother was deeply anxious, because in the pure faith of her heart, she was in greater labour to ensure my eternal salvation than she had been at my birth. Had I not quickly recovered, she would have hastened to see that I was admitted to the sacraments of salvation and washed clean by acknowledging you, Lord Jesus, for the pardon of my sins. So my washing in the waters of baptism was postponed, in the surmise that, if I continued to live, I should defile myself again with sin and, after baptism, the guilt of pollution would be greater and more dangerous. Even at that age I already believed in you, and so did my mother and the whole household except for my father. But, in my heart, he did not gain the better of my mother's piety and prevent me from believing in Christ just because he still disbelieved himself. For she did all that she could to see that you, my God, should be a Father to me rather than he. In this you helped her to turn the scales against her husband, whom she always obeyed because by obeying him she obeyed your law, thereby showing greater virtue than he did.

I ask you, my God – for, if it is your will, I long to know – for what purpose was my baptism postponed at that time? Was it for my good that the reins which held me from sin were slackened? Or is it untrue that they were slackened? If not, why do we continually hear people say, even nowadays, 'Leave him alone and let him do it. He is not yet baptized'? Yet when the health of the body is at stake, no one says 'Let him get worse. He is not yet cured.' It would, then, have been much better if I had been healed at once and if all that I and my family could do had been done to make sure that once my soul had received its salvation, its safety should be left in your keeping, since its salvation had come from you. This would surely have been the better course. But my mother well knew how many great tides of temptation threatened me before I grew up, and she chose to let them beat upon the as yet unmoulded clay rather than upon the finished image which had received the stamp of baptism.

12

These temptations were thought to be less of a danger in boyhood than in adolescence. But even as a boy I did not care for lessons and I disliked being forced to study. All the same I was compelled to learn and good came to me as a result, although it was not of my own making. For I would not have studied at all if I had not been obliged to do so, and what a person does against his will is not to his own credit, even if what he does is good in itself. Nor was the good which came of it due to those who compelled me to study, but to you, my God. For they had not the insight to see that I might put the lessons which they forced me to learn to any other purpose than the satisfaction of man's insatiable desire for the poverty he calls wealth and the infamy he knows as fame. But you, who *take every hair of our heads into your reckoning*,[1] used for my benefit the mistaken ideas of all those who insisted on making me study; and you used the mistake I made myself, in not wishing to study, as a punishment which I deserved to pay, for I was a great sinner for so small a boy. In this way you turned their faults to my advantage and justly punished me for my own. For this is what you have ordained and so it is with us, that every soul that sins brings its own punishment upon itself.

13

Even now I cannot fully understand why the Greek language, which I learned as a child, was so distasteful to me. I loved Latin, not the elementary lessons but those which I studied later under teachers of literature. The first lessons in Latin were reading, writing, and counting, and they were as much of an irksome imposition as any studies in Greek. But this, too, was due to the sinfulness and vanity of life, since I was *flesh and blood, no better than a breath of wind that passes by and never returns*.[2] For these elementary lessons were far more valuable than those which followed, because the subjects were practical. They gave me the power, which I still have, of reading whatever is set before me and writing whatever I wish to write. But in the later lessons I was obliged to memorize the wanderings of a hero named Aeneas, while in the meantime I failed to remember my own erratic ways. I learned to lament the death of Dido, who killed herself for love, while all the time, in the midst of these things, I was dying, separated from you, my God and my Life, and I shed no tears for my own plight.

What can be more pitiful than an unhappy wretch unaware of his

1 Matt. 10: 30.   2 Ps. 77: 39 (78: 39).

own sorry state, bewailing the fate of Dido, who died for love of Aeneas, yet shedding no tears for himself as he dies for want of loving you? O God, you are the Light of my heart, the Bread of my inmost soul, and the Power that weds my mind and the thoughts of my heart. But I did not love you. *I broke my troth with you*[1] and embraced another while applause echoed about me. For to love this world is to break troth with you,[2] yet men applaud and are ashamed to be otherwise. I did not weep over this, but instead I wept for Dido, who surrendered her life to the sword, while I forsook you and surrendered myself to the lowest of your created things. And if I were forbidden to read these books, I was sad not to be able to read the very things that made me sad. Such folly is held to be a higher and more fruitful form of study than learning to read and write.

But now, my God, let your voice ring in my soul and let your truth proclaim to me that it is wrong to think this. Tell me that reading and writing are by far the better study. This must be true, for I would rather forget the wanderings of Aeneas and all that goes with them, than how to read and write. It is true that curtains are hung over the entrances to the schools where literature is taught, but they are not so much symbols in honour of mystery as veils concealing error. The schoolmasters need not exclaim at my words, for I no longer go in fear of them now that I confess my soul's desires to you, my God, and gladly blame myself for my evil ways so that I may enjoy the good ways you have shown me. Neither those who traffic in literature nor those who buy their wares need exclaim against me. For if I put to them the question whether it is true, as the poet says, that Aeneas once came to Carthage, the less learned will plead ignorance and the better informed will admit that it is not true. But if I ask how the name of Aeneas is spelt, anyone who has learnt to read will give me the right answer, based on the agreed convention which fixes the alphabet for all of us. If I next ask them whether a man would lose more by forgetting how to read and write or by forgetting the fancies dreamed up by the poets, surely everyone who is not out of his wits can see the answer they would give. So it was wrong of me as a boy to prefer empty romances to more valuable studies. In fact it would be truer to say that I loved the one and hated the other. But in those days 'one and one are two, two and two are four' was a

[1] Ps. 72: 27 (73: 27).　　[2] See James 4: 4.

loathsome jingle, while the wooden horse and its crew of soldiers, the burning of Troy and even the ghost of Creusa made a most enchanting dream, futile though it was.

14

If this was so, why did I dislike Greek literature, which tells these tales, as much as the Greek language itself? Homer, as well as Virgil, was a skilful spinner of yarns and he is most delightfully imaginative. Nevertheless, as a boy, I found him little to my taste. I suppose that Greek boys think the same about Virgil when they are forced to study him as I was forced to study Homer. There was of course the difficulty which is found in learning any foreign language, and this soured the sweetness of the Greek romances. For I understood not a single word and I was constantly subjected to violent threats and cruel punishments to make me learn. As a baby, of course, I knew no Latin either, but I learned it without fear and fret, simply by keeping my ears open while my nurses fondled me and everyone laughed and played happily with me. I learned it without being forced by threats of punishment, because it was my own wish to be able to give expression to my thoughts. I could never have done this if I had not learnt a few words, not from schoolmasters, but from people who spoke to me and listened when I delivered to their ears whatever thoughts I had conceived. This clearly shows that we learn better in a free spirit of curiosity than under fear and compulsion. But your law, O God, permits the free flow of curiosity to be stemmed by force. From the schoolmaster's cane to the ordeals of martyrdom, your law prescribes bitter medicine to retrieve us from the noxious pleasures which cause us to desert you.

15

Grant my prayer, O Lord, and do not allow my soul to wilt under the discipline which you prescribe. Let me not tire of thanking you for your mercy in rescuing me from all my wicked ways, so that you may be sweeter to me than all the joys which used to tempt me; so that I may love you most intensely and clasp your hand with all the power of my devotion; so that you may save me from all temptation until the end of my days.

You, O Lord, are my King and my God, and in your service I want to use whatever good I learned as a boy. I can speak and write, read and count, and I want these things to be used to serve you, because when I studied other subjects you checked me and forgave me the sins I committed by taking pleasure in such worthless things. It is true that these studies taught me many useful words, but the same words can be learnt by studying something that matters, and this is the safe course for a boy to follow.

16

But we are carried away by custom to our own undoing and it is hard to struggle against the stream. Will this torrent never dry up? How much longer will it sweep the sons of Adam down to that vast and terrible sea which cannot easily be passed, even by those who climb upon the ark of the Cross?

This traditional education taught me that Jupiter punishes the wicked with his thunderbolts and yet commits adultery himself. The two roles are quite incompatible. All the same he is represented in this way, and the result is that those who follow his example in adultery can put a bold face on it by making false pretences of thunder. But can any schoolmaster in his gown listen unperturbed to a man who challenges him on his own ground and says 'Homer invented these stories and attributed human sins to the gods. He would have done better to provide men with examples of divine goodness'?[1] It would be nearer the truth to say that Homer certainly invented the tales but peopled them with wicked human characters in the guise of gods. In this way their wickedness would not be reckoned a crime, and all who did as they did could be shown to follow the example of the heavenly gods, not that of sinful mortals.

And yet human children are pitched into this hellish torrent, together with the fees which are paid to have them taught lessons like these. Much business is at stake, too, when these matters are publicly debated, because the law decrees that teachers should be paid a salary in addition to the fees paid by their pupils. And the roar of the torrent beating upon its boulders seems to say 'This is the school where men are made masters of words. This is where they learn the art of per-

[1] Cicero, *Tusculanae disputationes* I, 26.

suasion, so necessary in business and debate' – as much as to say that, but for a certain passage in Terence, we should never have heard of words like 'shower', 'golden', 'lap', 'deception', 'sky', and the other words which occur in the same scene. Terence brings on to the stage a dissolute youth who excuses his own fornication by pointing to the example of Jupiter. He looks at a picture painted on the wall, which 'shows how Jupiter is said to have deceived the girl Danae by raining a golden shower into her lap'.[1] These are the words with which he incites himself to lechery, as though he had heavenly authority for it: 'What a god he is! His mighty thunder rocks the sky from end to end. You may say that I am only a man, and thundering is beyond my power. But I played the rest of the part well enough, and willingly too'![1]

The words are certainly not learnt any the more easily by reason of the filthy moral, but filth is committed with greater confidence as a result of learning the words. I have nothing against the words themselves. They are like choice and costly glasses, but they contain the wine of error which had already gone to the heads of the teachers who poured it out for us to drink. If we refused to drink, we were beaten for it, without the right to appeal to a sober judge. With your eyes upon me, my God, my memory can safely recall those days. But it is true that I learned all these things gladly and took a sinful pleasure in them. And for this very reason I was called a promising boy.

17

Let me tell you, my God, how I squandered the brains you gave me on foolish delusions. I was set a task which troubled me greatly, for if I were successful, I might win some praise: if not, I was afraid of disgrace or a beating. I had to recite the speech of Juno,[2] who was pained and angry because she could not prevent Aeneas from sailing to Italy. I had been told that Juno had never really spoken the words, but we were compelled to make believe and follow the flight of the poet's fancy by repeating in prose what he had said in verse. The contest was to be won by the boy who found the best words to suit the meaning and best expressed feelings of sorrow and anger appropriate to the majesty of the character he impersonated.

[1] Terence, *Eunuchus* III, 5.   [2] Virgil, *Aeneid* I, 37–49.

What did all this matter to me, my God, my true Life? Why did my recitation win more praise than those of the many other boys in my class? Surely it was all so much smoke without fire? Was there no other subject on which I might have sharpened my wits and my tongue? I might have used them, O Lord, to praise you in the words of your Scriptures, which could have been a prop to support my heart, as if it were a young vine, so that it would not have produced this crop of worthless fruit, fit only for the birds to peck at. For offerings can be made to those birds of prey, the fallen angels, in more ways than one.

18

But was it surprising that I was lured into these fruitless pastimes and wandered away from you, my God? I was expected to model myself upon men who were disconcerted by the rebukes they received if they used outlandish words or strange idioms to tell of some quite harmless thing they might have done, but revelled in the applause they earned for the fine flow of well-ordered and nicely balanced phrases with which they described their own acts of indecency. You see all these things, Lord, and yet you keep silence, because you are patient and full of compassion and can tell no lie.[1] Will you be silent for ever? This very day you are ready to rescue from this fearsome abyss any soul that searches for you, any man who says from the depths of his heart, *I have eyes only for you; I long, Lord, for your presence;*[2] for the soul that is blinded by wicked passions is far from you and cannot see your face. The path that leads us away from you and brings us back again is not measured by footsteps or milestones. The prodigal son of the Scriptures went to live in a distant land to waste in dissipation all the wealth which his father had given him when he set out. But, to reach that land, he did not hire horses, carriages, or ships; he did not take to the air on real wings or set one foot before the other. For you were the Father who gave him riches. You loved him when he set out and you loved him still more when he came home without a penny. But he set his heart on pleasure and his soul was blinded, and this blindness was the measure of the distance he travelled away from you, so that he could not see your face.

O Lord my God, be patient, as you always are, with the men of

1 See Ps. 85: 15 (86: 15).   2 Ps. 26: 8 (27: 8).

this world as you watch them and see how strictly they obey the rules of grammar which have been handed down to them, and yet ignore the eternal rules of everlasting salvation which they have received from you. A man who has learnt the traditional rules of pronunciation, or teaches them to others, gives greater scandal if he breaks them by dropping the aitch from 'human being' than if he breaks your rules and hates another human, his fellow man. This is just as perverse as to imagine that our enemies can do us more harm than we do to ourselves by hating them, or that by persecuting another man we can damage him more fatally than we damage our own hearts in the process. O God, alone in majesty, high in the silence of heaven, unseen by man! we can see how your unremitting justice punishes unlawful ambition with blindness, for a man who longs for fame as a fine speaker will stand up before a human judge, surrounded by a human audience, and lash his opponent with malicious invective, taking the greatest care not to say "uman' instead of 'human' by a slip of the tongue, and yet the thought that the frenzy in his own mind may condemn a human being to death disturbs him not at all.

19

It was at the threshold of a world such as this that I stood in peril as a boy. I was already being prepared for its tournaments by a training which taught me to have a horror of faulty grammar instead of teaching me, when I committed these faults, not to envy others who avoided them. All this, my God, I admit and confess to you. By these means I won praise from the people whose favour I sought, for I thought that the right way to live was to do as they wished. I was blind to the whirlpool of debasement in which I had been plunged away from the sight of your eyes. For in your eyes nothing could be more debased than I was then, since I was even troublesome to the people whom I set out to please. Many and many a time I lied to my tutor, my masters, and my parents, and deceived them because I wanted to play games or watch some futile show or was impatient to imitate what I saw on the stage. I even stole from my parents' larder and from their table, either from greed or to get something to give to other boys in exchange for their favourite toys, which they were willing to barter with me. And in the games I played with them

I often cheated in order to come off the better, simply because a vain desire to win had got the better of me. And yet there was nothing I could less easily endure, nothing that made me quarrel more bitterly, than to find others cheating me as I cheated them. All the same, if they found me out and blamed me for it, I would lose my temper rather than give in.

Can this be the innocence of childhood? Far from it, O Lord! But I beg you to forgive it. For commanders and kings may take the place of tutors and schoolmasters, nuts and balls and pet birds may give way to money and estates and servants, but these same passions remain with us while one stage of life follows upon another, just as more severe punishments follow upon the schoolmaster's cane. It was, then, simply because they are small that you used children to symbolize humility when, as our King, you commended it by saying that *the kingdom of heaven belongs to such as these.*[1]

20

And yet, Lord, even if you had willed that I should not survive my childhood, I should have owed you gratitude, because you are our God, the supreme Good, the Creator and Ruler of the universe. For even as a child I existed, I was alive, I had the power of feeling; I had an instinct to keep myself safe and sound, to preserve my own being, which was a trace of the single unseen Being from whom it was derived; I had an inner sense which watched over my bodily senses and kept them in full vigour; and even in the small things which occupied my thoughts I found pleasure in the truth. I disliked finding myself in the wrong; my memory was good; I was acquiring the command of words; I enjoyed the company of friends; and I shrank from pain, ignorance, and sorrow. Should I not be grateful that so small a creature possessed such wonderful qualities? But they were all gifts from God, for I did not give them to myself. His gifts are good and the sum of them all is my own self. Therefore, the God who made me must be good and all the good in me is his. I thank him and praise him for all the good in my life, even my life as a boy. But my sin was this, that I looked for pleasure, beauty, and truth not in him but in myself and his other creatures, and the search led me instead

[1] Matt. 19: 14.

to pain, confusion, and error. My God, in whom is my delight, my glory, and my trust, I thank you for your gifts and beg you to preserve and keep them for me. Keep me, too, and so your gifts will grow and reach perfection and I shall be with you myself, for I should not even exist if it were not by your gift.

BOOK II

1

I MUST now carry my thoughts back to the abominable things I did in those days, the sins of the flesh which defiled my soul. I do this, my God, not because I love those sins, but so that I may love you. For love of your love I shall retrace my wicked ways. The memory is bitter, but it will help me to savour your sweetness, the sweetness that does not deceive but brings real joy and never fails. For love of your love I shall retrieve myself from the havoc of disruption which tore me to pieces when I turned away from you, whom alone I should have sought, and lost myself instead on many a different quest. For as I grew to manhood I was inflamed with desire for a surfeit of hell's pleasures. Foolhardy as I was, I ran wild with lust that was manifold and rank. In your eyes my beauty vanished and I was foul to the core, yet I was pleased with my own condition and anxious to be pleasing in the eyes of men.

2

I cared for nothing but to love and be loved. But my love went beyond the affection of one mind for another, beyond the arc of the bright beam of friendship. Bodily desire, like a morass, and adolescent sex welling up within me exuded mists which clouded over and obscured my heart, so that I could not distinguish the clear light of true love from the murk of lust. Love and lust together seethed within me. In my tender youth they swept me away over the precipice of my body's appetites and plunged me in the whirlpool of sin. More and more I angered you, unawares. For I had been deafened by the clank of my chains, the fetters of the death which was my due to punish the pride in my soul. I strayed still farther from you and you did not restrain me. I was tossed and spilled, floundering in the broiling sea of my fornication, and you said no word. How long it was before I learned that you were my true joy! You were silent then, and I went on my way, farther and farther from you, proud in my distress and restless in fatigue, sowing more and more seeds whose only crop was grief.

Was there no one to lull my distress, to turn the fleeting beauty of these new-found attractions to good purpose and set up a goal for their charms, so that the high tide of my youth might have rolled in upon the shore of marriage? The surge might have been calmed and contented by the procreation of children, which is the purpose of marriage, as your law prescribes, O Lord. By this means you form the offspring of our fallen nature, and with a gentle hand you prune back the thorns that have no place in your paradise. For your almighty power is not far from us, even when we are far from you. Or, again, I might have listened more attentively to your voice from the clouds, saying of those who marry that they will *meet with outward distress, but I leave you your freedom;*[1] that *a man does well to abstain from all commerce with women,*[2] and that *he who is unmarried is concerned with God's claim, asking how he is to please God; whereas the married man is concerned with the world's claim, asking how he is to please his wife.*[3] These were the words to which I should have listened with more care, and if I had made myself a *eunuch for love of the kingdom of heaven,*[4] I should have awaited your embrace with all the greater joy.

But, instead, I was in a ferment of wickedness. I deserted you and allowed myself to be carried away by the sweep of the tide. I broke all your lawful bounds and did not escape your lash. For what man can escape it? You were always present, angry and merciful at once, strewing the pangs of bitterness over all my lawless pleasures to lead me on to look for others unallied with pain. You meant me to find them nowhere but in yourself, O Lord, for you teach us by inflicting pain,[5] you smite so that you may heal,[6] and you kill us so that we may not die away from you. Where was I then and how far was I banished from the bliss of your house in that sixteenth year of my life? This was the age at which the frenzy gripped me and I surrendered myself entirely to lust, which your law forbids but human hearts are not ashamed to sanction. My family made no effort to save me from my fall by marriage. Their only concern was that I should learn how to make a good speech and how to persuade others by my words.

[1] 1 Cor. 7: 28. [2] 1 Cor. 7: 1. [3] 1 Cor. 7: 32, 33. [4] Matt. 19: 12.
[5] See Ps. 93: 20 (94: 20). [6] See Deut. 32: 39.

3

In the same year my studies were interrupted. I had already begun to go to the near-by town of Madaura to study literature and the art of public speaking, but I was brought back home while my father, a modest citizen of Thagaste whose determination was greater than his means, saved up the money to send me farther afield to Carthage. I need not tell all this to you, my God, but in your presence I tell it to my own kind, to those other men, however few, who may perhaps pick up this book. And I tell it so that I and all who read my words may realize the depths from which we are to cry to you. Your ears will surely listen to the cry of a penitent heart which lives the life of faith.

No one had anything but praise for my father who, despite his slender resources, was ready to provide his son with all that was needed to enable him to travel so far for the purpose of study. Many of our townsmen, far richer than my father, went to no such trouble for their children's sake. Yet this same father of mine took no trouble at all to see how I was growing in your sight or whether I was chaste or not. He cared only that I should have a fertile tongue, leaving my heart to bear none of your fruits, my God, though you are the only Master, true and good, of its husbandry.

In the meanwhile, during my sixteenth year, the narrow means of my family obliged me to leave school and live idly at home with my parents. The brambles of lust grew high above my head and there was no one to root them out, certainly not my father. One day at the public baths he saw the signs of active virility coming to life in me and this was enough to make him relish the thought of having grand-children. He was happy to tell my mother about it, for his happiness was due to the intoxication which causes the world to forget you, its Creator, and to love the things you have created instead of loving you, because the world is drunk with the invisible wine of its own perverted, earthbound will. But in my mother's heart you had already begun to build your temple and laid the foundations of your holy dwelling, while my father was still a catechumen and a new one at that. So, in her piety, she became alarmed and apprehensive, and although I had not yet been baptized, she began to dread that I might follow in the crooked path of those who do not keep their eyes on you but turn their backs instead.

How presumptuous it was of me to say that you were silent, my God, when I drifted farther and farther away from you! Can it be true that you said nothing to me at that time? Surely the words which rang in my ears, spoken by your faithful servant, my mother, could have come from none but you? Yet none of them sank into my heart to make me do as you said. I well remember what her wishes were and how she most earnestly warned me not to commit fornication and above all not to seduce any man's wife. It all seemed womanish advice to me and I should have blushed to accept it. Yet the words were yours, though I did not know it. I thought that you were silent and that she was speaking, but all the while you were speaking to me through her, and when I disregarded her, your handmaid, I was disregarding you, though I was both her son and your servant. But I did this unawares and continued headlong on my way. I was so blind to the truth that among my companions I was ashamed to be less dissolute than they were. For I heard them bragging of their depravity, and the greater the sin the more they gloried in it, so that I took pleasure in the same vices not only for the enjoyment of what I did, but also for the applause I won.

Nothing deserves to be despised more than vice; yet I gave in more and more to vice simply in order not to be despised. If I had not sinned enough to rival other sinners, I used to pretend that I had done things I had not done at all, because I was afraid that innocence would be taken for cowardice and chastity for weakness. These were the companions with whom I walked the streets of Babylon. I wallowed in its mire as if it were made of spices and precious ointments, and to fix me all the faster in the very depths of sin the unseen enemy trod me underfoot and enticed me to himself, because I was an easy prey for his seductions. For even my mother, who by now had escaped from the centre of Babylon, though she still loitered in its outskirts, did not act upon what she had heard about me from her husband with the same earnestness as she had advised me about chastity. She saw that I was already infected with a disease that would become dangerous later on, but if the growth of my passions could not be cut back to the quick, she did not think it right to restrict them to the bounds of married love. This was because she was afraid that the bonds of marriage might be a hindrance to my hopes for the future – not of course the hope of the life to come, which she reposed in you, but my hopes of success at my studies. Both my parents were unduly eager for me to learn, my father because he gave next to no thought to you and only shallow thought to me, and my mother because she thought that the usual course of study would certainly not hinder me, but would even help me, in my approach to you. To the best of my memory this is how I construe the characters of my parents. Furthermore, I was given a free rein to amuse myself beyond the strict limits of discipline, so that I lost myself in many kinds of evil ways, in all of which a pall of darkness hung between me and the bright light of your truth, my God. What malice proceeded from my pampered heart![1]

4

It is certain, O Lord, that theft is punished by your law, the law that is written in men's hearts and cannot be erased however sinful they are. For no thief can bear that another thief should steal from him, even if he is rich and the other is driven to it by want. Yet I was willing to steal, and steal I did, although I was not compelled by any lack, unless it were the lack of a sense of justice or a distaste for what was right and a greedy love of doing wrong. For of what I stole I already had plenty, and much better at that, and I had no wish to enjoy the things I coveted by stealing, but only to enjoy the theft itself and the sin. There was a pear-tree near our vineyard, loaded with fruit that was attractive neither to look at nor to taste. Late one night a band of ruffians, myself included, went off to shake down the fruit and carry it away, for we had continued our games out of doors until well after dark, as was our pernicious habit. We took away an enormous quantity of pears, not to eat them ourselves, but simply to throw them to the pigs. Perhaps we ate some of them, but our real pleasure consisted in doing something that was forbidden.

Look into my heart, O God, the same heart on which you took pity when it was in the depths of the abyss. Let my heart now tell you what prompted me to do wrong for no purpose, and why it was only my own love of mischief that made me do it. The evil in me was foul, but I loved it. I loved my own perdition and my own faults, not the things for which I committed wrong, but the wrong itself. My soul was vicious and broke away from your safe keeping to seek its

[1] See Ps. 72: 7 (73: 7).

own destruction, looking for no profit in disgrace but only for disgrace itself.

5

The eye is attracted by beautiful objects, by gold and silver and all
such things. There is great pleasure, too, in feeling something agreeable to the touch, and material things have various qualities to please
each of the other senses. Again, it is gratifying to be held in esteem by
other men and to have the power of giving them orders and gaining
the mastery over them. This is also the reason why revenge is sweet.
But our ambition to obtain all these things must not lead us astray
from you, O Lord, nor must we depart from what your law allows.
The life we live on earth has its own attractions as well, because it has
a certain beauty of its own in harmony with all the rest of this world's
beauty. Friendship among men, too, is a delightful bond, uniting
many souls in one. All these things and their like can be occasions of
sin because, good though they are, they are of the lowest order of
good, and if we are too much tempted by them we abandon those
higher and better things, your truth, your law, and you yourself, O
Lord our God. For these earthly things, too, can give joy, though not
such joy as my God, who made them all, can give, because *honest men
will rejoice in the Lord; upright hearts will not boast in vain.*[1]

When there is an inquiry to discover why a crime has been committed, normally no one is satisfied until it has been shown that the
motive might have been either the desire of gaining, or the fear of
losing, one of those good things which I said were of the lowest order.
For such things are attractive and have beauty, although they are
paltry trifles in comparison with the worth of God's blessed treasures.
A man commits murder and we ask the reason. He did it because he
wanted his victim's wife or estates for himself, or so that he might
live on the proceeds of robbery, or because he was afraid that the
other might defraud him of something, or because he had been
wronged and was burning for revenge. Surely no one would believe
that he would commit murder for no reason but the sheer delight of
killing? Sallust tells us that Catiline was a man of insane ferocity, 'who
chose to be cruel and vicious without apparent reason';[2] but we are
also told that his purpose was 'not to allow his men to lose heart or

[1] Ps. 63: 11 (64: 10). [2] Sallust, *Catilina* XVI.

waste their skill through lack of practice'.[1] If we ask the reason for this, it is obvious that he meant that once he had made himself master of the government by means of this continual violence, he would obtain honour, power, and wealth and would no longer go in fear of the law because of his crimes or have to face difficulties through lack of funds. So even Catiline did not love crime for crime's sake. He loved something quite different, for the sake of which he committed his crimes.

6

If the crime of theft which I committed that night as a boy of sixteen were a living thing, I could speak to it and ask what it was that, to my shame, I loved in it. I had no beauty because it was a robbery. It is true that the pears which we stole had beauty, because they were created by you, the good God, who are the most beautiful of all beings and the Creator of all things, the supreme Good and my own true Good. But it was not the pears that my unhappy soul desired. I had plenty of my own, better than those, and I only picked them so that I might steal. For no sooner had I picked them than I threw them away, and tasted nothing in them but my own sin, which I relished and enjoyed. If any part of one of those pears passed my lips, it was the sin that gave it flavour.

And now, O Lord my God, now that I ask what pleasure I had in that theft, I find that it had no beauty to attract me. I do not mean beauty of the sort that justice and prudence possess, nor the beauty that is in man's mind and in his memory and in the life that animates him, nor the beauty of the stars in their allotted places or of the earth and sea, teeming with new life born to replace the old as it passes away. It did not even have the shadowy, deceptive beauty which makes vice attractive – pride, for instance, which is a pretence of superiority, imitating yours, for you alone are God, supreme over all; or ambition, which is only a craving for honour and glory, when you alone are to be honoured before all and you alone are glorious for ever. Cruelty is the weapon of the powerful, used to make others fear them: yet no one is to be feared but God alone, from whose power nothing can be snatched away or stolen by any man at any time or place or by any means. The lustful use caresses to win the love

[1] Sallust, *Catilina* XVI.

they crave for, yet no caress is sweeter than your charity and no love is more rewarding than the love of your truth, which shines in beauty above all else. Inquisitiveness has all the appearance of a thirst for knowledge, yet you have supreme knowledge of all things. Ignorance, too, and stupidity choose to go under the mask of simplicity and innocence, because you are simplicity itself and no innocence is greater than yours. You are innocent even of the harm which overtakes the wicked, for it is the result of their own actions. Sloth poses as the love of peace: yet what certain peace is there besides the Lord? Extravagance masquerades as fullness and abundance: but you are the full, unfailing store of never-dying sweetness. The spendthrift makes a pretence of liberality: but you are the most generous dispenser of all good. The covetous want many possessions for themselves: you possess all. The envious struggle for preferment: but what is to be preferred before you? Anger demands revenge: but what vengeance is as just as yours? Fear shrinks from any sudden, unwonted danger which threatens the things that it loves, for its only care is safety: but to you nothing is strange, nothing unforeseen. No one can part you from the things that you love, and safety is assured nowhere but in you. Grief eats away its heart for the loss of things which it took pleasure in desiring, because it wants to be like you, from whom nothing can be taken away.

So the soul defiles itself with unchaste love when it turns away from you and looks elsewhere for things which it cannot find pure and unsullied except by returning to you. All who desert you and set themselves up against you merely copy you in a perverse way; but by this very act of imitation they only show that you are the Creator of all nature and, consequently, that there is no place whatever where man may hide away from you.

What was it, then, that pleased me in that act of theft? Which of my Lord's powers did I imitate in a perverse and wicked way? Since I had no real power to break his law, was it that I enjoyed at least the pretence of doing so, like a prisoner who creates for himself the illusion of liberty by doing something wrong, when he has no fear of punishment, under a feeble hallucination of power? Here was the slave who ran away from his master and chased a shadow instead! What an abomination! What a parody of life! What abysmal death! Could I enjoy doing wrong for no other reason than that it was wrong?

7

What return shall I make to the Lord[1] for my ability to recall these things with no fear in my soul? I will love you, Lord, and thank you, and praise your name, because you have forgiven me such great sins and such wicked deeds. I acknowledge that it was by your grace and mercy that you melted away my sins like ice. I acknowledge, too, that by your grace I was preserved from whatever sins I did not commit, for there was no knowing what I might have done, since I loved evil even if it served no purpose. I avow that you have forgiven me all, both the sins which I committed of my own accord and those which by your guidance I was spared from committing.

What man who reflects upon his own weakness can dare to claim that his own efforts have made him chaste and free from sin, as though this entitled him to love you the less, on the ground that he had less need of the mercy by which you forgive the sins of the penitent? There are some who have been called by you and because they have listened to your voice they have avoided the sins which I here record and confess for them to read. But let them not deride me for having been cured by the same Doctor who preserved them from sickness, or at least from such grave sickness as mine. Let them love you just as much, or even more, than I do, for they can see that the same healing hand which rid me of the great fever of my sins protects them from falling sick of the same disease.

8

It brought me no happiness, for *what harvest did I reap from acts which now make me blush,*[2] particularly from that act of theft? I loved nothing in it except the thieving, though I cannot truly speak of that as a 'thing' that I could love, and I was only the more miserable because of it. And yet, as I recall my feelings at the time, I am quite sure that I would not have done it on my own. Was it then that I also enjoyed the company of those with whom I committed the crime? If this is so, there was something else I loved besides the act of theft; but I cannot call it 'something else', because companionship, like theft, is not a thing at all.

[1] Ps. 115: 12 (116: 12).   [2] Rom. 6: 21.

No one can tell me the truth of it except my God, who enlightens my mind and dispels its shadows. What conclusion am I trying to reach from these questions and this discussion? It is true that if the pears which I stole had been to my taste, and if I had wanted to get them for myself, I might have committed the crime on my own if I had needed to do no more than that to win myself the pleasure. I should have had no need to kindle my glowing desire by rubbing shoulders with a gang of accomplices. But as it was not the fruit that gave me pleasure, I must have got it from the crime itself, from the thrill of having partners in sin.

9

How can I explain my mood? It was certainly a very vile frame of mind and one for which I suffered; but how can I account for it? *Who knows his own frailties?*[1]

We were tickled to laughter by the prank we had played, because no one suspected us of it although the owners were furious. Why was it, then, that I thought it fun not to have been the only culprit? Perhaps it was because we do not easily laugh when we are alone. True enough: but even when a man is all by himself and quite alone, sometimes he cannot help laughing if he thinks or hears or sees something especially funny. All the same, I am quite sure that I would never have done this thing on my own.

My God, I lay all this before you, for it is still alive in my memory. By myself I would not have committed that robbery. It was not the takings that attracted me but the raid itself, and yet to do it by myself would have been no fun and I should not have done it. This was friendship of a most unfriendly sort, bewitching my mind in an inexplicable way. For the sake of a laugh, a little sport, I was glad to do harm and anxious to damage another; and that without thought of profit for myself or retaliation for injuries received! And all because we are ashamed to hold back when others say 'Come on! Let's do it!'

10

Can anyone unravel this twisted tangle of knots? I shudder to look at it or think of such abomination. I long instead for innocence and justice, graceful and splendid in eyes whose sight is undefiled. My

[1] Ps. 18: 13 (19: 12).

longing fills me and yet it cannot cloy. With them is certain peace and life that cannot be disturbed. The man who enters their domain goes to *share the joy of his Lord*.[1] He shall know no fear and shall lack no good. In him that is goodness itself he shall find his own best way of life. But I deserted you, my God. In my youth I wandered away, too far from your sustaining hand, and created of myself a barren waste.

[1] Matt. 25: 21.

BOOK III

I

I WENT to Carthage, where I found myself in the midst of a hissing cauldron of lust. I had not yet fallen in love, but I was in love with the idea of it, and this feeling that something was missing made me despise myself for not being more anxious to satisfy the need. I began to look around for some object for my love, since I badly wanted to love something. I had no liking for the safe path without pitfalls, for although my real need was for you, my God, who are the food of the soul, I was not aware of this hunger. I felt no need for the food that does not perish, not because I had had my fill of it, but because the more I was starved of it the less palatable it seemed. Because of this my soul fell sick. It broke out in ulcers and looked about desperately for some material, worldly means of relieving the itch which they caused. But material things, which have no soul, could not be true objects for my love. To love and to have my love returned was my heart's desire, and it would be all the sweeter if I could also enjoy the body of the one who loved me.

So I muddied the stream of friendship with the filth of lewdness and clouded its clear waters with hell's black river of lust. And yet, in spite of this rank depravity, I was vain enough to have ambitions of cutting a fine figure in the world. I also fell in love, which was a snare of my own choosing. My God, my God of mercy, how good you were to me, for you mixed much bitterness in that cup of pleasure! My love was returned and finally shackled me in the bonds of its consummation. In the midst of my joy I was caught up in the coils of trouble, for I was lashed with the cruel, fiery rods of jealousy and suspicion, fear, anger, and quarrels.

2

I was much attracted by the theatre, because the plays reflected my own unhappy plight and were tinder to my fire. Why is it that men enjoy feeling sad at the sight of tragedy and suffering on the stage, although they would be most unhappy if they had to endure the same fate themselves? Yet they watch the plays because they hope to be made to feel sad, and the feeling of sorrow is what they enjoy. What miserable delirium this is! The more a man is subject to such suffering himself, the more easily he is moved by it in the theatre. Yet when he suffers himself, we call it misery: when he suffers out of sympathy with others, we call it pity. But what sort of pity can we really feel for an imaginary scene on the stage? The audience is not called upon to offer help but only to feel sorrow, and the more they are pained the more they applaud the author. Whether this human agony is based on fact or is simply imaginary, if it is acted so badly that the audience is not moved to sorrow, they leave the theatre in a disgruntled and critical mood; whereas, if they are made to feel pain, they stay to the end watching happily.

This shows that sorrow and tears can be enjoyable. Of course, everyone wants to be happy; but even if no one likes being sad, is there just the one exception that, because we enjoy pitying others, we welcome their misfortunes, without which we could not pity them? If so, it is because friendly feelings well up in us like the waters of a spring. But what course do these waters follow? Where do they flow? Why do they trickle away to join that stream of boiling pitch, the hideous flood of lust? For by their own choice they lose themselves and become absorbed in it. They are diverted from their true course and deprived of their original heavenly calm.

Of course this does not mean that we must arm ourselves against compassion. There are times when we must welcome sorrow on behalf of others. But for the sake of our souls we must beware of uncleanness. My God must be the Keeper of my soul, the God of our fathers, who is to be exalted and extolled for ever more. My soul must guard against uncleanness.

I am not nowadays insensible to pity. But in those days I used to share the joy of stage lovers and their sinful pleasure in each other even though it was all done in make-believe for the sake of entertainment; and when they were parted, pity of a sort led me to share their grief. I enjoyed both these emotions equally. But now I feel more pity for a man who is happy in his sins than for one who has to endure the ordeal of forgoing some harmful pleasure or being deprived of some enjoyment which was really an affliction. Of the two, this sort of pity is certainly the more genuine, but the sorrow which it causes is not a source of pleasure. For although a man who is sorry for the sufferings of others deserves praise for his charity, nevertheless, if his pity is genuine, he would prefer that there should be no cause for his sorrow. If the impossible could happen and kindness were unkind, a man whose sense of pity was true and sincere might want others to suffer so that he could pity them. Sorrow may therefore be commendable but never desirable. For it is powerless to stab you, Lord God, and this is why the love you bear for our souls and the compassion you show for them are pure and unalloyed, far purer than the love and pity which we feel ourselves. But *who can prove himself worthy of such a calling?*[1]

However, in those unhappy days I enjoyed the pangs of sorrow. I always looked for things to wring my heart and the more tears an actor caused me to shed by his performance on the stage, even though he was portraying the imaginary distress of others, the more delightful and attractive I found it. Was it any wonder that I, the unhappy sheep who strayed from your flock, impatient of your shepherding, became infected with a loathsome mange? Hence my love of things which made me sad. I did not seek the kind of sorrow which would wound me deeply, for I had no wish to endure the sufferings which I saw on the stage; but I enjoyed fables and fictions, which could only graze the skin. But where the fingers scratch, the skin becomes inflamed. It swells and festers with hideous pus. And the same happened to me. Could the life I led be called true life, my God?

3

Yet all the while, far above, your mercy hovered faithfully about me. I exhausted myself in depravity, in the pursuit of an unholy curiosity. I deserted you and sank to the bottom-most depths of scepticism and the mockery of devil-worship. My sins were a sacrifice to the devil, and for all of them you chastised me. I defied you even so far as to relish the thought of lust, and gratify it too, within the walls of your church during the celebration of your mysteries. For such a deed I deserved to pluck the fruit of death, and you punished me for it with

[1] II Cor. 2: 16.

a heavy lash. But, compared with my guilt, the penalty was nothing. How infinite is your mercy, my God! You are my Refuge from the terrible dangers amongst which I wandered, head on high, intent upon withdrawing still further from you. I loved my own way, not yours, but it was a truant's freedom that I loved.

Besides these pursuits I was also studying for the law. Such ambition was held to be honourable and I determined to succeed in it. The more unscrupulous I was, the greater my reputation was likely to be, for men are so blind that they even take pride in their blindness. By now I was at the top of the school of rhetoric. I was pleased with my superior status and swollen with conceit. All the same, as you well know, Lord, I behaved far more quietly than the 'Wreckers', a title of ferocious devilry which the fashionable set chose for themselves. I had nothing whatever to do with their outbursts of violence, but I lived amongst them, feeling a perverse sense of shame because I was not like them. I kept company with them and there were times when I found their friendship a pleasure, but I always had a horror of what they did when they lived up to their name. Without provocation they would set upon some timid newcomer, gratuitously affronting his sense of decency for their own amusement and using it as fodder for their spiteful jests. This was the devil's own behaviour or not far different. 'Wreckers' was a fit name for them, for they were already adrift and total wrecks themselves. The mockery and trickery which they loved to practise on others was a secret snare of the devil, by which they were mocked and tricked themselves.

4

These were the companions with whom I studied the art of eloquence at that impressionable age. It was my ambition to be a good speaker, for the unhallowed and inane purpose of gratifying human vanity. The prescribed course of study brought me to a work by an author named Cicero, whose writing nearly everyone admires, if not the spirit of it. The title of the book is *Hortensius* and it recommends the reader to study philosophy. It altered my outlook on life. It changed my prayers to you, O Lord, and provided me with new hopes and aspirations. All my empty dreams suddenly lost their charm and my heart began to throb with a bewildering passion for the wisdom of eternal truth. I began to climb out of the depths to which I had sunk, in order to return to you. For I did not use the book as a whetstone to sharpen my tongue. It was not the style of it but the contents which won me over, and yet the allowance which my mother paid me was supposed to be spent on putting an edge on my tongue. I was now in my nineteenth year and she supported me, because my father had died two years before.

My God, how I burned with longing to have wings to carry me back to you, away from all earthly things, although I had no idea what you would do with me! For *yours is the wisdom*.[1] In Greek the word 'philosophy' means 'love of wisdom', and it was with this love that the *Hortensius* inflamed me. There are people for whom philosophy is a means of misleading others, for they misuse its great name, its attractions, and its integrity to give colour and gloss to their own errors. Most of these so-called philosophers who lived in Cicero's time and before are noted in the book. He shows them up in their true colours and makes quite clear how wholesome is the admonition which the Holy Spirit gives in the words of your good and true servant, Paul: *Take care not to let anyone cheat you with his philosophizings, with empty fantasies drawn from human tradition, from worldly principles; they were never Christ's teaching. In Christ the whole plenitude of Deity is embodied and dwells in him.*[2]

But, O Light of my heart, you know that at that time, although Paul's words were not known to me, the only thing that pleased me in Cicero's book was his advice not simply to admire one or another of the schools of philosophy, but to love wisdom itself, whatever it might be, and to search for it, pursue it, hold it, and embrace it firmly. These were the words which excited me and set me burning with fire, and the only check to this blaze of enthusiasm was that they made no mention of the name of Christ. For by your mercy, Lord, from the time when my mother fed me at the breast my infant heart had been suckled dutifully on his name, the name of your Son, my Saviour. Deep inside my heart his name remained, and nothing could entirely captivate me, however learned, however neatly expressed, however true it might be, unless his name were in it.

[1] Job 12: 13. [2] Col. 2: 8, 9.

5

So I made up my mind to examine the holy Scriptures and see what kind of books they were. I discovered something that was at once beyond the understanding of the proud and hidden from the eyes of children. Its gait was humble, but the heights it reached were sublime. It was enfolded in mysteries, and I was not the kind of man to enter into it or bow my head to follow where it led. But these were not the feelings I had when I first read the Scriptures. To me they seemed quite unworthy of comparison with the stately prose of Cicero, because I had too much conceit to accept their simplicity and not enough insight to penetrate their depths. It is surely true that as the child grows these books grow with him. But I was too proud to call myself a child. I was inflated with self-esteem, which made me think myself a great man.

6

I fell in with a set of sensualists, men with glib tongues who ranted and raved and had the snares of the devil in their mouths. They baited the traps by confusing the syllables of the names of God the Father, God the Son Our Lord Jesus Christ, and God the Holy Ghost, the Paraclete, who comforts us. These names were always on the tips of their tongues, but only as sounds which they mouthed aloud, for in their hearts they had no inkling of the truth. Yet 'Truth and truth alone' was the motto which they repeated to me again and again, although the truth was nowhere to be found in them. All that they said was false, both what they said about you, who truly are the Truth, and what they said about this world and its first principles, which were your creation. But I ought not to have been content with what the philosophers said about such things, even when they spoke the truth. I should have passed beyond them for love of you, my supreme Father, my good Father, in whom all beauty has its source.

Truth! Truth! How the very marrow of my soul within me yearned for it as they dinned it in my ears over and over again! To them it was no more than a name to be voiced or a word to be read in their libraries of huge books. But while my hunger was for you, for Truth itself, these were the dishes on which they served me up the sun and the moon, beautiful works of yours but still only your works, not you yourself nor even the greatest of your created things.[1] For your spiritual works are greater than these material things, however brightly they may shine in the sky.

But my hunger and thirst were not even for the greatest of your works, but for you, my God, because you are Truth itself *with whom there can be no change, no swerving from your course.*[2] Yet the dishes they set before me were still loaded with dazzling fantasies, illusions with which the eye deceives the mind. It would have been better to love the sun itself, which at least is real as far as we can see. But I gulped down this food, because I thought that it was you. I had no relish for it, because the taste it left in my mouth was not the taste of truth – it could not be, for it was not you but an empty sham. And it did not nourish me, but starved me all the more. The food we dream of is very like the food we eat when we are awake, but it does not nourish because it is only a dream. Yet the things they gave me to eat were not in the least like you, as now I know since you have spoken to me. They were dream-substances, mock realities, far less true than the real things which we see with the sight of our eyes in the sky or on the earth. These things are seen by bird and beast as well as by ourselves, and they are far more certain than any image we conceive of them. And in turn we can picture them to ourselves with greater certainty than the vaster, infinite things which we surmise from them. Such things have no existence at all, but they were the visionary foods on which I was then fed but not sustained.

But you, O God whom I love and on whom I lean in weakness so that I may be strong, you are not the sun and the moon and the stars, even though we see these bodies in the heavens; nor are you those other bodies which we do not see in the sky, for you created them and, in your reckoning, they are not even among the greatest of your works. How far, then, must you really be from those fantasies of mine, those imaginary material things which do not exist at all! The images we form in our mind's eye, when we picture things that really do exist, are far better founded than these inventions; and the things themselves are still more certain than the images we form of them. But you are not these things. Neither are you the soul,

[1] Saint Augustine is here speaking of the Manichees, for whom astronomy was a part of theology.
[2] James 1: 17.

which is the life of bodies and, since it gives them life, must be better and more certain than they are themselves. But you are the life of souls, the life of lives. You live, O Life of my soul, because you are life itself, immutable.

Where were you in those days? How far away from me? I was wandering far from you and I was not even allowed to eat the husks on which I fed the swine. For surely the fables of the poets and the penmen are better than the traps which those impostors set! There is certainly more to be gained from verses and poems and tales like the flight of Medea than from their stories of the five elements disguised in various ways because of the five dens of darkness. These things simply do not exist and they are death to those who believe in them. Verses and poems can provide real food for thought, but although I used to recite verses about Medea's flight through the air, I never maintained that they were true; and I never believed the poems which I heard others recite. But I did believe the tales which these men told.

These were the stages of my pitiful fall into the depths of hell, as I struggled and strained for lack of the truth. My God, you had mercy on me even before I had confessed to you; but I now confess that all this was because I tried to find you, not through the understanding of the mind, by which you meant us to be superior to the beasts, but through the senses of the flesh. Yet you were deeper than my inmost understanding and higher than the topmost height that I could reach. I had blundered upon that woman in Solomon's parable who, ignorant and unabashed, sat at her door and said *Stolen waters are sweetest, and bread is better eating when there is none to see*.[1] She inveigled me because she found me living in the outer world that lay before my eyes, the eyes of the flesh, and dwelling upon the food which they provided for my mind.

7

There is another reality besides this, though I knew nothing of it. My own specious reasoning induced me to give in to the sly arguments of fools who asked me what was the origin of evil, whether God was confined to the limits of a bodily shape, whether he had hair and nails, and whether men could be called just if they had more than one wife at the same time, or killed other men, or sacrificed living animals.

[1] Prov. 9: 17.

My ignorance was so great that these questions troubled me, and while I thought I was approaching the truth, I was only departing the further from it. I did not know that evil is nothing but the removal of good until finally no good remains. How could I see this when with the sight of my eyes I saw no more than material things and with the sight of my mind no more than their images? I did not know that God is a spirit, a being without bulk and without limbs defined in length and breadth. For bulk is less in the part than in the whole, and if it is infinite, it is less in any part of it which can be defined within fixed limits than it is in its infinity. It cannot, therefore, be everywhere entirely whole, as a spirit is and as God is. Nor had I the least notion what it is in us that gives us our being, or what the Scriptures mean when they say that we are made in God's image.

I knew nothing of the true underlying justice which judges, not according to convention, but according to the truly equitable law of Almighty God. This is the law by which each age and place forms rules of conduct best suited to itself, although the law itself is always and everywhere the same and does not differ from place to place or from age to age. I did not see that by the sanction of this law Abraham and Isaac, Jacob, Moses, David, and the others whom God praised were just men, although they have been reckoned sinners by men who are not qualified to judge, for they try them by human standards and assess all the rights and wrongs of the human race by the measure of their own customs. Anyone who does this behaves like a man who knows nothing about armour and cannot tell which piece is meant for which part of the body, so that he tries to cover his head with a shin-piece and fix a helmet on his foot, and then complains because they will not fit; or like a shopkeeper who is allowed to sell his wares in the morning, but grumbles because the afternoon is a public holiday and he is not allowed to trade; or like a man who sees one of the servants in a house handling things which the cellar-man is not allowed to touch, or finds something being done in the stableyard which is not allowed in the dining-room, and is then indignant because the members of the household, living together in one house, are not all given the same privileges in all parts of the house.

The people of whom I am speaking have the same sort of grievance when they hear that things which good men could do without sin in days gone by are not permitted in ours, and that God gave them one commandment and has given us another. He has done this because the times have demanded it, although men were subject to the same justice in those days as we are in these. Yet those who complain about this understand that when we are dealing with a single man, a single day, or a single house, each part of the whole has a different function suited to it. What may be done at one time of day is not allowed at the next, and what may be done, or must be done, in one room is forbidden and punished in another. This does not mean that justice is erratic or variable, but that the times over which it presides are not always the same, for it is the nature of time to change. Man's life on earth is short and he cannot, by his own perception, see the connexion between the conditions of earlier times and of other nations, which he has not experienced himself, and those of his own times, which are familiar to him. But when only one individual, one day, or one house is concerned, he can easily see what is suitable for each part of the whole and for each member of the household, and what must be done at which times and places. These things he accepts: but with the habits of other ages he finds fault.

I knew nothing of this at that time. I was quite unconscious of it, quite blind to it, although it stared me in the face. When I composed verses, I could not fit any foot in any position that I pleased. Each metre was differently scanned and I could not put the same foot in every position in the same line. And yet the art of poetry, by which I composed, does not vary from one line to another: it is the same for all alike. But I did not discern that justice, which those good and holy men obeyed, in a far more perfect and sublime way than poetry contains in itself at one and the same time all the principles which it prescribes, without discrepancy; although, as times change, it prescribes and apportions them, not all at once, but according to the needs of the times. Blind to this, I found fault with the holy patriarchs not only because, in their own day, they acted as God commanded and inspired them, but also because they predicted the future as he revealed it to them.

8

Surely it is never wrong at any time or in any place for a man to *love God with his whole heart and his whole soul and his whole mind* and to

love his neighbour as himself?[1] Sins against nature, therefore, like the
sin of Sodom, are abominable and deserve punishment wherever and
whenever they are committed. If all nations committed them, all
alike would be held guilty of the same charge in God's law, for our
Maker did not prescribe that we should use each other in this way.
In fact the relationship which we ought to have with God is itself
violated when our nature, of which he is the Author, is desecrated
by perverted lust.

On the other hand, offences against human codes of conduct vary
according to differences of custom, so that no one, whether he is a
native or a foreigner, may, to suit his own pleasure, violate the con-
ventions established by the customary usage or the law of the community or the state. For any part that is out of keeping with the whole is at
fault. But if God commands a nation to do something contrary to its
customs or constitutions, it must be done even if it has never been
done in that country before. If it is a practice which has been dis-
continued, it must be resumed, and if it was not a law before, it must
be enacted. In his own kingdom a king has the right to make orders
which neither he nor any other has ever made before. Obedience to
his orders is not against the common interest of the community; in
fact, if they were disobeyed, the common interest would suffer,
because it is the general agreement in human communities that the
ruler is obeyed. How much more right, then, has God to give commands, since he is the Ruler of all creation and all his creatures must
obey his commandments without demur! For all must yield to God
just as, in the government of human society, the lesser authority must
yield to the greater.

With sins of violence the case is the same as with sins against nature.
Here the impulse is to injure others, either by word or by deed, but
by whichever means it is done, there are various reasons for doing it.
A man may injure his enemy for the sake of revenge; a robber may
assault a traveller to secure for himself something that is not his own;
or a man may attack someone whom he fears in order to avoid
danger to himself. Or the injury may be done from envy, which will
cause an unhappy man to harm another more fortunate than himself
or a rich man to harm someone whose rivalry he fears for the future
or already resents. Again, it may be done for the sheer joy of seeing

[1] Matt. 22: 37, 39.

others suffer, as is the case with those who watch gladiators or make fun of other people and jeer at them.

These are the main categories of sin. They are hatched from the lust for power, from gratification of the eye, and from gratification of corrupt nature – from one or two of these or from all three together. Because of them, O God most high, most sweet, our lives offend against your *ten-stringed harp*,[1] your commandments, the three which proclaim our duty to you and the seven which proclaim our duty to men.

But how can sins of vice be against you, since you cannot be marred by perversion? How can sins of violence be against you, since nothing can injure you? Your punishments are for the sins which men commit against themselves, because although they sin against you, they do wrong to their own souls and their malice is self-betrayed.[2] They corrupt and pervert their own nature, which you made and for which you shaped the rules, either by making wrong use of the things which you allow, or by becoming inflamed with passion to make unnatural use of things which you do not allow. Or else their guilt consists in raving against you in their hearts and with their tongues and *kicking against the goad*,[3] or in playing havoc with the restrictions of human society and brazenly exulting in private feuds and factions, each according to his fancies or his fads.

This is what happens, O Fountain of life, when we abandon you, who are the one true Creator of all that ever was or is, and each of us proudly sets his heart on some one part of your creation instead of on the whole. So it is by the path of meekness and devotion that we must return to you. You rid us of our evil habits and forgive our sins when we confess to you. You *listen to the groans of the prisoners*[4] and free us from the chains which we have forged for ourselves. This you do for us unless we toss our heads against you in the illusion of liberty and in our greed for gain, at the risk of losing all, love our own good better than you yourself, who are the common good of all.

9

Among these vices and crimes and all the endless ways in which men do wrong there are also the sins of those who follow the right path

[1] Ps. 143: 9 (144: 9). [2] See Ps. 26: 12 (27: 12). [3] Acts, 9: 5.
[4] Ps. 101: 21 (102: 20).

but go astray. By the rule of perfection these lapses are condemned, if we judge them aright, but the sinners may yet be praised, for they give promise of better fruit to come, like the young shoots which later bear the ears of corn. Sometimes we also do things which have every appearance of being sins against nature or against our fellow men, but are not sins because they offend neither you, the Lord our God, nor the community in which we live. For example, a man may amass a store of goods to meet the needs of life or some contingency, but it does not necessarily follow that he is a miser. Or he may be punished by those whose duty it is to correct misdemeanours, but it is by no means certain that they do it out of wanton cruelty. Many of the things we do may therefore seem wrong to men but are approved in the light of your knowledge, and many which men applaud are condemned in your eyes. This is because the appearance of what we do is often different from the intention with which we do it, and the circumstances at the time may not be clear.

But when you suddenly command us to do something strange and unforeseen, even if you had previously forbidden it, none can doubt that the command must be obeyed, even though, for the time being, you may conceal the reason for it and it may conflict with the established rule of custom in some forms of society; for no society is right and good unless it obeys you. But happy are they who know that the commandment was yours. For all that your servants do is done as an example of what is needed for the present or as a sign of what is yet to come.

10

I was ignorant of this and derided those holy servants and prophets of yours. But all that I achieved by deriding them was to earn your derision for myself, for I was gradually led to believe such nonsense as that a fig wept when it was plucked, and that the tree which bore it shed tears of mother's milk. But if some sanctified member of the sect were to eat the fig – someone else, of course, would have committed the sin of plucking it – he would digest it and breathe it out again in the form of angels or even as particles of God, retching them up as he groaned in prayer. These particles of the true and supreme God were supposed to be imprisoned in the fruit and could only be released by means of the stomach and teeth of one of the elect. I was foolish enough to believe that we should show more kindness to the fruits of the earth than to mankind, for whose use they were intended. If a starving man, not a Manichee, were to beg for a mouthful, they thought it a crime worthy of mortal punishment to give him one.

11

But *you sent down your help from above*[1] and rescued my soul from the depths of this darkness because my mother, your faithful servant, wept to you for me, shedding more tears for my spiritual death than other mothers shed for the bodily death of a son. For in her faith and in the spirit which she had from you she looked on me as dead. You heard her and did not despise the tears which streamed down and watered the earth in every place where she bowed her head in prayer. You heard her, for how else can I explain the dream with which you consoled her, so that she agreed to live with me and eat at the same table in our home? Lately she had refused to do this, because she loathed and shunned the blasphemy of my false beliefs.

She dreamed that she was standing on a wooden rule, and coming towards her in a halo of splendour she saw a young man who smiled at her in joy, although she herself was sad and quite consumed with grief. He asked her the reason for her sorrow and her daily tears, not because he did not know, but because he had something to tell her, for this is what happens in visions. When she replied that her tears were for the soul I had lost, he told her to take heart for, if she looked carefully, she would see that where she was, there also was I. And when she looked, she saw me standing beside her on the same rule.

Where could this dream have come from, unless it was that you listened to the prayer of her heart? For your goodness is almighty; you take good care of each of us as if you had no others in your care, and you look after all as you look after each. And surely it was for the same reason that, when she told me of the dream and I tried to interpret it as a message that she need not despair of being one day such as I was then, she said at once and without hesitation 'No! He did not say "Where he is, you are", but "Where you are, he is".'

I have often said before and, to the best of my memory, I now declare to you, Lord, that I was much moved by this answer, which

[1] Ps. 143: 7 (144: 7).

you gave me through my mother. She was not disturbed by my interpretation of her dream, plausible though it was, but quickly saw the
true meaning, which I had not seen until she spoke. I was more deeply
moved by this than by the dream itself, in which the joy for which this
devout woman had still so long to wait was foretold so long before
to comfort her in the time of her distress. For nearly nine years were
yet to come during which I wallowed deep in the mire and the darkness of delusion. Often I tried to lift myself, only to plunge the deeper.
Yet all the time this chaste, devout, and prudent woman, a widow
such as is close to your heart, never ceased to pray at all hours and to
offer you the tears she shed for me. The dream had given new spirit
to her hope, but she gave no rest to her sighs and her tears. *Her
prayers reached your presence*[1] and yet you still left me to twist and turn
in the dark.

12

I remember that in the meantime you gave her another answer to her
prayers, though there is much besides this that escapes my memory
and much too that I must omit, because I am in haste to pass on to
other things, which I am more anxious to confess to you.

This other answer you gave her through the mouth of one of your
priests, a bishop who had lived his life in the Church and was well
versed in the Scriptures. My mother asked him, as a favour, to have a
talk with me, so that he might refute my errors, drive the evil out of
my mind, and replace it with good. He often did this when he found
suitable pupils, but he refused to do it for me – a wise decision, as I
afterwards realized. He told her that I was still unripe for instruction
because, as she had told him, I was brimming over with the novelty of
the heresy and had already upset a great many simple people with my
casuistry. 'Leave him alone', he said. 'Just pray to God for him. From
his own reading he will discover his mistakes and the depth of his
profanity.'

At the same time he told her that when he was a child his misguided
mother had handed him over to the Manichees. He had not only read
almost all their books, but had also made copies of them, and even
though no one argued the case with him or put him right, he had
seen for himself that he ought to have nothing to do with the sect;

[1] Ps. 87: 3 (88: 2).

and accordingly he had left it. Even after she had heard this my mother still would not be pacified, but persisted all the more with her tears and her entreaties that he should see me and discuss the matter. At last he grew impatient and said 'Leave me and go in peace. It cannot be that the son of these tears should be lost.'

In later years, as we talked together, she used to say that she accepted these words as a message from heaven.

BOOK IV

1

DURING the space of those nine years, from the nineteenth to the twenty-eighth year of my life, I was led astray myself and led others astray in my turn. We were alike deceivers and deceived in all our different aims and ambitions, both publicly when we expounded our so-called liberal ideas, and in private through our service to what we called religion. In public we were cocksure, in private superstitious, and everywhere void and empty. On the one hand we would hunt for worthless popular distinctions, the applause of an audience, prizes for poetry, or quickly fading wreaths won in competition. We loved the idle pastimes of the stage and in self-indulgence we were unrestrained. On the other hand we aspired to be purged of these lowly pleasures by taking food to the holy elect, as they were called, so that in their paunches it might pass through the process of being made into angels and gods who would set us free. These were the objects I pursued and the tasks I performed together with friends who, like myself and through my fault, were under the same delusion.

Let the proud deride me, O God, and all whom you have not yet laid low and humiliated for the salvation of their souls; but let me still confess my sins to you for your honour and glory. Allow me, I beseech you, to trace again in memory my past deviations and to offer you a sacrifice of joy. Without you I am my own guide to the brink of perdition. And even when all is well with me, what am I but a creature suckled on your milk and feeding on yourself, the food that never perishes? And what is any man, if he is only man? Let the strong and mighty laugh at men like me: let us, the weak and the poor, confess our sins to you.

2

During those years I was a teacher of the art of public speaking. Love of money had gained the better of me and for it I sold to others the means of coming off the better in debate. But you know, Lord, that I preferred to have honest pupils, in so far as honesty has any meaning nowadays, and I had no evil intent when I taught the tricks of pleading, for I never meant them to be used to get the innocent condemned but, if the occasion arose, to save the lives of the guilty. From a distance, my God, you saw me losing my foothold on this treacherous ground, but through clouds of smoke you also saw a spark of good faith in me; for though, as I schooled my pupils, I was merely abetting their futile designs and their schemes of duplicity, nevertheless I did my best to teach them honestly.

In those days I lived with a woman, not my lawful wedded wife but a mistress whom I had chosen for no special reason but that my restless passions had alighted on her. But she was the only one and I was faithful to her. Living with her I found out by my own experience the difference between the restraint of the marriage alliance, contracted for the purpose of having children, and a bargain struck for lust, in which the birth of children is begrudged, though, if they come, we cannot help but love them.

I remember too that once, when I had decided to enter a competition for reciting dramatic verse, a sorcerer sent to ask me how much I would pay him to make certain that I won. I loathed and detested these foul rites and told him that even if the prize were a crown of gold that would last for ever, I would not let even a fly be killed to win it. For he would have slaughtered living animals in his ritual, and by means of these offerings he would have pretended to invoke the aid of his demons in my favour. But, O God of my heart, it was not from a pure love of you that I rejected this wickedness. I had not learnt how to love you, for when I thought of you I imagined you as some splendid being, but entirely physical. Does not the soul which pines for such fantasies *break its troth with you*?[1] Does it not trust in false hopes and *play shepherd to the wind*?[2] But while I would not let this man offer sacrifice for me to his devils, all the time I was offering myself as a sacrifice to them because of my false beliefs. For if we play shepherd to the wind, we find pasture for the devils, because by straying from the truth we give them food for laughter and fill their cup of pleasure.

---

[1] Ps. 72: 27 (73: 27). [2] Osee (Hosea) 12: 1.

3

The same reasoning did not prevent me from consulting those impostors, the astrologers, because I argued that they offered no sacrifices and said no prayers to any spirit to aid their divination. Nevertheless, true Christian piety rightly rejects and condemns what they do. For *sweet it is to praise the Lord*[1] and say *Have mercy on me; bring healing to a soul that has sinned against you.*[2] And it is wrong to impose upon your readiness to forgive, taking it as licence to commit sin. Instead we must remember Our Lord's words to the cripple: *You have recovered your strength. Do not sin any more, for fear that worse should befall you.*[3] This truth is our whole salvation, but the astrologers try to do away with it. They tell us that the cause of sin is determined in the heavens and we cannot escape it, and that this or that is the work of Venus or Saturn or Mars. They want us to believe that man is guiltless, flesh and blood though he is and doomed to die despite his pride. Instead they have it that the blame is to be laid on the Creator and Ruler of the heavens and the stars, none other than our God, himself the very source of justice, from whom its sweetness is derived – on you, O God, who *will award to every man what his acts have deserved*,[4] you who *will never disdain a heart that is humbled and contrite.*[5]

There was at that time a man of deep understanding, who had an excellent reputation for his great skill as a doctor. As he was pro-consul at the time, his was the hand that laid upon my head the wreath I won in the poetry competition, but it was not a doctor's hand that could cure my disordered state of mind. This is a disease that only you can cure, you who *thwart the proud and keep your grace for the humble.*[6] But you did not fail to use even that old man to help me, nor did you cease to give my soul through him the medicine which it needed. He and I became better acquainted and I listened intently and without fail to what he had to say, for though he was not a gifted speaker, his lively mind gave weight and charm to his words. In the course of our conversation he learned that I was an enthusiast for books of astrology, and in a kind and fatherly way he advised me to throw them away and waste no further pains upon such rubbish, because there were other more valuable things to be done. He said

[1] Ps. 91: 2 (92: 1).   [2] Ps. 40: 5 (41: 4).   [3] John 5: 14.
[4] Rom. 2: 6.   [5] Ps. 50: 19 (51: 17).   [6] 1 Pet. 5: 5.

that as a young man he had studied astrology himself, intending to make a living by it, and that if he could understand Hippocrates I need not doubt that he had been able to master these textbooks as well. All the same, after a time he had given them up and taken to medicine instead, for the very good reason that he had found out that they were entirely wrong, and, being an honest man, he had no wish to earn his living by deception. 'But you can support yourself by your rhetoric', he went on. 'Your interest in this trickery is mere curiosity and you do not have to depend upon it for a living. All the more reason, then, why you should believe what I say, because, as it was to be my only means of support, I tried to learn as much about it as I could.'

I asked him why it was then that the future was often correctly foretold by means of astrology. He gave me the only possible answer, that it was all due to the power of chance, a force that must always be reckoned with in the natural order. He said that people sometimes opened a book of poetry at random, and although the poet had been thinking, as he wrote, of some quite different matter, it often happened that the reader placed his finger on a verse which had a remarkable bearing on his problem. It was not surprising, then, that the mind of man, quite unconsciously, through some instinct not within its own control, should hit upon some thing that answered to the circumstances and the facts of a particular question. If so, it would be due to chance not to skill.

This answer which he gave me, or rather which I heard from his lips, must surely have come from you, my God. By means of it you imprinted on my mind doubts which I was to remember later, when I came to argue these matters out for myself. But at that time neither he nor my great friend, Nebridius – a young man of high principles and unexceptionable character, who ridiculed the whole business of soothsaying – could persuade me to give it up. I thought that the authors of the books made out a better case, and I had as yet found no evidence as positive as I required to prove beyond doubt that when the astrologers were found to be right, it was due to luck or pure chance and not to their skill in reading the stars.

4

During those years, when I first began to teach in Thagaste, my native town, I had found a very dear friend. We were both the same age, both together in the heyday of youth, and both absorbed in the same interests. We had grown up together as boys, gone to school together, and played together. Yet ours was not the friendship which should be between true friends, either when we were boys or at this later time. For though they cling together, no friends are true friends unless you, my God, bind them fast to one another through that love which is sown in our hearts by the Holy Ghost, who is given to us. Yet there was sweetness in our friendship, mellowed by the interests we shared. As a boy he had never held firmly or deeply to the true faith and I had drawn him away from it to believe in the same superstitious, soul-destroying fallacies which brought my mother to tears over me. Now, as a man, he was my companion in error and I was utterly lost without him. Yet in a moment, before we had reached the end of the first year of a friendship that was sweeter to me than all the joys of life as I lived it then, you took him from this world. For you are the God of vengeance[1] as well as the fountain of mercy. You follow close behind the fugitive and recall us to yourself in ways we cannot understand.

No man can count your praises, even though he is but one man and reckons only the blessings he has received in his own life. How can I understand what you did at that time, my God? How can I plumb the unfathomable depth of your judgement? My friend fell gravely ill of a fever. His senses were numbed as he lingered in the sweat of death, and when all hope of saving him was lost, he was baptized as he lay unconscious. I cared nothing for this, because I chose to believe that his soul would retain what it had learnt from me, no matter what was done to his body when it was deprived of sense. But no such thing happened. New life came into him and he recovered. And as soon as I could talk to him – which was as soon as he could talk to me, for I never left his side since we were so dependent on each other – I tried to chaff him about his baptism, thinking that he too would make fun of it, since he had received it when he was quite incapable of thought or feeling. But by this time he had

[1] See Ps. 93: 1 (94: 1).

been told of it. He looked at me in horror as though I were an enemy, and in a strange, new-found attitude of self-reliance he warned me that if I wished to be his friend, I must never speak to him like that again. I was astonished and confused, but I did not tell him what I felt, hoping that when he was better and had recovered his strength, he would be in a condition to listen to what I had to say. But he was rescued from my folly and taken into your safe keeping, for my later consolation. For a few days after this, while I was away from him, the fever returned and he died.

My heart grew sombre with grief, and wherever I looked I saw only death. My own country became a torment and my own home a grotesque abode of misery. All that we had done together was now a grim ordeal without him. My eyes searched everywhere for him, but he was not there to be seen. I hated all the places we had known together, because he was not in them and they could no longer whisper to me 'Here he comes!'as they would have done had he been alive but absent for a while. I had become a puzzle to myself, asking my soul again and again 'Why are you downcast? Why do you distress me?'[1] But my soul had no answer to give. If I said 'Wait for God's help',[1] she did not obey. And in this she was right because, to her, the well-loved man whom she had lost was better and more real than the shadowy being in whom I would have her trust. Tears alone were sweet to me, for in my heart's desire they had taken the place of my friend.

5

But now, O Lord, all this is past and time has healed the wound. Let the ears of my heart move close to your lips, and let me listen to you, who are the Truth, so that you may tell me why tears are sweet to the sorrowful. Can it be that though you are present everywhere, you have thrust aside our troubles? You are steadfast, constant in yourself; but we are tossed on a tide that puts us to the proof, and if we could not sob our troubles in your ear, what hope should we have left to us? How then can it be that there is sweetness in the fruit we pluck from the bitter crop of life, in the mourning and the tears, the wailing and the sighs? Does their sweetness spring from hope, the hope that you will hear them? When we pray, this is truly so, because

[1] See Ps. 41: 12 (42: 12).

it is the purpose of prayer to reach your ear. But is it also true of sorrow for the things we lose and mourning such as then became my cloak? I had no hope that he would come to life again, nor was this what I begged for through my tears: I simply grieved and wept, for I was heartbroken and had lost my joy. Or is weeping, too, a bitter thing, becoming a pleasure only when the things we once enjoyed turn loathsome and only as long as our dislike for them remains?

6

But why do I talk of these things? It is time to confess, not to question. I lived in misery, like every man whose soul is tethered by the love of things that cannot last and then is agonized to lose them. Only then does he realize the sorry state he is in, and was in even before his loss. In such a state was I at that time, as I wept bitter tears and found my only consolation in their very bitterness. This was the misery in which I lived, and yet my own wretched life was dearer to me than the friend I had lost. Gladly though I would have changed it, I was more loth to lose my life than I had been to lose my friend. True or not, the story goes that Orestes and Pylades were ready to die together for each other's sake, because each would rather die than live without the other. But I doubt whether I should have been willing, as they were, to give my life for my friend. I was obsessed by a strange feeling, quite the opposite of theirs, for I was sick and tired of living and yet afraid to die. I suppose that the great love which I had for my friend made me hate and fear death all the more, as though it were the most terrible of enemies, because it had snatched him away from me. I thought that, just as it had seized him, it would seize all others too without warning. I still remember how these thoughts filled my mind.

My heart lies before you, O my God. Look deep within. See these memories of mine, for you are my hope. You cleanse me when unclean humours such as these possess me, by drawing my eyes to yourself and *saving my feet from the snare*.[1]

I wondered that other men should live when he was dead, for I had loved him as though he would never die. Still more I wondered that he should die and I remain alive, for I was his second self. How well

[1] Ps. 24: 15 (25: 15).

the poet put it when he called his friend the half of his soul![1] I felt that our two souls had been as one, living in two bodies, and life to me was fearful because I did not want to live with only half a soul. Perhaps this, too, is why I shrank from death, for fear that one whom I had loved so well might then be wholly dead.

7

What madness, to love a man as something more than human! What folly, to grumble at the lot man has to bear! I lived in a fever, convulsed with tears and sighs that allowed me neither rest nor peace of mind. My soul was a burden, bruised and bleeding. It was tired of the man who carried it, but I found no place to set it down to rest. Neither the charm of the countryside nor the sweet scents of a garden could soothe it. It found no peace in song or laughter, none in the company of friends at table or in the pleasures of love, none even in books or poetry. Everything that was not what my friend had been was dull and distasteful. I had heart only for sighs and tears, for in them alone I found some shred of consolation. But if I tried to stem my tears, a heavy load of misery weighed me down. I knew, Lord, that I ought to offer it up to you, for you would heal it. But this I would not do, nor could I, especially as I did not think of you as anything real and substantial. It was not you that I believed in, but some empty figment. The god I worshipped was my own delusion, and if I tried to find in it a place to rest my burden, there was nothing there to uphold it. It only fell and weighed me down once more, so that I was still my own unhappy prisoner, unable to live in such a state yet powerless to escape from it. Where could my heart find refuge from itself? Where could I go, yet leave myself behind? Was there any place where I should not be a prey to myself? None. But I left my native town. For my eyes were less tempted to look for my friend in a place where they had not grown used to seeing him. So from Thagaste I went to Carthage.

8

Time never stands still, nor does it idly pass without effect upon our feelings or fail to work its wonders on the mind. It came and went,

[1] Horace, *Odes* I, 3: 8.

day after day, and as it passed it filled me with fresh hope and new thoughts to remember. Little by little it pieced me together again by means of the old pleasures which I had once enjoyed. My sorrow gave way to them. But it was replaced, if not by sorrow of another kind, by things which held the germ of sorrow still to come. For the grief I felt for the loss of my friend had struck so easily into my inmost heart simply because I had poured out my soul upon him, like water upon sand, loving a man who was mortal as though he were never to die. My greatest comfort and relief was in the solace of other friends who shared my love of the huge fable which I loved instead of you, my God, the long-drawn lie which our minds were always *itching to hear*,[1] only to be defiled by its adulterous caress.

But if one of my friends died, the fable did not die with him. And friendship had other charms to captivate my heart. We could talk and laugh together and exchange small acts of kindness. We could join in the pleasure that books can give. We could be grave or gay together. If we sometimes disagreed, it was without spite, as a man might differ with himself, and the rare occasions of dispute were the very spice to season our usual accord. Each of us had something to learn from the others and something to teach in return. If any were away, we missed them with regret and gladly welcomed them when they came home. Such things as these are heartfelt tokens of affection between friends. They are signs to be read on the face and in the eyes, spoken by the tongue and displayed in countless acts of kindness. They can kindle a blaze to melt our hearts and weld them into one.

9

This is what we cherish in friendship, and we cherish it so dearly that in conscience we feel guilty if we do not return love for love, asking no more of our friends than these expressions of goodwill. This is why we mourn their death, which shrouds us in sorrow and turns joy into bitterness, so that the heart is drenched in tears and life becomes a living death because a friend is lost. Blessed are those who love you, O God, and love their friends in you and their enemies for your sake. They alone will never lose those who are dear to them, for they love them in one who is never lost, in God, our God who

[1] II Tim. 4: 3.

made heaven and earth and fills them with his presence, because by filling them he made them. No one can lose you, my God, unless he forsakes you. And if he forsakes you, where is he to go? If he abandons your love, his only refuge is your wrath. Wherever he turns, he will find your law to punish him, for your law is the truth and the truth is yourself.

10

O God of hosts, restore us to our own; smile upon us, and we shall find deliverance.[1] For wherever the soul of man may turn, unless it turns to you, it clasps sorrow to itself. Even though it clings to things of beauty, if their beauty is outside God and outside the soul, it only clings to sorrow.

Yet these things of beauty would not exist at all unless they came from you. Like the sun, they rise and set. At their rise they have their first beginning; they grow until they reach perfection; but, once they have reached it, they grow old and die. Not all reach old age, but all alike must die. When they rise, therefore, they are set upon the course of their existence, and the faster they climb towards its zenith, the more they hasten towards the point where they exist no more. This is the law they obey. This is all that you have appointed for them, because they are parts of a whole. Not all the parts exist at once, but some must come as others go, and in this way together they make up the whole of which they are the parts. Our speech follows the same rule, using sounds to signify a meaning. For a sentence is not complete unless each word, once its syllables have been pronounced, gives way to make room for the next. Let my soul praise you for these things, O God, Creator of them all; but the love of them, which we feel, through the senses of the body, must not be like glue to bind my soul to them. For they continue on the course that is set for them and leads to their end, and if the soul loves them and wishes to be with them and find its rest in them, it is torn by desires that can destroy it. In these things there is no place to rest, because they do not last. They pass away beyond the reach of our senses. Indeed, none of us can lay firm hold of them even when they are with us. For the senses of the body are sluggish, because they are the senses of flesh and blood. They are limited by their own nature. They are sufficient for the purposes

[1] Ps. 79: 8 (80: 7).

for which they were made, but they cannot halt the progress of transient things, which pass from their allotted beginning to their allotted end. All such things are created by your word, which tells them 'Here is your beginning and here your end'.

11

My soul, you too must listen to the word of God. Do not be foolish; do not let the din of your folly deafen the ears of your heart. For the Word himself calls you to return. In him is the place of peace that cannot be disturbed, and he will not withhold himself from your love unless you withhold your love from him. In this world one thing passes away so that another may take its place and the whole be preserved in all its parts. 'But do I pass away elsewhere?' says the Word of God. Make your dwelling in him, my soul. Entrust to him whatever you have, for all that you have is from him. Now, at last, tired of being misled, entrust to the Truth all that the Truth has given to you and nothing will be lost. All that is withered in you will be made to thrive again. All your sickness will be healed. Your mortal body will be refashioned and renewed and firmly bound to you, and when it dies it will not drag you with it to the grave, but will endure and abide with you before God, who abides and endures for ever.

My soul, why do you face about and follow the lead of the flesh? Turn forward, and let it follow you! Whatever you feel through the senses of the flesh you only feel in part. It delights you, but it is only a part and you have no knowledge of the whole. To punish you this just limit has been fixed for the senses of your body. But if this were not so and they could comprehend the whole, you would wish that whatever exists in the present should pass on, so that you might gain greater pleasure from the whole. It is one of these same bodily senses that enables you to hear the words I speak, but you do not want the syllables to sound for ever in my mouth: you want them to fly from my tongue and give place to others, so that you may hear the whole of what I have to say. It is always the same with the parts that together make a whole. They are not present at the same time, but if they can all be felt as one, together they give more pleasure than each single part. But far better than these is he who made them all, our God. He does not pass away, because there is none to take his place.

If the things of this world delight you, praise God for them but turn your love away from them and give it to their Maker, so that in the things that please you you may not displease him. If your delight is in souls, love them in God, because they too are frail and stand firm only when they cling to him. If they do not, they go their own way and are lost. Love them, then, in him and draw as many with you to him as you can. Tell them 'He is the one we should love. He made the world and he stays close to it.' For when he made the world he did not go away and leave it. By him it was created and in him it exists. Wherever we taste the truth, God is there. He is in our very inmost hearts, but our hearts have strayed from him. *Think well on it, unbelieving hearts*[1] and cling to him who made you. Stand with him and you shall not fall; rest in him and peace shall be yours. What snags and pitfalls lie before you? Where do your steps lead you? The good things which you love are all from God, but they are good and sweet only as long as they are used to do his will. They will rightly turn bitter if God is spurned and the things that come from him are wrongly loved. Why do you still choose to travel by this hard and arduous path? There is no rest to be found where you seek it. In the land of death you try to find a happy life: it is not there. How can life be happy where there is no life at all?

Our Life himself came down into this world and took away our death. He slew it with his own abounding life, and with thunder in his voice he called us from this world to return to him in heaven. From heaven he came down to us, entering first the Virgin's womb, where humanity, our mortal flesh, was wedded to him so that it might not be for ever mortal. Then *as a bridegroom coming from his bed, he exulted like some great runner who sees the track before him.*[2] He did not linger on his way but ran, calling us to return to him, calling us by his words and deeds, by his life and death, by his descent into hell and his ascension into heaven. He departed from our sight, so that we should turn to our hearts and find him there. He departed, but he is here with us. He would not stay long with us, but he did not leave us. He went back to the place which he had never left, because *he, through whom the world was made, was in the world*[3] and he *came into the world to save*

---

[1] Is. 46: 8.   [2] Ps. 18: 6 (19: 5).   [3] John 1: 10.

sinners.[1] To him my soul confesses and he is its Healer, because the wrong it did was against him. *Great ones of the world, will your hearts always be hardened?*[2] Your Life has come down from heaven: will you not now at last rise with him and live? But how can you rise if you are in high places and your *clamour reaches heaven?*[3] Come down from those heights, for then you may climb and, this time, climb to God. To climb against him was your fall.

My soul, tell this to the souls that you love. Let them weep in this valley of tears, and so take them with you to God. For if, as you speak, the flame of charity burns in you, it is by his Spirit that you tell them this.

13

I did not know this then. I was in love with beauty of a lower order and it was dragging me down. I used to ask my friends 'Do we love anything unless it is beautiful? What, then, is beauty and in what does it consist? What is it that attracts us and wins us over to the things we love? Unless there were beauty and grace in them, they would be powerless to win our hearts.' When I looked at things, it struck me that there was a difference between the beauty of an object considered by itself as one whole and the beauty to be found in a proper proportion between separate things, such as the due balance between the whole of the body and any of its limbs, or between the foot and the shoe with which it is shod, and so on. This idea burst from my heart like water from a spring. My mind was full of it and I wrote a book called *Beauty and Proportion*, in two or three volumes as far as I remember. You know how many there were, O Lord. I have forgotten, because by some chance the book was lost and I no longer have it.

14

O Lord, my God, what induced me to dedicate my book to Hierius, the great public speaker at Rome? I had never even seen him, but I admired his brilliant reputation for learning and had been greatly struck by what I had heard of his speeches. Even more than this I was impressed by the admiration which other people had for him. They overwhelmed him with praise, because it seemed extraordinary that

[1] 1 Tim. 1: 15. [2] Ps. 4: 3 (4: 2). [3] Ps. 72: 9 (73: 9).

a man born in Syria and originally trained to speak in Greek had later become so remarkable a speaker in Latin, and had also such a wealth of knowledge of the subjects studied by philosophers.

We can admire persons whom we have never seen, if we hear them praised, though this does not mean that simply to hear their praises will make us admire them. But enthusiasm in one man will kindle the same fire in another, for we admire the person whose praises we hear only if we believe that they are sincerely uttered – in other words that the person who utters them genuinely admires the man whom he praises.

In those days I admired people in this way, according to the judgements I heard of them from others, not according to your judgement my God, in whom no one is deceived. But I did not admire Hierius, in the way that I might have admired a famous charioteer or a popular contestant in the amphitheatre. My feeling for him and others like him was quite different. It was something quite serious, the kind of admiration that I should have liked to win for myself. Why was this? Though I liked actors and openly admired them, I should not have wanted their fame and popularity for myself. I would rather have been entirely unknown than known in the way that they were known. I would rather have been hated than loved as they were.

How can one soul contain within itself feelings so much at variance, in such conflict with each other? How does it balance them in the scale? Suppose that I like a certain quality in another man. Is it not inconsistent to loathe it in myself and reject it, since this can only mean that I detest it? Yet both of us are human beings. A man may admire a fine horse without wishing to be one himself, assuming that such a thing were possible. But with the actor the case is different, because both admirer and admired share the same nature. Can I, then, love in another what I should hate in myself, though both of us are human? Man is a great mystery, Lord. You even keep count of the hairs on his head and not one of them escapes your reckoning.[1] Yet his hairs are more easily counted than his feelings and the emotions of his heart.

But Hierius was the kind of man in whom I admired qualities that I would have been glad to possess. In my pride I was running adrift, at the mercy of every wind. You were guiding me as a helmsman steers a ship, but the course you steered was beyond my understanding. I know now, and confess it as the truth, that I admired Hierius

[1] See Matt. 10: 30.

more because others praised him than for the accomplishments for which they praised him. I know this because those same people, instead of praising him, might have abused him. They might have spoken of the same talents in him but found fault with them and despised them. If they had done this, my feelings would not have been aroused nor my admiration kindled. Yet his qualities would have been the same and he himself would have been no different. The only difference would have been in their attitude towards him.

We can see from this that the soul is weak and helpless unless it clings to the firm rock of truth. Men give voice to their opinions, but they are only opinions, like so many puffs of wind that waft the soul hither and thither and make it veer and turn. The light is clouded over and the truth cannot be seen, although it is there before our eyes. I thought it a matter of much importance to myself to bring my book and the work I had done to the notice of this great man. If he had approved of them, my fervour would have been all the more ardent. If he had found fault, my heart, which was empty and bereft of God's firm truth, would have suffered a cruel blow. Yet I found pleasure in giving my mind to the problem of beauty and proportion, the work which I had dedicated to him. Although I found no others to admire it, I was proud of it myself.

15

But I still did not see that the pivot upon which this important matter turns is the fact that it is all of your making, almighty God, for *you do wonderful deeds as none else.*[1] My thoughts ranged only amongst material forms. I defined them in two classes, those which please the eye because they are beautiful in themselves and those which do so because they are properly proportioned in relation to something else. I drew this distinction and illustrated it from material examples. I also gave some thought to the nature of the soul, but my misconception of spiritual things prevented me from seeing the truth, although it forced itself upon my mind if only I would see it. Instead I turned my pulsating mind away from the spiritual towards the material. I considered line and colour and shape, and since my soul had no such visible qualities, I argued that I could not see it.

[1] Ps. 71: 18 (72: 18).

I loved the peace that virtue brings and hated the discord that comes of vice. From this I concluded that in goodness there was unity, but in evil disunion of some kind. It seemed to me that this unity was the seat of the rational mind and was the natural state of truth and perfect goodness; whereas the disunion consisted of irrational life, which I thought of as a substance of some kind, and was the natural state of the ultimate evil. I was misguided enough to believe that evil, too, was not only a substance, but itself a form of life, although I did not think it had its origin in you, my God, *who are the origin of all things.*[1] I called the unity a 'monad', a kind of mind without sex, and the disunion a 'dyad', consisting of the anger that leads to crimes of violence and the lust that leads to sins of passion. But I did not know what I was saying, because no one had taught me, and I had not yet found out for myself, that evil is not a substance and man's mind is not the supreme good that does not vary.

Crimes against other men are committed when the emotions, which spur us to action, are corrupt and rise in revolt without control. Sins of self-indulgence are committed when the soul fails to govern the impulses from which it derives bodily pleasure. In the same way, if the rational mind is corrupt, mistaken ideas and false beliefs will poison life. In those days my mind was corrupt. I did not know that if it was to share in the truth, it must be illumined by another light, because the mind itself is not the essence of truth. For *it is you, Lord, that keep the lamp of my hopes still burning and shine on the darkness about me.*[2] *We have all received something out of your abundance.*[3] For *you are the true Light which enlightens every soul born into the world,*[4] because *with you there can be no change, no swerving from your course.*[5]

I was struggling to reach you, but you thrust me back so that I knew the taste of death. For *you thwart the proud.*[6] And what greater pride could there be than to assert, as I did in my strange madness, that by nature I was what you are? I was changeable, and I knew it; for if I wanted to be a learned man, it could only mean that I wanted to be better than I was. All the same I preferred to think that you too were changeable rather than suppose that I was not what you are. This was why you thrust me back and crushed my rearing pride,

[1] I Cor. 8: 6.　　[2] Ps. 17: 29 (18: 28).　　[3] John 1: 16.
[4] John 1: 9.　　[5] James: 17.　　[6] I Pet. 5: 5.

while my imagination continued to play on material forms. Myself a man of flesh and blood I blamed the flesh. I was as fickle as *a breath of wind*,[1] unable to return to you. I drifted on, making my way towards things that had no existence in you or in myself or in the body. They were not created for me by your truth but were the inventions of my own foolish imagination working on material things. Though I did not know it, I was in exile from my place in God's city among his faithful children, my fellow citizens. But I was all words, and stupidly I used to ask them, 'If, as you say, God made the soul, why does it err?' Yet I did not like them to ask me in return, 'If what you say is true, why does God err?' So I used to argue that your unchangeable substance, my God, was forced to err, rather than admit that my own was changeable and erred of its own free will, and that its errors were my punishment.

At the time when I wrote the book I was about twenty-six or twenty-seven years old. Sweet Truth, although I was straining to catch the sound of your secret melody, I deafened the ears of my heart by allowing my mind to twist and turn among these material inventions of my imagination. As I pondered over beauty and proportion, all the time I wanted to stand still and listen to you and *rejoice at hearing the bridegroom's voice*,[2] the voice of the Bridegroom of my soul; but this I could not do, because the voice of my own error called me away from him and I was dragged down and down by the weight of my own pride. You sent me no *tidings of good news and rejoicing*, nor did my body *thrill with pride*, for it had not been laid *in the dust*.[3]

16

When I was only about twenty years of age Aristotle's book on the 'Ten Categories' came into my hands. Whenever my teacher at Carthage and others who were reputed to be scholars mentioned this book, their cheeks would swell with self-importance, so that the title alone was enough to make me stand agape, as though I were poised over some wonderful divine mystery. I managed to read it and understand it without help, though I now ask myself what advantage I gained from doing so. Other people told me that they had understood it only with difficulty, after the most learned masters had not

[1] Ps. 77: 39 (78: 39).   [2] John 3: 29.   [3] Ps. 50: 10 (51: 8).

only explained it to them but also illustrated it with a wealth of diagrams. But when I discussed it with them, I found that they could tell me no more about it than I had already discovered by reading it on my own.

The meaning of the book seemed clear enough to me. It defined *substance*, such as man, and its attributes. For instance, a man has a certain shape; this is *quality*. He has height, measured in feet, which is *quantity*. He has *relation* to other men; for example, he is another man's brother. You may say *where* he is and *when* he was born, or describe his *position* as standing or sitting. You may name his *possessions* by saying that he has shoes or carries arms. You may define *what he does* and *what is done to him*. I have mentioned these examples, but there are countless others, all falling into these nine categories or the main category of substance.

What profit did this study bring me? None. In fact it made difficulties for me, because I thought that everything that existed could be reduced to these ten categories, and I therefore attempted to understand you, my God, in all your wonderful immutable simplicity, in these same terms, as though you too were substance, and greatness and beauty were your attributes in the same way that a body has attributes by which it is defined. But your greatness and beauty are your own self: whereas a body is not great or beautiful simply because it is a body. It would still be a body, even if it were less great or less beautiful. My conception of you was quite untrue, a mere falsehood. It was a fiction based on my own wretched state, not the firm foundation of your bliss. It was your command that *the ground should yield me thorns and thistles*[1] and that I should *earn my bread with the sweat of my brow*.[2] And your word was accomplished in me.

I read and understood by myself all the books that I could find on the so-called liberal arts, for in those days I was a good-for-nothing and a slave to sordid ambitions. But what advantage did I gain from them? I read them with pleasure, but I did not know the real source of such true and certain facts as they contained. I had my back to the light and my face was turned towards the things which it illumined, so that my eyes, by which I saw the things which stood in the light, were themselves in darkness. Without great difficulty and without

[1] Gen. 3: 18.   [2] Gen. 3: 19.

need of a teacher I understood all that I read on the arts of rhetoric and logic, on geometry, music, and mathematics. You know this, O Lord my God, because if a man is quick to understand and his perception is keen, he has these gifts from you. But since I made no offering of them to you, it did me more harm than good to struggle to keep in my own power so large a part of what you had given to me and, instead of preserving my strength for you,[1] to leave you and *go to a far country*[2] to squander your gifts on loves that sold themselves for money. For what good to me was my ability, if I did not use it well? And ability I had, for until I tried to instruct others I did not realize that these subjects are very difficult to master, even for pupils who are studious and intelligent, and a student who could follow my instruction without faltering was reckoned a very fine scholar.

But what value did I gain from my reading as long as I thought that you, Lord God who are the Truth, were a bright, unbounded body and I a small piece broken from it? What utter distortion of the truth! Yet this was my belief; and I do not now blush to acknowledge, my God, the mercies you have shown to me, nor to call you to my aid, just as in those days I did not blush to declare my blasphemies aloud and snarl at you like a dog. What, then, was the value to me of my intelligence, which could take these subjects in its stride, and all those books, with their tangled problems, which I unravelled without the help of any human tutor, when in the doctrine of your love I was lost in the most hideous error and the vilest sacrilege? And was it so great a drawback to your faithful children that they were slower than I to understand such things? For they did not forsake you, but grew like fledglings in the safe nest of your Church, nourishing the wings of charity on the food of the faith that would save them.

O Lord our God, let *the shelter of your wings*[3] give us hope. Protect us and uphold us. You will be the Support that upholds us from childhood till the hair on our heads is grey.[4] When you are our strength we are strong, but when our strength is our own we are weak. In you our good abides for ever, and when we turn away from it we turn to evil. Let us come home at last to you, O Lord, for fear

---

[1] See Ps. 58: 10 (59: 9).   [2] Luke 15: 13.   [3] Ps. 16: 8 (17: 8).
[4] See Is. 46: 4.

that we be lost. For in you our good abides and it has no blemish, since it is yourself. Nor do we fear that there is no home to which we can return. We fell from it; but our home is your eternity and it does not fall because we are away.

BOOK V

I

Accept my confessions, O Lord. They are a sacrifice offered by my tongue, for yours was the hand that fashioned it and yours the spirit that moved it to acknowledge you. Heal all my bones and let them say *Lord, there is none like you.*[1]

If a man confesses to you, he does not reveal his inmost thoughts to you as though you did not know them. For the heart may shut itself away, but it cannot hide from your sight. Man's heart may be hard, but it cannot resist the touch of your hand. Whenever you will, your mercy or your punishment can make it relent, and just as none can hide away from the sun, *none can escape your burning heat.*[2]

Let my soul praise you, so that it may show its love; and let it make avowal of your mercies, so that for these it may praise you. No part of your creation ever ceases to resound in praise of you. Man turns his lips to you in prayer and his spirit praises you. Animals too and lifeless things as well praise you through the lips of all who give them thought. For our souls lean for support upon the things which you have created, so that we may be lifted up to you from our weakness and use them to help us on our way to you who made them all so wonderfully. And in you we are remade and find true strength.

2

Let the wicked go upon their way and fly from you, for they know no rest. But your eye can pierce the darkness; you can see them. All the world about them teems with beauty and they alone defile it. What harm have they been able to inflict on you? Have they been able to bring disgrace upon your rule, which reaches in its indivisible justice from the heights of heaven to the meanest things of earth? Where did they find refuge when they turned from your face and

[1] Ps. 34: 10 (35: 10).   [2] Ps. 18: 7 (19: 6).

fled? What hiding place can they find where you cannot seek them out? They have fled and hidden their eyes from you, knowing that yours are on them. They are blind and do not see the God they have offended; but you are there, because you abandon no part of your creation. They have offended against your justice and for this they have justly suffered, because they have stolen away from your gentle mercy and sinned against your law, and so they have fallen down upon your anger.

Clearly the wicked do not know that you are everywhere. But you are not bound within the limits of any place. You alone are always present, even to those who set themselves apart from you. Let them then turn back and look for you. They will find that you have not deserted your creatures as they have deserted their Creator. Let them turn back, and they will find you in their hearts, in the hearts of all who confess to you and throw themselves upon your mercy, in the hearts of all who have left the hard path and come to weep upon your breast. Gently you wipe away their tears. They weep the more, but now their tears are tears of joy, because it is not some man of flesh and blood but you, O Lord, their Maker, who remakes them and consoles them.

But where was I when I looked for you? You were there before my eyes, but I had deserted even my own self. I could not find myself, much less find you.

3

In the sight of my God I will describe the twenty-ninth year of my age.

A Manichean bishop named Faustus had recently arrived at Carthage. He was a great decoy of the devil and many people were trapped by his charming manner of speech. This I certainly admired, but I was beginning to distinguish between mere eloquence and the real truth, which I was so eager to learn. The Manichees talked so much about this man Faustus that I wanted to see what scholarly fare he would lay before me, and I did not care what words he used to garnish the dish. I had already heard that he was very well versed in all the higher forms of learning and particularly in the liberal sciences.

I had read a great many scientific books which were still alive in my memory. When I compared them with the tedious tales of the

Manichees, it seemed to me that, of the two, the theories of the scientists were the more likely to be true. For *their thoughts could reach far enough to form a judgement about the world around them*, though *they found no trace of him who is Master of it.*[1] You, Lord, *who are so high above us, yet look with favour on the humble, look on the proud too, but from far off.*[2] You come close only to men who are humble at heart.[3] The proud cannot find you, even though by dint of study they have skill to number stars and grains of sand, to measure the tracts of constellations and trace the paths of planets.

The reason and understanding by which they investigate these things are gifts they have from you. By means of them they have discovered much and foretold eclipses of the sun and moon many years before they happened. They calculated the day and the hour of the eclipse, and whether it would be total or partial, and their reckonings were found correct because it all happened as they had predicted. They wrote down the principles which they had discovered, and their books are still read and used to forecast the year, the month, the day, and the hour of eclipses of the sun and moon, and the degree of their totality. And these eclipses will take place just as they foretell.

These powers are a source of wonder and astonishment to men who do not know the secrets. But the astronomers are flattered and claim the credit for themselves. They lapse into pride without respect for you, my God, and fall into shadow away from your light, but although they can predict an eclipse of the sun so far ahead, they cannot see that they themselves are already in the shadow of eclipse. This is because they ignore you and do not inquire how they come to possess the intelligence to make these researches. Even when they discover that it was you who made them, they do not submit to you so that you may preserve what you have made, nor, such as their own efforts have made them, do they offer themselves to you in sacrifice. Their conceit soars like a bird; their curiosity probes the deepest secrets of nature like a fish that swims in the sea; and their lust grows fat like a beast at pasture. But they slaughter none of these. Yet if they make this sacrifice to you, O God, you are the consuming fire that can burn away their love for these things and re-create the men in immortal life.

They do not know Christ, who is the Way and the Word of God,

[1] Wisdom 13: 9.   [2] Ps. 137: 6 (138: 6).   [3] See Ps. 33: 19 (34: 18).

by which you created all the things which they number and count, the very men who count them, the senses by which they are aware of what they count, and the intelligence by which they count them. *Your wisdom is inscrutable*,[1] but your only-begotten Son was given to us to be *our wisdom, our justification, and our sanctification*.[2] He was counted as one of our number and he paid his dues to Caesar. Yet these men do not know that he is the way by which they must come down from the heights where they have set themselves and rise again, with him, to be with him. They do not know this way, but think themselves as high and as bright as the stars; and this is why they have fallen to earth and *their senseless hearts grow benighted*.[3] Much of what they say about the created world is true, but they do not search with piety for the Truth, its Creator. This is why they do not find him; or, if they do find him and *have the knowledge of God, they do not honour him or give thanks to him as God; they become fantastic in their notions; they, who claim to be so wise*,[3] attribute to themselves what is yours, and in the same perverse blindness they try to ascribe their own qualities to you. They even attribute falsehoods to you who are Truth itself. *They exchange the glory of the imperishable God for representations of perishable man, of bird and beast and reptile. They exchange your truth for a lie, reverencing and worshipping the creature in preference to the Creator*.[3]

All the same I remembered many of the true things that they had said about the created world, and I saw that their calculations were borne out by mathematics, the regular succession of the seasons and the visible evidence of the stars. I compared it all with the teaching of Manes, who had written a great deal on these subjects, all of it extremely incoherent. But in his writings I could find no reasonable explanation of the solstices and the equinoxes or of eclipses and similar phenomena such as I had read about in books written by secular scientists. Yet I was expected to believe what he had written, although it was entirely at variance and out of keeping with the principles of mathematics and the evidence of my own eyes.

4

O Lord God of truth, if a man is to please you, surely it is not enough that he should know facts like these? Even if he knows them all, he is

[1] Ps. 146: 5 (147: 5).   [2] I Cor. 1: 30.   [3] Rom. 1: 21-5.

not happy unless he knows you; but the man who knows you is happy, even if he knows none of these things. And the man who knows you, and knows these things as well, is none the happier for his knowledge of them: he is happy only because he knows you, and then only if *he has knowledge of you and honours you and gives you thanks as God* and does not *become fantastic in his notions.*[1]

A man who knows that he owns a tree and thanks you for the use he has of it, even though he does not know its exact height or the width of its spread, is better than another who measures it and counts all its branches, but neither owns it nor knows and loves its Creator. In just the same way, a man who has faith in you owns all the wealth of the world, for if he clings to you, whom all things serve, though he has nothing yet he owns them all. It would be foolish to doubt that such a man, though he may not know the track of the Great Bear, is altogether better than another who measures the sky and counts the stars and weighs the elements, but neglects you who allot to all things their size, their number, and their weight.[2]

5

But who asked that any Manichee should write about science as well as religion, when we can learn our duty to God without a knowledge of these things? For you have told man that *wisdom is fearing the Lord.*[3] Even if Manes did not have this true wisdom, he could still have had a very good knowledge of science; but as he knew no science and yet had the effrontery to try to teach it, he could not possibly have had true wisdom. For it is sheer vanity for a man to profess his learning, even if it is well founded, whereas it is his duty to you, O God, to confess his sins. Manes departed from this duty. He wrote at great length on scientific subjects, only to be proved wrong by genuine scientists, thereby making perfectly clear the true nature of his insight into more abstruse matters. Because he did not want them to think lightly of him, he tried to convince his followers that the Holy Spirit, who comforts and enriches your faithful servants, was present in him personally and with full powers. Therefore, when he was shown to be wrong in what he said about the sky and the stars and the movements of the sun and the moon, it was obvious that he was guilty of

[1] Rom. 1: 21.   [2] See Wisdom 11: 21.   [3] Job 28: 28.

sacrilegious presumption, because, although these matters are no part of religious doctrine, he was not only ignorant of the subjects which he taught, but also taught what was false, yet was demented and conceited enough to claim that his utterances were those of a divine person.

Whenever I hear a brother Christian talk in such a way as to show that he is ignorant of these scientific matters and confuses one thing with another, I listen with patience to his theories and think it no harm to him that he does not know the true facts about material things, provided that he holds no beliefs unworthy of you, O Lord, who are the Creator of them all. The danger lies in thinking that such knowledge is part and parcel of what he must believe to save his soul and in presuming to make obstinate declarations about things of which he knows nothing. Yet, when a man first enters the cradle of the faith, Charity, his mother, will show indulgence even to failings of this sort, until the new man *reaches perfect manhood* and cannot be *driven before the wind of each new doctrine*.[1] But Manes dared to pose as teacher, sole authority, guide, and leader of all whom he could convince of his theories, leading his followers to believe that they were following no ordinary man, but your Holy Spirit. Surely, then, once he had been detected in error, everyone would agree that he was a madman and that his claims were repugnant and should be entirely rejected?

All the same I was not yet entirely satisfied that his writings might not contain a plausible explanation of the variations in the length of the day and the night, the alternation of night and day, eclipses, and the other phenomena of which I had read elsewhere. If his theories were admissible, I should have been undecided whether he or the scientists were right, but I might have chosen to accept his authority because of his reputed sanctity.

6

For almost the whole of those nine years during which my mind was unsettled and I was an aspirant of the Manichees, I awaited the coming of this man Faustus with the keenest expectation. Other members of the sect whom I happened to meet were unable to answer the questions I raised upon these subjects, but they assured me that once

[1] Eph. 4: 13, 14.

Faustus had arrived I had only to discuss them with him and he would have no difficulty in giving me a clear explanation of my queries and any other more difficult problems which I might put forward.

At last he arrived. I found him a man of agreeable personality, with a pleasant manner of speech, who pattered off the usual Manichean arguments with a great deal more than the usual charm. But my thirst was not to be satisfied in this way, however precious the cup and however exquisite the man who served it. My ears were already ringing with these tales and they seemed to me none the better for being better expressed, nor true simply because they were eloquently told. Neither did I think that a pleasant face and a gifted tongue were proof of a wise mind. Those who had given me such assurances about him must have been poor judges. They thought him wise and thoughtful simply because they were charmed by his manner of speech.

I have known men of another sort, who look on truth with suspicion and are unwilling to accept it if it is presented in fine, rounded phrases. But in your wonderful, secret way, my God, you had already taught me that a statement is not necessarily true because it is wrapped in fine language or false because it is awkwardly expressed. I believe that it was you who taught me this, because it is the truth and there is no other teacher of the truth besides yourself, no matter how or where it comes to light. You had already taught me this lesson and the converse truth, that an assertion is not necessarily true because it is badly expressed or false because it is finely spoken. I had learnt that wisdom and folly are like different kinds of food. Some are wholesome and others are not, but both can be served equally well on the finest china dish or the meanest earthenware. In just the same way, wisdom and folly can be clothed alike in plain words or the finest flowers of speech.

My long and eager expectation of Faustus's arrival was amply rewarded by the way in which he set about the task of disputation and the goodwill that he showed. The ease with which he found the right words to clothe his thoughts delighted me, and I was not the only one to applaud it, though perhaps I did so more than most. But I found it tiresome, when so many people assembled to hear him, not to be allowed to approach him with my difficulties and lay them before him in the friendly give-and-take of conversation. As soon as the opportunity arose I and some of my friends claimed his attention at a time when a private discussion would not be inappropriate. I mentioned some of my doubts, but soon discovered that except for a rudimentary knowledge of literature he had no claims to scholarship. He had read some of Cicero's speeches, one or two books of Seneca, some poetry, and such books as had been written in good Latin by members of his sect. Besides his daily practice as a speaker, this reading was the basis of his eloquence, which derived extra charm and plausibility from his attractive personality and his ability to make good use of his mental powers.

O Lord my God, is this not the truth as I remember it? You are the Judge of my conscience, and my heart and my memory lie open before you. The secret hand of your providence guided me then, and you set my abject errors before my eyes so that I might see them and detest them.

7

As soon as it became clear to me that Faustus was quite uninformed about the subjects in which I had expected him to be an expert, I began to lose hope that he could lift the veil and resolve the problems which perplexed me. Of course, despite his ignorance of these matters he might still have been a truly pious man, provided he were not a Manichee. The Manichean books are full of the most tedious fictions about the sky and the stars, the sun and the moon. I badly wanted Faustus to compare these with the mathematical calculations which I had studied in other books, so that I might judge whether the Manichean theories were more likely to be true or, at least, equally probable, but I now began to realize that he could not give me a detailed explanation. When I suggested that we should consider these problems and discuss them together, he was certainly modest enough not to undertake the task. He knew that he did not know the answers to my questions and was not ashamed to admit it, for unlike many other talkative people whom I have had to endure, he would not try to teach me a lesson when he had nothing to say. He had a heart, and though his approach to you was mistaken, he was not without discretion. He was not entirely unaware of his limitations and did not want to enter rashly into an argument which might force him into a position which he could not possibly maintain and from which he could not easily withdraw. I liked him all the better for this, because modesty and candour are finer equipment for the mind than scientific knowledge of the kind that I wished to possess. I found that his attitude towards all the more difficult and abstruse questions was the same.

The keen interest which I had had in Manichean doctrines was checked by this experience, and my confidence in the other teachers of the sect was further diminished when I saw that Faustus, of whom they spoke so much, was obviously unable to settle the numerous problems which troubled me. His enthusiasm for literature, which I was then teaching to students at Carthage, often brought us together, and I set out to read with him either the books which he knew by repute and was eager to study or such works as I thought suitable for a man of his intelligence. But once I had come to know him well all my endeavours to make progress in the sect, as I had intended, were abandoned. I did not cut myself off entirely from the Manichees, but as I could find nothing better than the beliefs which I had stumbled upon more or less by chance, I decided to be content with them for the time being, unless something preferable clearly presented itself to me.

So it was that, unwittingly and without intent, Faustus who had been a deadly snare to many now began to release me from the trap in which I had been caught. For in the mystery of your providence, my God, your guiding hand did not desert me. Night and day my mother poured out her tears to you and offered her heart-blood in sacrifice for me, and in the most wonderful way you guided me. It was you who guided me, my God, for *man's feet stand firm, if the Lord is with him to prosper his journey*.[1] What else can save us but your hand, remaking what you have made?

8

It was, then, by your guidance that I was persuaded to go to Rome and teach there the subjects which I taught at Carthage. I will not omit to confess to you how I was persuaded to do this, because even in matters like these we need to reflect upon your sublime secrets and the mercy which you are always ready to show to us.

It was not because I could earn higher fees and greater honours that

[1] Ps. 36: 23 (37: 23).

I wanted to go to Rome, though these were the rewards promised me by my friends, who urged me to go. Naturally these considerations influenced me, but the most important reason, and almost the only one, was that I had heard that the behaviour of young students at Rome was quieter. Discipline was stricter and they were not permitted to rush insolently and just as they pleased into the lecture-rooms of teachers who were not their own masters. In fact they were not admitted at all without the master's permission. At Carthage, on the other hand, the students are beyond control and their behaviour is disgraceful. They come blustering into the lecture-rooms like a troop of maniacs and upset the orderly arrangements which the master has made in the interest of his pupils. Their recklessness is unbelievable and they often commit outrages which ought to be punished by law, were it not that custom protects them. Nevertheless, it is a custom which only proves their plight the more grievous, because it supposedly sanctions behaviour which your eternal law will never allow. They think that they do these things with impunity, but the very blindness with which they do them is punishment in itself and they suffer far more harm than they inflict.

As a student I had refused to take part in this behaviour, but as a teacher I was obliged to endure it in others. This was why I was glad to go to a place where, by all accounts, such disturbances did not occur. But it was to save my soul that you obliged me to go and live elsewhere, you who are *my only Refuge, all that is left me in this world of living men.*[1] You applied the spur that would drive me away from Carthage and offered me enticements that would draw me to Rome, and for your purpose you made use of men whose hearts were set upon this life of death, some acting like madmen, others promising me vain rewards. In secret you were using my own perversity and theirs to set my feet upon the right course. For those who upset my leisure were blind in their shameless violence, and those who tempted me to go elsewhere knew only the taste of worldly things. As for myself, life at Carthage was a real misery and I loathed it: but the happiness I hoped to find at Rome was not real happiness.

You knew, O God, why it was that I left one city and went to the other. But you did not make the reason clear either to me or to my mother. She wept bitterly to see me go and followed me to the

---

[1] Ps. 141: 6 (142: 5).

water's edge, clinging to me with all her strength in the hope that I would either come home or take her with me. I deceived her with the excuse that I had a friend whom I did not want to leave until the wind rose and his ship could sail. It was a lie, told to my own mother – and to such a mother, too! But you did not punish me for it, because you forgave me this sin also when in your mercy you kept me safe from the waters of the sea, laden though I was with detestable impurities, and preserved me to receive the water of your grace. This was the water that would wash me clean and halt the flood of tears with which my mother daily watered the ground as she bowed her head, praying to you for me.

But she would not go home without me and it was all I could do to persuade her to stay that night in a shrine dedicated to Saint Cyprian, not far from the ship. During the night, secretly, I sailed away, leaving her alone to her tears and her prayers. And what did she beg of you, my God, with all those tears, if not that you would prevent me from sailing? But you did not do as she asked you then. Instead, in the depth of your wisdom, you granted the wish that was closest to her heart. You did with me what she had always asked you to do. The wind blew and filled our sails, and the shore disappeared from sight. The next morning she was wild with grief, pouring her sighs and sorrows in your ear, because she thought you had not listened to her prayer. But you were letting my own desires carry me away on a journey that was to put an end to those same desires, and you used her too jealous love for her son as a scourge of sorrow for her just punishment. For as mothers do, and far more than most, she loved to have me with her, and she did not know what joys you had in store for her because of my departure. It was because she did not know this that she wept and wailed, and the torments which she suffered were proof that she had inherited the legacy of Eve, seeking in sorrow what with sorrow she had brought into the world. But at last she ceased upbraiding me for my deceit and my cruelty and turned again to you to offer her prayers for me. She went back to her house, and I went on to Rome.

9

At Rome I was at once struck down by illness, which all but carried me off to hell loaded with all the evil that I had committed against you, against myself, and against other men, a host of grave offences over and above the bond of original sin, by which we *all have died with Adam.*[1] You had not yet forgiven me any of these sins in Christ nor, on his cross, had he dissolved the enmity which my sins had earned me in your sight. How could he dissolve it on the cross if he were a mere phantom, as I believed? In so far, then, as I thought the death of his body unreal, the death of my own soul was real; and the life of my soul, because it doubted his death, was as false as the death of his flesh was true.

My fever rose. I came close to dying, close to losing my soul. For if I left this life, where else would I go but to the fiery torments which my deeds deserved in the justice of your law? My mother did not know that I was ill, yet far away she continued to pray for me. But you are present everywhere. Where she was you listened to her prayers, and where I was you had mercy on me, so that I regained my bodily health, though my blasphemous heart was still diseased. For despite my great danger I had no desire to be baptized. As a boy I had been better, for I had appealed to my mother's piety and begged her to let me be baptized, as I have already recalled in these confessions. But I had grown up and grown more vicious with the years. I was a fool who laughed at the cure which you prescribed when you saved me, in my state of sin, from twofold death, the death of the body and the death of the soul.

If I had died in that state, my mother's heart would never have recovered from the blow. Words cannot describe how dearly she loved me or how much greater was the anxiety she suffered for my spiritual birth than the physical pain she had endured in bringing me into the world. I cannot see how she could ever have recovered if I had died in that condition, for my death would have pierced the very heart of her love. And what would have become of all the fervent prayers which she offered so often and without fail? They would have come to you, nowhere but to you. But would you, O God of mercy, have despised the contrite and humble heart of that chaste and gentle widow, so ready to give alms, so full of humble reverence for your saints, who never let a day go by unless she had brought an offering to your altar, and never failed to come to your church twice every day, each morning and night, not to listen to empty tales and old

[1] 1 Cor. 15: 22.

wive's gossip, but so that she might hear the preaching of your word and you might listen to her prayers? Could you deny your help to her, when it was by your grace that she was what she was, or despise her tears, when she asked not for gold or silver or any fleeting, short-lived favour, but that the soul of her son might be saved? Never would you have done this, O Lord. No, you were there to hear her prayer and do all, in due order, as you had determined it was to be done. It could not be that you would have deceived her in the visions you sent her and the answers you gave to her prayers, both those that I have recorded and the others which I have not set down. All these signs she cherished in her faithful heart, and in her ceaseless prayers she laid them before you as though they were pledges signed by your hand. For, since *your mercy endures for ever*,[1] by your promises you deign to become a debtor to those whom you release from every debt.

10

So it was that you healed my sickness. To the son of your servant you restored the health of his body, so that he might live to receive from you another far better and more certain kind of health.

In Rome I did not part company with those would-be saints, who were such frauds both to themselves and to others. I associated not only with aspirants, one of whom was my host during my illness and convalescence, but also with those whom they call the elect. I still thought that it is not we who sin but some other nature that sins within us. It flattered my pride to think that I incurred no guilt and, when I did wrong, not to confess it so that you might *bring healing to a soul that had sinned against you*.[2] I preferred to excuse myself and blame this unknown thing which was in me but was not part of me. The truth, of course, was that it was all my own self, and my own impiety had divided me against myself. My sin was all the more incurable because I did not think myself a sinner. It was abominable wickedness to prefer to defeat your ends and lose my soul rather than submit to you and gain salvation. You had not yet *set a guard on my mouth, posted a sentry before my lips, that my heart might not turn towards thoughts of evil, to cover sins with smooth names, and take part with the*

[1] Ps. 117: 1(118: 1). [2] Ps 40: 5 (41: 4).

wrong-doers.[1] This was why I still associated with the elect of the Manichees.

All the same, I had no hope of profit from their false doctrines and by now I was also becoming indifferent and inattentive to the theories with which I had resolved to be content unless I could find something better. I began to think that the philosophers known as Academics were wiser than the rest, because they held that everything was a matter of doubt and asserted that man can know nothing for certain. This is the common belief about their teaching and it seemed evident to me that it was what they thought, but I did not yet understand what they really meant. At the same time I did not scruple to discourage my host from placing too much confidence, as I saw that he did, in the tales which fill the pages of the Manichean books. Nevertheless I remained on more familiar terms with the Manichees than with others who did not share their heresy. I no longer advocated their cause with my old enthusiasm, but many of them were to be found in Rome, living unobtrusively, and their friendship made me slow to seek another, especially since I had lost hope of being able to find the truth in your Church, O Lord of heaven and earth, Creator of all things visible and invisible. The Manichees had turned me away from it: at the same time I thought it outrageous to believe that you had the shape of a human body and were limited within the dimensions of limbs like our own. When I tried to think of my God, I could think of him only as a bodily substance, because I could not conceive of the existence of anything else. This was the principal and almost the only cause of the error from which I could not escape.

For the same reason I believed that evil, too, was some similar kind of substance, a shapeless, hideous mass, which might be solid, in which case the Manichees called it earth, or fine and rarefied like air. This they imagine as a kind of evil mind filtering through the substance they call earth. And because such little piety as I had compelled me to believe that God, who is good, could not have created an evil nature, I imagined that there were two antagonistic masses, both of which were infinite, yet the evil in a lesser and the good in a greater degree.

All my other sacrilegious beliefs were the outcome of this first fatal mistake. For when I tried to fall back upon the Catholic faith,

[1] Ps. 140: 3, 4 (141: 3, 4).

my mind recoiled because the Catholic faith was not what I supposed it to be. My theories forced me to admit that you were finite in one point only, in so far as the mass of evil was able to oppose you; but, O my God, whose mercies I now aver, if I believed that you were infinite in all other ways, I thought that this was a more pious belief than to suppose that you were limited, in each and every way, by the outlines of a human body. And it seemed to me better to believe that you had created no evil than to suppose that evil, such as I imagined it to be, had its origin in you. For, ignorant as I was, I thought of evil not simply as some vague substance but as an actual bodily substance, and this was because I could not conceive of mind except as a rarefied body somehow diffused in space. I also thought of our Saviour, your only Son, as somehow extended or projected for our salvation from the mass of your transplendent body, and I was so convinced of this that I could believe nothing about him except such futile dreams as I could picture to myself. I did not believe that a nature such as his could have taken birth from the Virgin Mary unless it were mingled with her flesh; and, if it were such as I imagined it to be, I could not see how it could be mingled with her flesh without being defiled. So I dared not believe in his incarnation, for fear that I should be compelled to believe that the flesh had defiled him.

Those who have the gifts of your Holy Spirit will laugh at me, in all kindness and charity, if they read of this confusion in my mind. But this was the man that I was.

11

Besides this I thought that there could be no answer to the objections raised by the Manichees against the Scriptures. But there were times when I had a genuine wish to discuss these points one by one with someone who had a really profound knowledge of Scripture, so that I might hear his views on them. Even before I left Carthage I had listened to the speeches of a man named Elpidius, who used to join in open controversy with the Manichees, and I had been impressed when he put forward arguments from Scripture which were not easy to demolish. I thought that the Manichees' answer was weak and, in fact, they were chary of giving it in public and only mentioned it in private to adherents of the sect. They claimed that the books of the New

Testament had been tampered with by unnamed persons who wished to impose the Jewish law upon the Christian faith, but they could produce no uncorrupted copies.

But it was principally the idea of the two masses of good and evil that held me fast and stifled me, for I was unable to conceive of any but material realities. Under the weight of these two masses I gasped for the pure clear air of your truth, but I could draw no breath of it.

12

I began actively to set about the business of teaching literature and public speaking, which was the purpose for which I had come to Rome. At first I taught in my house, where I collected a number of pupils who had heard of me, and through them my reputation began to grow. But I now realized that there were difficulties in Rome with which I had not had to contend in Africa. True enough, I found that there was no rioting by young hooligans, but I was told that at any moment a number of students would plot together to avoid paying their master his fees and would transfer in a body to another. They were quite unscrupulous, and justice meant nothing to them compared with the love of money. There was hatred for them in my heart, and it was not unselfish hatred, for I suppose that I hated them more for what I should have to suffer from them than for the wrong they might do to any teacher. All the same, students like these are utterly dishonest. *They break their troth with you*[1] by setting their hearts on fleeting temporal delusions and tainted money which defiles the hands that grasp it, and by clinging to a world which they can never hold. And all the while they turn their backs on you who are always present, calling them back and ready to pardon man's adulterous soul when it returns to you. For their warped and crooked minds I still hate students like these, but I love them too, hoping to teach them to mend their ways, so that they may learn to love their studies more than money and love you, their God, still more, for you are the Truth, the Source of good that does not fail, and the Peace of purest innocence. But in those days I was readier to dislike them for fear of the harm they might cause me than to hope that they would become good for your sake.

[1] Ps. 72: 27 (73: 27).

13

So, when the Prefect of Rome received a request from Milan to find a teacher of literature and elocution for the city, with a promise that travelling expenses would be charged to public funds, I applied for the appointment, armed with recommendations from my friends who were so fuddled with the Manichean rigmarole. This journey was to mean the end of my association with them, though none of us knew it at the time. Eventually Symmachus, who was then Prefect, set me a test to satisfy himself of my abilities and sent me to Milan.

In Milan I found your devoted servant the bishop Ambrose, who was known throughout the world as a man whom there were few to equal in goodness. At that time his gifted tongue never tired of dispensing the richness of your corn, the joy of your oil, and the sober intoxication of your wine.[1] Unknown to me, it was you who led me to him, so that I might knowingly be led by him to you. This man of God received me like a father and, as bishop, told me how glad he was that I had come. My heart warmed to him, not at first as a teacher of the truth, which I had quite despaired of finding in your Church, but simply as a man who showed me kindness. I listened attentively when he preached to the people, though not with the proper intention; for my purpose was to judge for myself whether the reports of his powers as a speaker were accurate, or whether eloquence flowed from him more, or less, readily than I had been told. So while I paid the closest attention to the words he used, I was quite uninterested in the subject-matter and was even contemptuous of it. I was delighted with his charming delivery, but although he was a more learned speaker thar. Faustus, he had not the same soothing and gratifying manner. I am speaking only of his style for, as to content, there could be no comparison between the two. Faustus had lost his way among the fallacies of Manicheism, while Ambrose most surely taught the doctrine of salvation. But *your mercy is unknown to sinners*[2] such as I was then, though step by step, unwittingly, I was coming closer to it.

[1] These phrases are modifications of verses from the Psalms. Cf. Ps. 4: 8 (4: 7), 44: 8 (45: 7), and 80: 17 (81: 16). The words 'sober intoxication' are borrowed from Saint Ambrose's hymn 'Splendor paternae gloriae'.

[2] Ps. 118: 155 (119: 155).

14

For although I did not trouble to take what Ambrose said to heart, but only to listen to the manner in which he said it – this being the only paltry interest that remained to me now that I had lost hope that man could find the path that led to you – nevertheless his meaning, which I tried to ignore, found its way into my mind together with his words, which I admired so much. I could not keep the two apart, and while I was all ears to seize upon his eloquence, I also began to sense the truth of what he said, though only gradually. First of all it struck me that it was, after all, possible to vindicate his arguments. I began to believe that the Catholic faith, which I had thought impossible to defend against the objections of the Manichees, might fairly be maintained, especially since I had heard one passage after another in the Old Testament figuratively explained. These passages had been death[1] to me when I took them literally, but once I had heard them explained in their spiritual meaning I began to blame myself for my despair, at least in so far as it had led me to suppose that it was quite impossible to counter people who hated and derided the law and the prophets. But I did not feel that I ought to follow the Catholic path simply because it too had its learned men, ready to vouch for it and never at a loss for sound arguments in answer to objections. On the other hand I did not think that my own beliefs should be condemned simply because an equally good case could be made out for either side. For I thought the Catholic side unbeaten but still not victorious.

Next I tried my utmost to find some certain proof which would convict the Manichees of falsehood. If I had been able to conceive of a spiritual substance, all their inventions would at once have been disproved and rejected from my mind. But this I could not do. However, the more I thought about the material world and the whole of nature, as far as we can be aware of it through our bodily senses, and the more I took stock of the various theories, the more I began to think that the opinions of the majority of the philosophers were most likely to be true. So, treating everything as a matter of doubt, as the Academics are generally supposed to do, and hovering between one doctrine and another, I made up my mind at least to leave the Mani-

[1] See II Cor. 3: 6.

chees, for while I was in this state of indecision I did not think it right to remain in the sect now that I found the theories of some of the philosophers preferable. Nevertheless I utterly refused to entrust the healing of the maladies of my soul to these philosophers, because they ignored the saving name of Christ. I therefore decided to remain a catechumen in the Catholic Church, which was what my parents wanted, at least until I could clearly see a light to guide my steps.

BOOK VI

I

O GOD, *Hope of my youth*,[1] where were you all this time? Where were you hiding from me? Were you not my Creator and was it not you who made me different from the beasts that walk on the earth and wiser than the birds that fly in the air? Yet I was walking on a treacherous path, in darkness. I was looking for you outside myself and I did not find the God of my own heart. I had reached the depths of the ocean. I had lost all faith and was in despair of finding the truth.

By now my mother had come to me, for her piety had given her strength to follow me over land and sea, facing all perils in the sure faith she had in you. When the ship was in danger, it was she who put heart into the crew, the very men to whom passengers unused to the sea turn for reassurance when they are alarmed. She promised them that they would make the land in safety, because you had given her this promise in a vision. And she found that I too was in grave danger because of my despair of discovering the truth. I told her that I was not a Catholic Christian, but at least I was no longer a Manichee. Yet she did not leap for joy as though this news were unexpected. In fact, to this extent, her anxiety for me had already been allayed. For in her prayers to you she wept for me as though I were dead, but she also knew that you would recall me to life. In her heart she offered me to you as though I were laid out on a bier, waiting for you to say to the widow's son, 'Young man, I say to you, stand up.' And he would get up and begin to speak, and you would give him back to his mother.[2] So she felt no great surge of joy and her heart beat none the faster when she heard that the tears and the prayers which she had offered you day after day had at last, in great part, been rewarded. For I had been rescued from falsehood, even if I had not yet grasped the truth. Instead, because she was sure that if you had promised her all, you would also give her what remained to be given, she told me quite

[1] Ps. 70: 5 (71: 5).   [2] See Luke 7: 14, 15.

serenely, with her heart full of faith, that in Christ she believed that before she left this life she would see me a faithful Catholic. This was what she said to me. But to you, from whom all mercies spring, she poured out her tears and her prayers all the more fervently, begging you to speed your help and give me light in my darkness. She hurried all the more eagerly to church, where she listened with rapt attention to all that Ambrose said. For her his words were like *a spring of water within her, that flows continually to bring her everlasting life.*[1] She loved him *as God's angel,*[2] because she had learnt that it was through him that I had been led, for the time being, into a state of wavering uncertainty. She had no doubt that I must pass through this condition, which would lead me from sickness to health, but not before I had surmounted a still graver danger, much like that which doctors call the crisis.

2

It had been my mother's custom in Africa to take meal-cakes and bread and wine to the shrines of the saints on their memorial days, but the door-keeper would not allow her to do this in Milan. When she learned that the bishop had forbidden it, she accepted his ruling with such pious submission that I was surprised to see how willingly she condemned her own practice rather than dispute his command. For her heart was not beset by a craving for wine nor did the love of it goad her into hatred of the truth, as happens with so many men and women who are as disgusted to hear the praises of sobriety as drunkards to be offered water with their wine. She used to bring her basket full of the customary offerings of food, intending to taste a little and give the rest away. For herself she never poured more than a small cupful of wine, watered to suit her sober palate, and she drank only as much of it as was needed to do honour to the dead. If there were many shrines to be honoured in this way, she carried the same cup around with her to each one and shared its contents, by now well watered and quite lukewarm, with any of her friends who were present, allowing each to take only the smallest sip. For her purpose was to perform an act of piety, not to seek pleasure for herself.

But she willingly ceased this custom when she found that this great preacher, this holy bishop, had forbidden such ceremonies even to

[1] John 4: 14. [2] Gal. 4: 14.

those who performed them with sobriety, both for fear that to some they might be occasions for drunkenness and also because they bore so close a resemblance to the superstitious rites which the pagans held in honour of their dead. Instead of her basket full of the fruits of the earth she learned to bring to the shrines of the martyrs a heart full of prayers far purer than any of these gifts. In this way she was able to give what she could to the poor and the Communion of the Lord's Body was celebrated at the shrines of the saints, who had given their lives and earned the crown of martyrdom by following the example of his passion.

Yet it seems to me that my mother probably would not have given up this habit so readily, if the prohibition had come from another whom she loved less dearly than Ambrose. My heart lies open before you, O Lord my God, and this is what I believe. Because he could show me the way of salvation she was greatly devoted to Ambrose, and his heart too had warmed to her for her truly pious way of life, her zeal in good works, and her regular churchgoing. Often, when he saw me, he would break out in praise of her, congratulating me on having such a mother. But he little knew what sort of a son she had, one who doubted all these things and was convinced that man could not find the *road leading to life*.[1]

3

But although my mind was full of questions and I was restless to argue out my problems, I did not pour out my sorrows to you, praying for your help. I even thought of Ambrose simply as a man who was fortunate, as the world appraises fortune, because he was held in such high esteem by such important people. His celibacy seemed to me the only hardship which he had to bear. As for his secret hopes, his struggles against the temptations which must come to one so highly placed, the consolations he found in adversity, and the joy he knew in the depths of his heart when he fed upon your Bread, these were quite beyond my surmise for they lay outside my experience. For his part he did not know how I was tormented or how deeply I was engulfed in danger. I could not ask him the questions I wished to ask in the way that I wished to ask them, because so many people used to

[1] Prov. 6: 23.

keep him busy with their problems that I was prevented from talking to him face to face. When he was not with them, which was never for very long at a time, he was reviving his body with the food that it needed or refreshing his mind with reading. When he read, his eyes scanned the page and his heart explored the meaning, but his voice was silent and his tongue was still. All could approach him freely and it was not usual for visitors to be announced, so that often, when we came to see him, we found him reading like this in silence, for he never read aloud. We would sit there quietly, for no one had the heart to disturb him when he was so engrossed in study. After a time we went away again, guessing that in the short time when he was free from the turmoil of other men's affairs and was able to refresh his own mind, he would not wish to be distracted. Perhaps he was afraid that, if he read aloud, some obscure passage in the author he was reading might raise a question in the mind of an attentive listener, and he would then have to explain the meaning or even discuss some of the more difficult points. If he spent his time in this way, he would not manage to read as much as he wished. Perhaps a more likely reason why he read to himself was that he needed to spare his voice, which quite easily became hoarse. But whatever his reason, we may be sure it was a good one.

At all events I had no chance to probe the heart of this man, your holy oracle, with the questions that I wished to put to him, unless it was some matter that could be treated briefly. If I was to pour out my sea of troubles before him, I should need to find him truly at his leisure, but this I never did. Yet every Sunday I listened as he preached the word of truth to the people, and I grew more and more certain that it was possible to unravel the tangle woven by those who had deceived both me and others with their cunning lies against the Holy Scriptures. I learned that your spiritual children, whom by your grace you have made to be born again of our Catholic mother the Church, do not understand the words *God made man in his own image*[1] to mean that you are limited by the shape of a human body, and although I could form not the vaguest idea, even with the help of allegory, of how there could be substance that was spiritual, nevertheless I was glad that all this time I had been howling my complaints not against the Catholic faith but against something quite imaginary which I had

[1] Gen. 1: 27.

thought up in my own head. At the same time I was ashamed of myself, because I had certainly been both rash and impious in speaking out in condemnation of a matter on which I ought to have taken pains to be better informed.

O God, you who are so high above us and yet so close, hidden and yet always present, you have not parts, some greater and some smaller. You are everywhere, and everywhere you are entire. Nowhere are you limited by space. You have not the shape of a body like ours. Yet you made man in your own likeness, and man is plainly in space from head to foot.

4

Since I did not know what was meant by your likeness, I ought to have knocked at your door and asked how it was to be understood: I ought not to have derided and set myself against it as though it meant what I imagined it to mean. Anxiety about what I could believe as certain gnawed at my heart all the more sharply as I grew more and more ashamed that I had been misled and deluded by promises of certainty for so long, and had talked wildly, like an ignorant child, about so many unconfirmed theories as though they were beyond question. It was only later that I realized that they were false. But by now I was sure at least that there was no certainty in them, though I had taken them for true when I blindly attacked your Catholic Church. Though I had not yet discovered that what the Church taught was the truth, at least I had learnt that she did not teach the doctrines which I so sternly denounced. This bewildered me, but I was on the road to conversion and I was glad, my God, that the one Church, the Body of your only Son, in which the name of Christ had been put upon me as a child, had no liking for childish absurdities and there was nothing in the sound doctrine which she taught to show that you, the Creator of all things, were confined within a measure of space which, however high, however wide it might be, was yet strictly determined by the form of a human body.

I was glad too that at last I had been shown how to interpret the ancient Scriptures of the law and the prophets in a different light from that which had previously made them seem absurd, when I used to criticize your saints for holding beliefs which they had never really held at all. I was pleased to hear that in his sermons to the people

Ambrose often repeated the text: *The written law inflicts death, whereas the spiritual law brings life,*[1] as though this were a rule upon which he wished to insist most carefully. And when he lifted the veil of mystery and disclosed the spiritual meaning of texts which, taken literally, appeared to contain the most unlikely doctrines, I was not aggrieved by what he said, although I did not yet know whether it was true. I refused to allow myself to accept any of it in my heart, because I was afraid of a headlong fall, but I was hanging in suspense which was more likely to be fatal than a fall. I wanted to be just as certain of these things which were hidden from my sight as that seven and three make ten, for I was not so far out of my wits as to suppose that not even this could be known. But I wanted to be equally sure about everything else, both material things for which I could not vouch by my own senses, and spiritual things of which I could form no idea except in bodily form. If I had been able to believe I might have been cured, because in my mind's eye I should have had clearer vision, which by some means might have been directed towards your eternal, unfailing truth. But it is often the case that a man who has had experience of a bad doctor is afraid to trust himself even to a good one, and in the same way my sick soul, which could not be healed except through faith, refused this cure for fear of believing a doctrine that was false. My soul resisted your healing hand, for it was you who prepared and dispensed the medicine of faith and made it so potent a remedy for the diseases of the world.

5

From now on I began to prefer the Catholic teaching. The Church demanded that certain things should be believed even though they could not be proved, for if they could be proved, not all men could understand the proof, and some could not be proved at all. I thought that the Church was entirely honest in this and far less pretentious than the Manichees, who laughed at people who took things on faith, made rash promises of scientific knowledge, and then put forward a whole system of preposterous inventions which they expected their followers to believe on trust because they could not be proved. Then, O Lord, you laid your most gentle, most merciful finger on my heart

[1] II Cor. 3: 6.

and set my thoughts in order, for I began to realize that I believed countless things which I had never seen or which had taken place when I was not there to see – so many events in the history of the world, so many facts about places and towns which I had never seen, and so much that I believed on the word of friends or doctors or various other people. Unless we took these things on trust, we should accomplish absolutely nothing in this life. Most of all it came home to me how firm and unshakeable was the faith which told me who my parents were, because I could never have known this unless I believed what I was told. In this way you made me understand that I ought not to find fault with those who believed your Bible, which you have established with such great authority amongst almost all the nations of the earth, but with those who did not believe it; and that I ought to pay no attention to people who asked me how I could be sure that the Scriptures were delivered to mankind by the Spirit of the one true God who can tell no lie. It was precisely this that I most needed to believe, because in all the conflicting books of philosophy which I had read no misleading proposition, however contentious, had been able, even for one moment, to wrest from me my belief in your existence and in your right to govern human affairs; and this despite the fact that I had no knowledge of what you are.

My belief that you existed and that our well-being was in your hands was sometimes strong, sometimes weak, but I always held to it even though I knew neither what I ought to think about your substance nor which way would lead me to you or lead me back to you. And so, since we are too weak to discover the truth by reason alone and for this reason need the authority of sacred books, I began to believe that you would never have invested the Bible with such conspicuous authority in every land unless you had intended it to be the means by which we should look for you and believe in you. As for the passages which had previously struck me as absurd, now that I had heard reasonable explanations of many of them I regarded them as of the nature of profound mysteries; and it seemed to me all the more right that the authority of Scripture should be respected and accepted with the purest faith, because while all can read it with ease, it also has a deeper meaning in which its great secrets are locked away. Its plain language and simple style make it accessible to everyone, and yet it absorbs the attention of the learned. By this means it gathers all men in the wide sweep of its net, and some pass safely through the narrow mesh and come to you. They are not many, but they would be fewer still if it were not that this book stands out alone on so high a peak of authority and yet draws so great a throng in the embrace of its holy humility.

My mind dwelt on these thoughts and you were there to help me and listen to my sighs. You were my helmsman when I ran adrift, and you did not desert me as I travelled along the broad way of the world.

<h1 style="text-align:center">6</h1>

I was eager for fame and wealth and marriage, but you only derided these ambitions. They caused me to suffer the most galling difficulties, but the less you allowed me to find pleasure in anything that was not yourself, the greater, I know, was your goodness to me. Look into my heart, O Lord, for it was your will that I should remember these things and confess them to you. I pray now that my soul may cling to you, for it was you who released it from the deadly snare in which it was so firmly caught. It was in a state of misery and you probed its wound to the quick, pricking it on to leave all else and turn to you to be healed, to turn to you who are above all things and without whom nothing could exist.

My misery was complete and I remember how, one day, you made me realize how utterly wretched I was. I was preparing a speech in praise of the Emperor, intending that it should include a great many lies which would certainly be applauded by an audience who knew well enough how far from the truth they were. I was greatly pre-occupied by this task and my mind was feverishly busy with its harassing problems. As I walked along one of the streets in Milan I noticed a poor beggar who must, I suppose, have had his fill of food and drink, since he was laughing and joking. Sadly I turned to my companions and spoke to them of all the pain and trouble which is caused by our own folly. My ambitions had placed a load of misery on my shoulders and the further I carried it the heavier it became, but the only purpose of all the efforts we made was to reach the goal of peaceful happiness. This beggar had already reached it ahead of us, and perhaps we should never reach it at all. For by all my laborious contriving and intricate manoeuvres I was hoping to win the joy of worldly happiness, the very thing which this man had already secured at the cost of the few pence which he had begged.

Of course, his was not true happiness. But the state of felicity which I aimed to reach was still more false. He, at any rate, was cheerful, while I was unhappy: he had no worries, but I was full of apprehension. And if anyone had asked me whether I would rather be happy or afraid, I should have replied that I preferred to be happy. But if I had then been asked to choose between the life which that beggar led and my own, I should have chosen my own life, full of fears and worries though it was. This would have been an illogical choice and how could I have pretended that it was the right one? For I ought not to have preferred myself to the beggar simply because I was the more learned, since my learning was no source of happiness to me. I only made use of it to try to please others, and I only tried to please them, not to teach them. This was why you broke my bones with the rod of your discipline.

My soul, then, must beware of those who say that what matters is the reason why a man is happy. They will say that it was drunkenness that made the beggar happy, while my soul looked for happiness in honour. But what sort of honour did it hope to find? Not the kind which is to be found in you, O Lord. It was not true honour, any more than the beggar's joy was true joy, but it turned my head even more. That very night the beggar would sleep off his drunkenness, but mine had been with me night after night as I slept and was still with me in the morning when I woke, and would still be with me night and day after that.

Yet I know that it does matter why a man is happy. There is a world of difference between the joy of hope that comes from faith and the shallow happiness that I was looking for. There was a difference too between the beggar and myself. He was certainly the happier man, not only because he was flushed with cheerfulness while I was eaten away with anxiety, but also because he had earned his wine by wishing good day to passers-by while I was trying to feed my pride by telling lies.

On this occasion I told my friends much of what I felt about these things. Often, by observing them, I was made aware of my own state, and I was not pleased with what I saw. This made me sad and my misery was redoubled; and if, by chance, fortune smiled upon me, I was too disheartened to seize it, for it would take to flight just as my hand was ready to close upon it.

7

This was a constant subject of gloomy talk among my circle of friends, but I used to discuss it especially with Alypius and Nebridius. Alypius came from my own town and his people were one of the leading families. He was younger than I was and had been a student of mine both in our own town, when I first began to teach, and later on at Carthage. He was greatly attached to me because he thought that I was a good and learned man, and I was fond of him because, although he was still young, it was quite clear that he had much natural disposition to goodness. But he had been caught in the whirl of easy morals at Carthage, with its continual round of futile entertainments, and had lost his heart and his head to the games in the amphitheatre. At the time when he was so wrapped up in this wretched sport I had opened my school as professor of rhetoric in Carthage, but because of some difference of opinion which had occurred between his father and me he was not one of my pupils. I found out that he was fatally attracted by the games and it caused me grave anxiety to think that he was likely to ruin a future which promised so well, if he had not already done so. But I had no means of offering him advice or using any pressure to restrain him, for I could claim neither the privilege of a friend nor the right of a master. I thought that he shared his father's feelings about me, although, in fact, this was not the case for he ignored his father's wishes and treated me with courtesy when we met. He soon began to come and listen to some of my lectures, but he never stayed for long.

I had forgotten that I might use my influence with him to prevent him from wasting his talents in this thoughtless, impetuous enthusiasm for futile pastimes. But you, O Lord, who hold the reins of all you have created, had not forgotten this man who was one day to be a bishop and administer your sacrament to your children. You used me to set him on the right path, but so that we might recognize that it was all by your doing, you used me without my knowledge. One day as I sat in my usual place with my pupils before me, Alypius came in and after greeting me politely sat down and listened attentively to the lesson. It occurred to me that the passage which I happened to be reading could very well be explained by an illustration taken from the games in the arena. It would appeal to the students and make my meaning clearer, and it would also enable me to make a laughing-stock of those who were under the spell of this insane sport. You know, my God, that I was not thinking of Alypius, who so badly needed to be cured of this mania. But he took my words to heart, thinking that I had meant the allusion to apply to him alone. Anyone else would have taken this as a good reason to be angry with me, but this conscientious young man saw in it cause for anger with himself and warmer affection for me. Long ago you caused these words of yours to be inserted in your book: *The wise are grateful for a remonstrance.*[1]

I had not meant to rebuke him, but you use us all, whether we know it or not, for a purpose which is known to you, a purpose which is just. You made my heart and my tongue burn like coals to sear his mind, which was so full of promise, and cure it when it was sick of a wasting disease. Those who have no inkling of your mercy may be silent and offer you no word of praise, but from the depths of my heart I make avowal of your mercy. For after he had heard my words, Alypius hastened to drag himself out of the deep pitfall into which, dazzled by the allure of pleasure, he had plunged of his own accord. By a great effort of self-control he shook himself free of all the dirt of the arena and never went near it again. Then he managed to overcome his father's reluctance to allow him to become a pupil of mine. His father gave in and granted his request. But once he had started his studies with me he became involved in my superstitious beliefs. He particularly admired the Manichees for their ostensible continence, which he thought quite genuine, though of course it was merely a nonsensical and deceitful method of trapping precious souls which had not learnt to feel the depth of real virtue and were easily deceived by the appearance of virtue that was spurious and counter-feit.

8

But he did not abandon his career in the world, for his parents would not allow him to forget it. He went to Rome ahead of me to study

[1] Prov. 9: 8.

law and there, strange to relate, he became obsessed with an extra-ordinary craving for gladiatorial shows. At first he detested these displays and refused to attend them. But one day during the season for this cruel and bloodthirsty sport he happened to meet some friends and fellow-students returning from their dinner. In a friendly way they brushed aside his resistance and his stubborn protests and carried him off to the arena.

'You may drag me there bodily,' he protested, 'but do you imagine that you can make me watch the show and give my mind to it? I shall be there, but it will be just as if I were not present, and I shall prove myself stronger than you or the games.'

He did not manage to deter them by what he said, and perhaps the very reason why they took him with them was to discover whether he would be as good as his word. When they arrived at the arena, the place was seething with the lust for cruelty. They found seats as best they could and Alypius shut his eyes tightly, determined to have nothing to do with these atrocities. If only he had closed his ears as well! For an incident in the fight drew a great roar from the crowd, and this thrilled him so deeply that he could not contain his curiosity. Whatever had caused the uproar, he was confident that, if he saw it, he would find it repulsive and remain master of himself. So he opened his eyes, and his soul was stabbed with a wound more deadly than any which the gladiator, whom he was so anxious to see, had received in his body. He fell, and fell more pitifully than the man whose fall had drawn that roar of excitement from the crowd. The din had pierced his ears and forced him to open his eyes, laying his soul open to receive the wound which struck it down. This was presumption, not courage. The weakness of his soul was in relying upon itself instead of trusting in you.

When he saw the blood, it was as though he had drunk a deep draught of savage passion. Instead of turning away, he fixed his eyes upon the scene and drank in all its frenzy, unaware of what he was doing. He revelled in the wickedness of the fighting and was drunk with the fascination of bloodshed. He was no longer the man who had come to the arena, but simply one of the crowd which he had joined, a fit companion for the friends who had brought him.

Need I say more? He watched and cheered and grew hot with excitement, and when he left the arena, he carried away with him a

diseased mind which would leave him no peace until he came back
again, no longer simply together with the friends who had first
dragged him there, but at their head, leading new sheep to the
slaughter. Yet you stretched out your almighty, ever merciful hand,
O God, and rescued him from this madness. You taught him to trust
in you, not in himself. But this was much later.

9

Nevertheless, all this was stored away in his memory so that later on
he might turn the lesson to good account. And there was another
event in his life, too, which you, my God, must surely have allowed
to happen only because you knew that he was to be a great man in
later life and you wanted him to start in good time to learn that, in
judging cases, one man must not too easily condemn another through
being over-credulous.

While he was still studying under me at Carthage, you allowed
him to be arrested as a thief by the market officers. He was in the
market in the middle of the day thinking over an exercise of the sort
which is regularly given to students, a set piece which he had to recite.
He was strolling alone in front of the law courts carrying his pen and
his writing tablets, when the real thief, a young student like himself,
made his way without attracting the notice of Alypius towards the
leaden gratings which project over the moneylenders' shops. He
carried a hatchet, which he kept out of sight, and with this he began
to hack away the lead. But the moneylenders, in their shops below,
heard the noise. Quietly they discussed what to do, and sent some
men to arrest anyone they might find. At the sound of their voices the
thief dropped his hatchet and ran off, frightened that he might be
caught with it in his possession.

Alypius had not seen the thief arrive, but he saw him leave. He
noticed that he was in a hurry to get away, and went into the building
to discover the reason for this haste. He found the hatchet, and while
he stood wondering how it came to be there, the men who had been
sent to find the intruder arrived to find Alypius alone and in his hand
the tool which had caused the noise that had alarmed them and
brought them to the spot. They seized him and dragged him away,
proudly telling the crowd of shopkeepers who had by now assembled

that they had caught him in the act. Then they took him off to hand him over to the magistrates.

But this was the end of his lesson. You, O Lord, were the only witness of his innocence and at once you stood by his side to defend him. For as they were leading him away to be tortured or imprisoned, they met the architect in charge of public buildings. Alypius's captors were particularly glad to meet this official, because he had often suspected them of stealing goods missing from the market and now, at last, he would realize who was guilty of these crimes. But the architect had often seen Alypius at the house of one of the senators, whom he frequently visited. He recognized him at once and, taking him by the arm, led him aside to ask how he came to be in such trouble. When he heard what had happened, he turned to the excited onlookers, who were noisily threatening Alypius, and told them all to follow him. They passed by the house of the youth who had committed the crime. At the door they found a slave-boy, quite able to tell all he knew but too young to fear any consequences for his master. He had, in fact, been with his master in the market. Alypius remembered him and told the architect, who showed the hatchet to the boy and asked him whose it was. Without hesitation the boy answered 'Ours', and went on to tell the whole story in answer to the architect's questions. By this means the guilt was laid where it belonged, much to the confusion of the crowd, which had begun too soon to be jubilant over the arrest of Alypius. And Alypius, who was destined later to preach your word and judge many cases in your Church, went home all the wiser for this experience.

10

I found him in Rome when I arrived. He became very closely attached to me and came with me to Milan so that we need not part, and also because he wanted to put his legal studies into practice, though this was more his parents' wish than his own. He had already acted three times as assessor, with an integrity that was a source of wonder to his colleagues, though to him it was astonishing that anyone should prefer wealth before honesty. But it was not only by inducements of bribery that his character was put to the test; he was also subjected to intimidation. When he was in Rome acting as assessor to the controller of Italian provincial funds, there was a very influential senator who held large numbers of people in his power, either because he had granted them favours or because they had reason to fear him. In his usual domineering way he attempted to obtain some privilege to which he had no right in law. Alypius refused to grant it. A bribe was offered and he contemptuously turned it down. Threats followed and he rebuffed them. Everyone was amazed by his extraordinary self-possession, for although this formidable man had earned widespread notoriety for his innumerable methods of patronizing or injuring others, Alypius neither desired him as a friend nor feared him as an enemy. Even the judge for whom Alypius was acting as assessor agreed that the privilege should not be granted, though he would not openly refuse it. Declaring that he could do nothing in face of Alypius's attitude, he left the case in his hands; and, in fact, if he had acted himself, Alypius would have left the court.

There was only one temptation to which he nearly yielded through his love of literature, and this was to have books copied for him at the special rates available to government officers. But he conscientiously chose the better course and decided that honest principles, which forbade the deal, were more precious than the opportunity which made it possible. This is a small matter; but *he who is trustworthy over a little sum is trustworthy over a greater*.[1] The words of Christ, the Voice of your truth, can never be unmeaning, and it was he who said *If you, then, could not be trusted to use the base riches you had, who will put the true riches in your keeping? Who will give you property of your own, if you could not be trusted with what was only lent you?*[1]

These were the qualities I knew in Alypius, who was my close friend and, like myself, was perplexed to know what course of life we ought to follow. Nebridius was also with us. He had left his own town near Carthage and Carthage itself, where he had spent much of his time. He had given up his house and his family's rich estate in the country and had left his mother, who refused to come with him. He had come to Milan for no other purpose than to live with me, so that we might be together in our fervent search for truth and wisdom. His distress was not less than mine and, like me, he wavered between one course and another, desperately seeking the way of happiness and prying closely into the problems which troubled us most. We were

[1] Luke 16: 10-12.

like three hungry mouths, able only to gasp out our needs to one another, while our eyes were on you, waiting for you *to grant us, in due time, our nourishment*.[1] And in all the bitter disappointments which, by your mercy, thwarted our undertakings in this world, we tried to see the reason for our sufferings. But darkness overshadowed us and we turned away asking, 'How long is this to be?' Again and again we asked ourselves this question, but we did not relinquish our worldly aims, because we could not see the light of any truth that we might grasp in place of them.

II

I found much to bewilder me in my memories of the long time which had passed since I was nineteen, the age at which I had first begun to search in earnest for truth and wisdom and had promised myself that, once I had found them, I would give up all the vain hopes and mad delusions which sustained my futile ambitions. I realized that I was now thirty years old and was still floundering in the same quagmire, because I was greedy to enjoy what the world had to offer, though it only eluded me and wasted my strength. And all the time I had been telling myself one tale after another.

'Tomorrow I shall discover the truth. I shall see it quite plainly, and it will be mine to keep. . . .

'Faustus will come and explain everything. . . .

'The Academics! What wonderful men they are! Is it true that we can never know for certain how we ought to manage our lives . . .?

'No, not that! We must search all the more carefully and never despair. I can see now that the passages in Scripture which I used to think absurd are not absurd at all. They can be understood in another sense, quite fairly. I shall fix my foot firmly on the step where my parents set me as a boy, until I find the manifest truth. But where and when am I to look for it? Ambrose has no time to spare and I have no time for reading. Where am I to look for the books I need? Where and when can I buy them or get someone to lend them to me? I must plan my time and arrange my day for the good of my soul. . . .

'Great hope is born in me, because I have found that the doctrines of the Catholic faith are not what I thought them to be, and my

[1] Ps. 144: 15 (145: 15).

accusations were unfounded. The learned men of the Church hold it wrong to believe that God is limited by the shape of a human body. Why, then, do I hesitate to knock, so that the door may be opened to reveal what is still hidden from me . . .?

'My pupils keep me busy all the morning, but how do I use the rest of my day? Why should I not spend it knocking at God's door? Yet if I did, when could I visit my influential friends, whose patronage I need? When could I prepare the lessons for which I am paid by my students? When could I refresh my own mind by giving it a rest from the troubles which absorb it . . .?

'All this must go by the board. I must dismiss all these futile trifles from my mind and devote myself entirely to the search for truth. Life is a misery and I do not know when death may come. If it steals upon me, shall I be in a fit state to leave this world? Where could I then learn all that I have neglected to learn in this life? Is it not more probable that I should have to pay a heavy penalty for my negligence . . .?

'Suppose death puts an end to all care. Suppose that it cuts it off together with the senses of the body. This is another problem to be solved . . .

'But it is unthinkable that this could be true. It is not for nothing, not mere chance, that the towering authority of the Christian faith has spread throughout the world. God would never have done so much, such wonderful things for us if the life of the soul came to an end with the death of the body. Why then do I delay? Why do I not abandon my worldly hopes and give myself up entirely to the search for God and the life of true happiness . . .?

'But not so fast! This life too is sweet. It has its own charms. They are not of small account and a man must not lightly undertake to detach his mind from them, because to return to them later would be a disgrace. . . .

'It would need little effort to win myself a position of some standing in the world, and what more could a man ask? I have many influential friends, and if I press for nothing more, I may at least obtain a governor's post. I could marry a wife who would bring me a small dowry, so that the expense would be no burden, and this would be the limit of my ambitions. There have been many great men who have dedicated themselves to the pursuit of wisdom even though they were married, and I might do well to follow their example.'

As I reasoned with myself in this way, my heart was buffeted hither and thither by winds blowing from opposite quarters. Time was passing and I kept delaying my conversion to you, my God. Day after day I postponed living in you, but I never put off the death which I died each day in myself. I longed for a life of happiness but I was frightened to approach it in its own domain; and yet, while I fled from it, I still searched for it. I thought it would be too much for me to bear if I were to be deprived of woman's love. In your mercy you have given us a remedy to cure this weakness, but I gave it no thought because I had never tried it for myself. I believed that continence was to be achieved by man's own power, which I knew that I did not possess. Fool that I was, I did not know that no man *can be master of himself, except of God's bounty*,[1] as your Bible tells us. And you would have given me this strength, if I had allowed the cries of my soul to beat upon your ears and had had faith firm enough to shed my troubles on to you.

12

It was Alypius who prevented me from marrying, because he insisted that if I did so, we could not possibly live together in uninterrupted leisure, devoted to the pursuit of wisdom, as we had long desired to do. As for himself, even as a grown man he was quite remarkably self-controlled in matters of sex. In early adolescence he had had the experience of sexual intercourse, but it had not become habitual. In fact he had been ashamed of it and thought it degrading and, ever since, he had lived a life of the utmost chastity. For my part I answered his arguments by pointing to the example of married men who had been lovers of wisdom, had served God well, and had retained the affection of their friends, whom they had loyally loved in return. But I was far from being the equal of these noble spirits. I was bound down by this disease of the flesh. Its deadly pleasures were a chain that I dragged along with me, yet I was afraid to be freed from it; and I refused to accept the good advice of Alypius, repelling the hand that meant to loose my bonds, as though it only rubbed my sores.

[1] Wisdom 8: 21.

Moreover, the serpent used me as a mouthpiece to speak to Alypius himself. Satan twisted my words into snares that were meant to entice, and strewed them in the path to trap the feet of his victim, who walked in all innocence with no burden to bear.

Alypius could not understand how it was that I, of whom he thought so highly, could be so firmly caught in the toils of sexual pleasure as to assert, whenever we discussed the subject, that I could not possibly endure the life of a celibate. When I saw that he was puzzled by my words, I used to defend them by saying that there was a great difference between his own hasty, furtive experience and my enjoyment of a settled way of life. In his case, since he could scarcely remember the occasion, he might easily disparage it: but in mine, it required only the respectable name of marriage and he need no longer wonder why I found it impossible to turn my back upon it. As a result of what I said, he began to wish to be married himself, not because he had yielded to lust for pleasure of this kind, but simply out of curiosity. He explained that he was eager to find out what it was without which my life, which he thought so pleasant, would seem to me no life but a misery. His mind was free from the fetters by which mine was enchained. He was amazed at my state of bondage, and amazement led to the desire to test it for himself. If he made the experiment, he was likely to fall into the very state which was the object of his amazement, for he was willing *to make terms with death*,[1] and *danger loved is death won*.[2] Neither of us was greatly influenced by the thought of such honour as we should earn by fulfilling the duties of maintaining a well-ordered marriage and raising a family. For my part I was a prisoner of habit, suffering cruel torments through trying to satisfy a lust that could never be sated: while Alypius was being led by curiosity into a like state of captivity. This was the state in which we remained until you, O God most high, who formed us out of clay and never desert us, had pity on our misery and came to our aid in a wonderful way that we could not understand.

13

I was being urged incessantly to marry, and had already made my proposal and been accepted. My mother had done all she could to

<hr>

[1] Is. 28: 15.   [2] Ecclus. 3: 27.

help, for it was her hope that, once I was married, I should be washed clean of my sins by the saving waters of baptism. She was delighted that, day by day, I was becoming more fitted for baptism, and in my acceptance of the faith she saw the answer to her prayers and the fulfilment of your promises. At my request and by her own desire she daily beseeched you with heartfelt prayers to send her some revelation in a vision about my future marriage, but this you would not do. She had some vague and fanciful dreams, which were the result of her preoccupation with these thoughts, and when she told me about them, she treated them as of no importance and did not speak with the assurance that she always had when you sent her visions. She always said that by some sense, which she could not describe in words, she was able to distinguish between your revelations and her own natural dreams. All the same, the plans for my marriage were pushed ahead and the girl's parents were asked for their consent. She was nearly two years too young for marriage, but I liked her well enough and was content to wait.

14

A group of my friends who detested the bustle and worry of life had all but decided to live a life of peace away from the crowd. We had thought over this project and discussed it together a great deal. The plan was to arrange this life of leisure by pooling our possessions and using such money as we had between us to create a common fund. In the spirit of sincere friendship none of us would claim this or that as his own, but all would be thrown together and the whole would belong to each and to all. We thought that there might be about ten members of our community. Some of them were very wealthy, especially Romanianus, who came from my own town. He had been one of my closest friends since boyhood and had come to Milan on some urgent legal business connected with his affairs. He was most enthusiastic about our project, and as he was far richer than the rest of us, his opinions carried great weight. We had agreed that two leaders should be chosen each year to deal with day-to-day problems, while the rest of us were to be left to live in peace.

But I was hoping to get married and some of the others already had wives, and when we began to ask ourselves whether the women would agree to the plan, all our carefully made arrangements collapsed and broke to pieces in our hands and were discarded. Once more we turned to our sighs and groans. Again we trod the wide, well-beaten tracks of the world, and *thought jostled thought in our hearts*.[1] But *your will stands firm*[1] and in the wisdom of your plan you made light of ours and prepared the way you had chosen for us. You were ready *to grant us, in due time, our nourishment, ready to open your hand and fill* our souls *with your blessing*.[2]

15

Meanwhile I was sinning more and more. The woman with whom I had been living was torn from my side as an obstacle to my marriage and this was a blow which crushed my heart to bleeding, because I loved her dearly. She went back to Africa, vowing never to give herself to any other man, and left with me the son whom she had borne me. But I was too unhappy and too weak to imitate this example set me by a woman. I was impatient at the delay of two years which had to pass before the girl whom I had asked to marry became my wife, and because I was more a slave of lust than a true lover of marriage, I took another mistress, without the sanction of wedlock. This meant that the disease of my soul would continue unabated, in fact it would be aggravated, and under the watch and ward of uninterrupted habit it would persist into the state of marriage. Furthermore the wound that I had received when my first mistress was wrenched away showed no signs of healing. At first the pain was sharp and searing, but then the wound began to fester, and though the pain was duller there was all the less hope of a cure.

16

Praise and honour be yours, O Fountain of mercy! As my misery grew worse and worse, you came the closer to me. Though I did not know it, your hand was poised ready to lift me from the mire and wash me clean. Nothing prevented me from plunging still deeper into the gulf of carnal pleasure except the fear of death and your

[1] Prov. 19: 21. [2] Ps. 144: 15, 16 (145: 15, 16).

judgement to come. Through all my changing opinions this fear never left my heart.

With my friends Alypius and Nebridius I often discussed the nature of good and evil. In my judgement Epicurus would have won all the honours, were it not that I believed that the soul lived on after death and received the reward or punishment which it deserved. Epicurus had refused to believe this. If we were immortal, I used to say, and could live in a perpetual state of bodily pleasure, with no fear of losing it, why should we not be happy? What else could we desire? I did not realize that the very root of my misery was that I had sunk to such depths and was so blind that I could not discern the light of virtue and of beauty that is loved for its own sake, for true beauty is seen by the inner eye of the soul, not by the eye of the flesh. And I never wondered what was the source of my pleasure in discussing these topics, shameful as they were, with my friends, nor did I ask myself why, however great my indulgence in sensual pleasure, I could not find happiness, even in the sense in which I then conceived of it, unless I had these friends. And yet I certainly loved them for their own sakes, and I felt that they loved me for my sake in return.

What crooked paths I trod! What dangers threatened my soul when it rashly hoped that by abandoning you it would find something better! Whichever way it turned, on front or back or sides, it lay on a bed that was hard, for in you alone the soul can rest. You are there to free us from the misery of error which leads us astray, to set us on your own path and to comfort us by saying, 'Run on, for I shall hold you up. I shall lead you and carry you on to the end.'

BOOK VII

I

By now my adolescence, with all its shameful sins, was dead. I was approaching mature manhood, but the older I grew, the more disgraceful was my self-delusion. I could imagine no kind of substance except such as is normally seen by the eye. But I did not think of you, my God, in the shape of a human body, for I had rejected this idea ever since I had first begun to study philosophy, and I was glad to find that our spiritual mother, your Catholic Church, also rejected such beliefs. But I did not know how else to think of you.

I was only a man, and a weak man at that, but I tried to think of you as the supreme God, the only God, the true God. With all my heart I believed that you could never suffer decay or hurt or change, for although I did not know how or why this should be, I understood with complete certainty that what is subject to decay is inferior to that which is not, and without hesitation I placed that which cannot be harmed above that which can, and I saw that what remains constant is better than that which is changeable. My heart was full of bitter protests against the creations of my imagination, and this single truth was the only weapon with which I could try to drive from my mind's eye all the unclean images which swarmed before it. But hardly had I brushed them aside than, in the flicker of an eyelid, they crowded upon me again, forcing themselves upon my sight and clouding my vision, so that although I did not imagine you in the shape of a human body, I could not free myself from the thought that you were some kind of bodily substance extended in space, either permeating the world or diffused in infinity beyond it. This substance I thought of as something not subject to decay or harm or variation and therefore better than any that might suffer corruption or damage or change. I reasoned in this way because, if I tried to imagine something without dimensions of space, it seemed to me that nothing, absolutely nothing, remained, not even a void. For if a body were removed from the space which it occupied, and that space remained empty of any body whatsoever, whether of earth, water, air, or sky, there would still remain an empty space. Nothing would be there, but it would still be a space.

My wits were so blunt and I was so completely unable even to see clearly into my own mind, that I thought that whatever had no dimensions in space must be absolutely nothing at all. If it did not, or could not, have qualities related to space, such as density, sparseness, or bulk, I thought it must be nothing. For my mind ranged in imagination over shapes and forms such as are familiar to the eye, and I did not realize that the power of thought, by which I formed these images, was itself something quite different from them. And yet it could not form them unless it were itself something, and something great enough to do so.

So I thought of you too, O Life of my life, as a great being with dimensions extending everywhere, throughout infinite space, permeating the whole mass of the world and reaching in all directions beyond it without limit, so that the earth and the sky and all creation were full of you and their limits were within you, while you had no limits at all. For the air, that is, the atmosphere which covers the earth, is a material body, but it does not block out the light of the sun. The light passes through it and penetrates it, not by breaking it or splitting it, but by filling it completely. In the same way I imagined that you were able to pass through material bodies, not only the air and the sky and the sea, but also the earth, and that you could penetrate to all their parts, the greatest and the smallest alike, so that they were filled with your presence, and by this unseen force you ruled over all that you had created, from within and from without.

This was the theory to which I held, because I could imagine you in no other way. But it was a false theory. For if it were true, it would mean that a greater part of the earth would contain a greater part of you, and a smaller part less in proportion. Everything would be filled with your presence, but in such a way that the body of an elephant would contain more of you than the body of a sparrow, because the one is larger than the other and occupies more space. So you would distribute your parts piecemeal among the parts of the world, to each more or less according to its size. This, of course, is quite untrue. But at that time you had not yet given me light in my darkness.

2

As for the Manichees, O Lord, those frauds who deceived both themselves and others and, for all their talk, were no better than mutes because it was not your holy Word which spoke from their lips, I could answer them well enough by using the argument which Nebridius used to put forward long ago when we were at Carthage. We had all been deeply impressed when we heard it. He used to ask what the imaginary powers of darkness, which the Manichees always describe as a force in conflict with you, would have done if you had refused to join battle with them. If they answered that this force could have done you some harm, they would, in effect, be saying that you were subject to hurt and corruption. If on the other hand they said that the powers of darkness could not harm you, there would be no purpose in a battle which was supposed to result in some part or member of you, some offshoot of your substance, becoming intermingled with opposing powers whose nature was not of your creation, and being corrupted and degraded to such an extent that its bliss was turned to misery and it needed your help if it was to be rescued and purged of evil. This offshoot of your substance, they claimed, was man's soul. It had been taken captive, made impure, and corrupted, while the Word of God, which was to come to its assistance, was free, pure, and incorrupt. Yet, if this was so, the Word of God must also have been subject to corruption, because it came of one and the same substance as the soul.

Therefore, whatever you are – that is, whatever the substance by which you are what you are – if they admitted that you were incorruptible, all their theories were proved to be false and repugnant. If they said you were corruptible, it would be an obvious falsehood, no sooner uttered than rejected in horror. Nebridius' argument was therefore a sufficient answer to the Manichees, and I ought to have disgorged these men like vomit from my over-laden system, because if they thought of you and spoke of you like this, they could not extricate themselves without committing a horrible sacrilege of heart and tongue.

3

But although I declared and firmly believed that you, our Lord God, the true God who made not only our souls but also our bodies and not only our souls and bodies but all things, living and inanimate, as well, although I believed that you were free from corruption or mutation or any degree of change, I still could not find a clear explanation, without complications, of the cause of evil. Whatever the cause might be, I saw that it was not to be found in any theory that would oblige me to believe that the immutable God was mutable. If I believed this, I should myself become a cause of evil, the very thing which I was trying to discover. So I continued the search with some sense of relief, because I was quite sure that the theories of the Manichees were wrong. I repudiated these people with all my heart, because I could see that while they were inquiring into the origin of evil they were full of evil themselves, since they preferred to think that yours was a substance that could suffer evil rather than that theirs was capable of committing it.

I was told that we do evil because we choose to do so of our own free will, and suffer it because your justice rightly demands that we should. I did my best to understand this, but I could not see it clearly. I tried to raise my mental perceptions out of the abyss which engulfed them, but I sank back into it once more. Again and again I tried, but always I sank back. One thing lifted me up into the light of your day. It was that I knew that I had a will, as surely as I knew that there was life in me. When I chose to do something or not to do it, I was quite certain that it was my own self, and not some other person, who made this act of will, so that I was on the point of understanding that herein lay the cause of my sin. If I did anything against my will, it seemed to me to be something which happened to me rather than something which I did, and I looked upon it not as a fault, but as a punishment. And because I thought of you as a just God, I admitted at once that your punishments were not unjust.

But then I would ask myself once more: 'Who made me? Surely it was my God, who is not only good but Goodness itself. How, then, do I come to possess a will that can choose to do wrong and refuse to do good, thereby providing a just reason why I should be punished? Who put this will into me? Who sowed this seed of bitterness in me, when all that I am was made by my God, who is Sweetness itself? If it was the devil who put it there, who made the devil? If he was a good angel who became a devil because of his own wicked will, how did he come to possess the wicked will which made him a devil, when the Creator, who is entirely good, made him a good angel and nothing else?'

These thoughts swept me back again into the gulf where I was being stifled. But I did not sink as far as that hell of error where no one confesses to you his own guilt, choosing to believe that you suffer evil rather than that man does it.

4

Now that I had realized that what is incorruptible is better than that which is not, I took this as the basis for further research and acknowledged that, whatever your nature might be, you must be incorruptible. For no soul has ever been, or ever will be, able to conceive of anything better than you, who are the supreme, the perfect Good. And since, as I now believed, there could be no possible doubt that the incorruptible is better than the corruptible, it followed that you must be incorruptible; otherwise I should be able to think of something that was better than my God. So, once I had seen that the incorruptible is superior to the corruptible, I had to search for you in the light of this truth and make it the starting point of my inquiry into the origin of evil, that is, the origin of corruption, by which your substance cannot possibly be violated. For there is no means whatsoever by which corruption can injure our God, whether by an act of will, by necessity, or by chance. This is because he is God and what he wills is good and he is himself that same Good: whereas to be corrupted is not good. And you are never compelled, my God, to do or suffer anything against your will, because your will is not greater than your power. It would be greater only if you were greater than yourself, for the will and power of God are God himself. Neither can anything unforeseen happen to you, because you know all things and nothing, whatever its nature, exists except by reason of the very fact that you know it. Need I say more to prove that the substance which is God cannot be corruptible since, if it were, it would not be God?

5

I was trying to find the origin of evil, but I was quite blind to the evil in my own method of research. In my mind's eye I pictured the whole of creation, both the things which are visible to us, such as the earth and the sea, the air and the stars, the trees and the animals which live their lives and die, and the things which we cannot see, such as the firmament of Heaven above, with all its angels and everything in it that is spiritual – for I thought of spiritual things, too, as material bodies, each in its allotted place. I imagined the whole of your creation as a vast mass made up of different kinds of bodies, some of them real, some of them only the bodies which in my imagination took the place of spirits. I thought of this mass as something huge. I could not, of course, know how big it really was, but I made it as large as need be, though finite in all directions. I pictured you, O Lord, as encompassing this mass on all sides and penetrating it in every part, yet yourself infinite in every dimension. It was as though there were sea everywhere, nothing but an immense, an infinite sea, and somewhere within it a sponge, as large as might be but not infinite, filled through and through with the water of this boundless sea. In some such way as this I imagined that your creation, which was finite, was filled by you, who were infinite. I said to myself, 'Here is God, and here is what he has created. God is good, utterly and entirely better than the things which he has made. But, since he is good, the things that he has made are also good. This is how he contains them all in himself and fills them all with his presence.

'Where then is evil? What is its origin? How did it steal into the world? What is the root or seed from which it grew? Can it be that there simply is no evil? If so, why do we fear and guard against something which is not there? If our fear is unfounded, it is itself an evil, because it stabs and wrings our hearts for nothing. In fact the evil is all the greater if we are afraid when there is nothing to fear. Therefore, either there is evil and we fear it, or the fear itself is evil.

'Where then does evil come from, if God made all things and, because he is good, made them good too? It is true that he is the supreme Good, that he is himself a greater Good than these lesser goods which he created. But the Creator and all his creation are both good. Where then does evil come from?

'Can it be that there was something evil in the matter from which he made the universe? When he shaped this matter and fitted it to his purpose, did he leave in it some part which he did not convert to good? But why should he have done this? Are we to believe that, although he is omnipotent, he had not the power to convert the whole of this matter to good and change it so that no evil remained in it? Why, indeed, did he will to make anything of it at all? Why did he not instead, by this same omnipotence, destroy it utterly and entirely? Could it have existed against his will? If it had existed from eternity, why did he allow it to exist in that state through the infinite ages of the past and then, after so long a time, decide to make something of it? If he suddenly determined to act, would it not be more likely that he would use his almighty power to abolish this evil matter, so that nothing should exist besides himself, the total, true, supreme, and infinite Good? Or, if it was not good that a God who was good should not also create and establish something good, could he not have removed and annihilated the evil matter and replaced it with good, of which he could create all things? For he would not be omnipotent if he could not create something good without the help of matter which he had not created himself.'

These were the thoughts which I turned over and over in my unhappy mind, and my anxiety was all the more galling for the fear that death might come before I had found the truth. But my heart clung firmly to the faith in Christ your Son, our Lord and Saviour, which it had received in the Catholic Church. There were many questions on which my beliefs were still indefinite and wavered from the strict rule of doctrine, yet my mind never relinquished the faith but drank it in more deeply day by day.

6

By this time I had also turned my back upon the astrologers with their illusory claims to predict the future and their insane and impious ritual. In this too, my God, let me acknowledge your mercy from the deepest depths of my soul! For you, and you alone, are the life that recalls us from the death we die each time we err. You alone are the life which never dies and the wisdom that needs no light besides itself, but illumines all who need to be enlightened, the wisdom that governs the world, down to the leaves that flutter on the trees.

You provided me with a friend who cured my stubborn resistance both to that wise old man Vindicianus[1] and to Nebridius who, for all his youth, was gifted with spiritual qualities that I greatly admired. Vindicianus was quite outspoken on the subject of astrology. Nebridius was not so ready to declare himself, although he too repeated often enough that there was no art by which the future could be foretold. They said that guesswork was often borne out by mere chance. If a man made a great many predictions, several of them would later prove to be true, but he could not know it at the time and would only hit upon them by chance, simply by opening his mouth to speak.

So to cure my obstinacy you found me a friend who was usually ready enough to consult the astrologers. He had made no real study of their lore but, as I have said, he used to make inquiries of them out of curiosity. He did this although he was perfectly well aware of certain facts about them which he said he had heard from his father. If only he had realized it, these facts would have been quite enough to destroy his belief in astrology.

This man, whose name was Firminus, had been educated in the liberal arts and had received a thorough training in rhetoric. He came to consult me, as his closest friend, about some business matters of which he had high hopes, and asked me what prospects I could see in his horoscope, as they call it. I was already beginning to change my mind in favour of Nebridius's opinions on astrology, but I did not refuse outright to read the stars for him and tell him what I saw, though I had little faith in it myself. Nevertheless I added that I was almost convinced that it was all absurd and quite meaningless. He then told me that his father had studied books of astrology with the greatest interest and had had a friend who shared his enthusiasm for the subject. Each was as intent upon this nonsense as the other, and by pooling their experiences they whetted their enthusiasm to the point that, even when their domestic animals had litters, they would note the exact moment of birth and record the position of the stars, intending to use these observations for their experiments in this so-called art.

[1] The doctor previously mentioned in Book IV, chapter 3.

Firminus went on to tell me a story about his own birth. His father had told him that when his mother was pregnant, a female slave in the household of this friend was also expecting a child. Her master was of course aware of her condition, because he used to take very great care to find out even when his dogs were due to have puppies. The two men made the most minute calculations to determine the time of labour of both the women, counting the days, the hours, and even the minutes, and it so happened that both gave birth at exactly the same moment. This meant that the horoscopes which they cast for the two babies had to be exactly the same, down to the smallest particular, though one was the son of the master of the house and the other a slave. For as soon as labour began, each man informed the other of the situation in his house, and each had a messenger waiting, ready to be sent to the other as soon as the birth was announced. As the confinements took place in their own houses, they could easily arrange to be told without delay. The messengers, so Firminus told me, crossed paths at a point which was exactly half way between the two houses, so that each of the two friends inevitably made an identical observation of the stars and could not find the least difference in the time of birth. Yet Firminus, who was born of a rich family, strode along the smoother paths of life. His wealth increased and high honours came his way. But the slave continued to serve his masters. Firminus, who knew him, said that his lot had been in no way bettered.

I believed this story when I heard it, because Firminus was a man whom I could trust. It marked the final end of all my doubts, and my first reaction was to try to redeem Firminus from his interest in astrology. I told him that if I had cast his horoscope and my reading of the stars was correct, I could only have seen in them that his parents were important people, that he belonged to one of the noble families of his town, that he was a freeman by birth, that his upbringing suited his rank, and that his education was liberal. But the slave was born under the very same constellations, and if he had asked me to tell him their meaning, my interpretation of them could not have been true unless I saw in them a family of the meanest sort, the status of a slave, and various other details entirely different from and inconsistent with those which applied to Firminus. This proved that if I were to say what was actually the truth, I should give a different answer to each, though the stars I read were the same; whereas, if I gave the same answer to each, I should be wrong in fact. It was there-fore perfectly clear to me that when predictions based on observa-tions of the stars turn out to be true, it is a matter of luck, not of skill. When they turn out to be wrong, it is not due to lack of skill, but to the perversity of chance.

Taking this as my starting point I began to think the matter over in my mind, so that I should have an answer ready if the eccentrics who made their living at this trade should raise the objection that the story, as Firminus told it, was untrue, or that he had been misin-formed by his father. By now I was eager to move to the attack and reduce these people to silence by ridicule. So I turned my attention to the case of twins, who are generally born within a short time of each other. Whatever significance in the natural order the astrologers may attribute to this interval of time, it is too short to be appreciated by human observation and no allowance can be made for it in the charts which an astrologer has to consult in order to cast a true horo-scope. His predictions, then, will not be true, because he would have consulted the same charts for both Esau and Jacob and would have made the same predictions for each of them, whereas it is a fact that the same things did not happen to them both. Therefore, either he would have been wrong in his predictions or, if his forecast was cor-rect, he would not have predicted the same future for each. And yet he would have consulted the same chart in each case. This proves that if he had foretold the truth, it would have been by luck, not by skill. For, O Lord, though neither the astrologers nor those who consult them know it, by your secret prompting each man, when he seeks their advice, hears what it is right for him to hear. For you rule the universe with the utmost justice, and in the inscrutable depths of your just judgement you know what is right for him, because you can see the hidden merits of our souls. And let no man question the why or the wherefore of your judgement. This he must not do, for he is only a man.

7

By now, O God my Help, you had released me by this means from the bondage of astrology. But I was still trying to discover the origin of evil, and I could find no solution to the problem. My ideas were always changing, like the ebb and flow of the tide, but you never allowed them to sweep me away from the faith by which I believed that you were, that your substance was unchangeable, and that it was yours to care for and to judge mankind. I believed too that it was in Christ your Son, our Lord, and in the Holy Scriptures, which are affirmed by the authority of your Catholic Church, that you had laid the path of man's salvation, so that he might come to that other life which is to follow this our life in death. These beliefs remained intact and firmly rooted in my mind, but I was still burning with anxiety to find the source from which evil comes.

What agony I suffered, my God! How I cried out in grief, while my heart was in labour! But, unknown to me, you were there, listening. Even when I bore the pain of my search valiantly, in silence, the mute sufferings of my soul were loud voices calling to your mercy. You knew what I endured, but no man knew. How little of it could I find words to tell, even to my closest friends! Could they catch a sound of the turmoil in my soul? Time did not suffice to tell them and words failed me. But as *I groaned aloud in the weariness of my heart*,[1] all my anguish reached your ears. *You knew all my longings; the very light that shone in my eyes was mine no longer*.[1] For the light was within, while I looked on the world outside. The light was not in space, but I thought only of things that are contained in space, and in them I found no place where I might rest. They offered me no haven where I could own myself satisfied and content, nor would they let me turn back where I might find contentment and satisfaction. For I was a creature of a higher order than these things, though I was lower than you. You were my true Joy while I was subject to you, and you had made subject to me all the things that you had created inferior to me. This was the right mean, the middle path that led to my salvation, if only I remained true to your likeness and, by serving you, became the master of my own body. But when I rose in pride against you and *made onslaught* against my Lord, *proud of my strong sinews*,[2] even those lower things became my masters and oppressed me, and nowhere could I find respite or time to draw my breath. Everywhere I looked they loomed before my eyes in swarms and clusters, and when I set myself to thinking and tried to escape from them, images of these selfsame things blocked my way, as though they were asking where I meant to go, unclean and undeserving as I was. All this had grown

[1] Ps. 37: 9–11 (38: 8–10). [2] Job 15: 26.

143

from my wound, for the proud *lie wounded at your feet*,[1] and I was separated from you by the swelling of my pride, as though my cheeks were so puffed with conceit that they masked the sight of my eyes.

8

O Lord, you are eternal but you will not *always be indignant with us*,[2] because you take pity on our dust and ashes. You saw me and it pleased you to transform all that was misshapen in me. Your goad was thrusting at my heart, giving me no peace until the eye of my soul could discern you without mistake. Under the secret touch of your healing hand my swelling pride subsided, and day by day the pain I suffered brought me health, like an ointment which stung but cleared the confusion and darkness from the eye of my mind.

9

First of all it was your will to make me understand how *you thwart the proud and keep your grace for the humble*[3] and what a great act of your mercy it was to show mankind the way of humility when *the Word was made flesh and came to dwell*[4] among the men of this world. So you made use of a man, one who was bloated with the most outrageous pride, to procure me some of the books of the Platonists, translated from the Greek into Latin. In them I read – not, of course, word for word, though the sense was the same and it was supported by all kinds of different arguments – that *at the beginning of time the Word already was; and God had the Word abiding with him, and the Word was God. He abode, at the beginning of time, with God. It was through him that all things came into being, and without him came nothing that has come to be. In him there was life, and that life was the light of men. And the light shines in darkness, a darkness which was not able to master it.* I read too that the soul of man, although it *bears witness of the light, is not the Light.* But the Word, who is himself God, *is the true Light, which enlightens every soul born into the world. He, through whom the world was made, was in the world, and the world treated him as a stranger.* But I did not find it written in those books that *he came to what was his own, and they who*

---

[1] Ps. 88: 11 (89: 10). [2] Ps. 84: 6 (85: 5). [3] 1 Pet. 5: 5.
[4] John 1: 14.

were his own gave him no welcome. But all those who did welcome him he empowered to become the children of God, all those who believe in his name.[1]

In the same books I also read of the Word, God, that his *birth came not from human stock, not from nature's will or man's, but from God.*[1] But I did not read in them that *the Word was made flesh and came to dwell among us.*[1]

Though the words were different and the meaning was expressed in various ways, I also learned from these books that God the Son, being himself, like the Father, of divine nature, *did not see, in the rank of Godhead, a prize to be coveted.*[2] But they do not say that *he dispossessed himself, and took the nature of a slave, fashioned in the likeness of men, and presenting himself to us in human form; and then he lowered his own dignity, accepted an obedience which brought him to death, death on a cross;* and *that is why God has raised him from the dead, given him that name which is greater than any other name; so that everything in heaven and on earth and under the earth must bend the knee before the name of Jesus, and every tongue must confess Jesus Christ as the Lord, dwelling in the glory of God the Father.*[3]

The books also tell us that your only-begotten Son abides for ever in eternity with you; that before all time began, he was; that he is above all time and suffers no change; that of his plenty our souls receive their part[4] and hence derive their blessings; and that by partaking of the Wisdom which abides in them they are renewed, and this is the source of their wisdom. But there is no word in those books to say that *in his own appointed time he underwent death for us sinners*[5] and that *you did not even spare your own Son, but gave him up for us all.*[6] For *you have hidden all this from the wise and revealed it to little children*, so that *all that labour and are burdened may come to him and he will give them rest*, because *he is gentle and humble of heart*;[7] and *in his own laws he will train the humble, in his own paths the humble he will guide*,[8] for he sees how we are *restless and forlorn* and is *merciful to our sins.*[9] But some hold their heads so high in the clouds of learning that they do not hear him saying *Learn from me; I am gentle and humble of heart; and you shall find rest for your souls.*[10] Although they have the knowledge of God,

---

[1] John 1: 1–14.   [2] Philipp. 2: 6.   [3] Philipp. 2: 7–11.   [4] See John 1: 16.
[5] Rom. 5: 6.   [6] Rom. 8: 32.   [7] Matt. 11: 25, 28, 29.   [8] Ps. 24: 9 (25: 9).
[9] Ps. 24: 18 (25: 18).   [10] Matt. 11: 29.

they do not honour him or give thanks to him as God; they become fantastic in their notions, and their senseless hearts grow benighted; they, who claim to be so wise, turn fools.[1]

I read too in the same books that *they had exchanged the glory of the imperishable God*[1] for idols and all kinds of make-believe, *for representations of perishable man, of bird and beast and reptile,*[1] in fact for that Egyptian food for which Esau lost his birthright, since your firstborn people worshipped the head of a four-footed beast instead of you and, *turning their thoughts towards Egypt,*[2] bowed down their souls, those images made in your likeness, before the *semblance of a bullock at grass.*[3] All this I found in those books, but I did not feed upon this fare. For it pleased you, Lord, to rid Jacob of the reproach of inferiority so that *the elder should be the servant of the younger,*[4] and you have called the Gentiles into your inheritance. It was from the Gentiles that I had come to you, and I set my mind upon the gold which you willed your people to carry away from Egypt for, wherever it was, it was yours. Through your apostle you told the Athenians that *it is in you that we live and move and have our being, as some of their own poets have told us.*[5] And, of course, the books I was reading were written in Athens. But your people had used the gold that was yours to serve the idols of the Egyptians, for *they had exchanged God's truth for a lie, reverencing and worshipping the creature in preference to the Creator,*[1] and it was not upon these idols that I set my mind.

10

These books served to remind me to return to my own self. Under your guidance I entered into the depths of my soul, and this I was able to do because *your aid befriended me.*[6] I entered, and with the eye of my soul, such as it was, I saw the Light that never changes casting its rays over the same eye of my soul, over my mind. It was not the common light of day that is seen by the eye of every living thing of flesh and blood, nor was it some more spacious light of the same sort, as if the light of day were to shine far, far brighter than it does and fill all space with a vast brilliance. What I saw was something quite, quite different from any light we know on earth. It shone above my mind,

---

[1] Rom. 1: 21–3, 25.　[2] Acts 7: 39.　[3] Ps. 105: 20 (106: 20).
[4] Rom. 9: 12.　[5] Acts 17: 28.　[6] Ps. 29: 11 (30: 10).

but not in the way that oil floats above water or the sky hangs over the earth. It was above me because it was itself the Light that made me, and I was below because I was made by it. All who know the truth know this Light, and all who know this Light know eternity. It is the Light that charity knows.

Eternal Truth, true Love, beloved Eternity – all this, my God, you are, and it is to you that I sigh by night and day. When first I knew you, you raised me up so that I could see that there was something to be seen, but also that I was not yet able to see it. I gazed on you with eyes too weak to resist the dazzle of your splendour. Your light shone upon me in its brilliance, and I thrilled with love and dread alike. I realized that I was far away from you. It was as though I were in a land where all is different from your own and I heard your voice calling from on high, saying 'I am the food of full-grown men. Grow and you shall feed on me. But you shall not change me into your own substance, as you do with the food of your body. Instead you shall be changed into me.' I realized too that you have chastened man for his sins[1]; you made my life melt away like gossamer,[1] and I asked myself 'Is truth then nothing at all, simply because it has no extension in space, with or without limits?' And, far off, I heard your voice saying *I am the God who IS.*[2] I heard your voice, as we hear voices that speak to our hearts, and at once I had no cause to doubt. I might more easily have doubted that I was alive than that Truth had being. For we catch sight of the Truth, as he is known through his creation.[3]

11

Also I considered all the other things that are of a lower order than yourself, and I saw that they have not absolute being in themselves, nor are they entirely without being. They are real in so far as they have their being from you, but unreal in the sense that they are not what you are. For it is only that which remains in being without change that truly is. As for me, *I know no other content but clinging to God,*[4] because unless my being remains in him, it cannot remain in me. But *himself ever unchanged, he makes all things new.*[5] *I own him as my God; he has no need of aught that is mine.*[6]

[1] See Ps. 38: 12 (39: 11).   [2] Ex. 3: 14.   [3] See Rom. 1: 20.
[4] Ps. 72: 28 (73: 28).   [5] Wisdom 7: 27.   [6] Ps. 15: 2 (16: 2).

12

It was made clear to me also that even those things which are subject
to decay are good. If they were of the supreme order of goodness,
they could not become corrupt; but neither could they become
corrupt unless they were in some way good. For if they were
supremely good, it would not be possible for them to be corrupted.
On the other hand, if they were entirely without good, there would be
nothing in them that could become corrupt. For corruption is harmful, but unless it diminished what is good, it could do no harm. The
conclusion then must be either that corruption does no harm – which
is not possible; or that everything which is corrupted is deprived of
good – which is beyond doubt. But if they are deprived of all good,
they will not exist at all. For if they still exist but can no longer be
corrupted, they will be better than they were before, because they
now continue their existence in an incorruptible state. But could anything be more preposterous than to say that things are made better by
being deprived of all good?

So we must conclude that if things are deprived of all good, they
cease altogether to be; and this means that as long as they are, they are
good. Therefore, whatever is, is good; and evil, the origin of which
I was trying to find, is not a substance, because if it were a substance,
it would be good. For either it would be an incorruptible substance
of the supreme order of goodness, or it would be a corruptible substance which would not be corruptible unless it were good. So it
became obvious to me that all that you have made is good, and that
there are no substances whatsoever that were not made by you. And
because you did not make them all equal, each single thing is good
and collectively they are very good, for our God made his whole
creation *very good*.[1]

13

For you evil does not exist, and not only for you but for the whole of
your creation as well, because there is nothing outside it which could
invade it and break down the order which you have imposed on it.
Yet in the separate parts of your creation there are some things which
we think of as evil because they are at variance with other things. But

[1] Gen. 1: 31.

there are other things again with which they are in accord, and then they are good. In themselves, too, they are good. And all these things which are at variance with one another are in accord with the lower part of creation which we call the earth. The sky, which is cloudy and windy, suits the earth to which it belongs. So it would be wrong for me to wish that these earthly things did not exist, for even if I saw nothing but them, I might wish for something better, but still I ought to praise you for them alone. For all things *give praise to the Lord on earth, monsters of the sea and all its depths; fire and hail, snow and mist, and the storm-wind that executes his decree; all you mountains and hills, all you fruit trees and cedars; all you wild beasts and cattle, creeping things and birds that fly in air; all you kings and peoples of the world, all you that are princes and judges on earth; young men and maids, old men and boys together; let them all give praise to the Lord's name.*[1] The heavens, too, ring with your praises, O God, for you are the God of us all. *Give praise to the Lord in heaven; praise him, all that dwells on high. Praise him, all you angels of his, praise him, all his armies. Praise him, sun and moon; praise him, every star that shines. Praise him, you highest heavens, you waters beyond the heavens. Let all these praise the Lord.*[2] And since this is so, I no longer wished for a better world, because I was thinking of the whole of creation, and in the light of this clearer discernment I had come to see that though the higher things are better than the lower, the sum of all creation is better than the higher things alone.

14

Those who find fault with any part of your creation are bereft of reason, just as I was when I decried many of the things which you had made. My soul did not dare to find fault with my God, and therefore it would not admit that what it found distasteful had been created by you. This was why it went astray and accepted the theory of the two substances. This, too, was why it could find no rest and talked so foolishly. Then it had turned away from this error and had imagined for itself a god extended through all space to infinity. Thinking that this god was you, it had enshrined this idol in its heart and, once again, had made of itself a temple abominable to you. But, unknown to me, you soothed my head and closed my eyes so that

[1] Ps. 148: 7–13.   [2] Ps. 148: 1–5.

they should not look upon *vain phantoms*,[1] and I became drowsy and slept away my madness. I awoke in you and saw that you were infinite, but not in the way I had supposed. This I saw, but it was not with the sight of the flesh that I saw it.

15

I looked at other things too and saw that they owe their being to you. I saw that all finite things are in you, not as though you were a place that contained them, but in a different manner. They are in you because you hold all things in your truth as though they were in your hand, and all things are true in so far as they have being. Falsehood is nothing but the supposed existence of something which has no being.

I saw too that all things are fit and proper not only to the places but also to the times in which they exist, and that you, who are the only eternal Being, did not begin to work only after countless ages of time had elapsed, because no age of time, past or still to come, could either come or go if it were not that you abide for ever and cause time to come and go.

16

From my own experience I knew that there was nothing strange in the fact that a man who finds bread agreeable to the taste when he is well finds it hard to eat when he is sick, and that light is hateful to sore eyes, although we welcome it when our sight is hale and clear. In the same way the wicked find your justice disagreeable, just as they find vipers and worms unpleasant. Yet these animals were created good by you. They were created to suit the lower order of your creation. Thus the wicked themselves are suited to this lower order in as much as they are unlike you, whereas they are suited to the higher order in so far as they become more like you. And when I asked myself what wickedness was, I saw that it was not a substance but perversion of the will when it turns aside from you, O God, who are the supreme substance, and veers towards things of the lowest order, being *bowelled alive*[2] and becoming inflated with desire for things outside itself.

[1] Ps. 118: 37 (119: 37).　[2] Ecclus. 10: 10.

17

I was astonished that although I now loved you and not some phantom in your place, I did not persist in enjoyment of my God. Your beauty drew me to you, but soon I was dragged away from you by my own weight and in dismay I plunged again into the things of this world. The weight I carried was the habit of the flesh. But your memory remained with me and I had no doubt at all that you were the one to whom I should cling, only I was not yet able to cling to you. For *ever the soul is weighed down by a mortal body, earth-bound cell that clogs the manifold activity of its thought.*[1] I was most certain, too, that *from the foundations of the world men have caught sight of your invisible nature, your eternal power, and your divineness, as they are known through your creatures.*[2] For I wondered how it was that I could appreciate beauty in material things on earth or in the heavens, and what it was that enabled me to make correct decisions about things that are subject to change and to rule that one thing ought to be like this, another like that. I wondered how it was that I was able to judge them in this way, and I realized that above my own mind, which was liable to change, there was the never changing, true eternity of truth. So, step by step, my thoughts moved on from the consideration of material things to the soul, which perceives things through the senses of the body, and then to the soul's inner power, to which the bodily senses communicate external facts. Beyond this dumb animals cannot go. The next stage is the power of reason, to which the facts communicated by the bodily senses are submitted for judgement.

This power of reason, realizing that in me it too was liable to change, led me on to consider the source of its own understanding. It withdrew my thoughts from their normal course and drew back from the confusion of images which pressed upon it, so that it might discover what light it was that had been shed upon it when it proclaimed for certain that what was immutable was better than that which was not, and how it had come to know the immutable itself. For unless, by some means, it had known the immutable, it could not possibly have been certain that it was preferable to the mutable. And so, in an instant of awe, my mind attained to the sight of the God who IS. Then, at last, *I caught sight of your invisible nature, as it is*

[1]Wisdom 9: 15. [2] Rom. 1: 20.

151

known through your creatures.[1] But I had no strength to fix my gaze upon them. In my weakness I recoiled and fell back into my old ways, carrying with me nothing but the memory of something that I loved and longed for, as though I had sensed the fragrance of the fare but was not yet able to eat it.

18

I began to search for a means of gaining the strength I needed to enjoy you, but I could not find this means until I embraced the *mediator between God and men, Jesus Christ, who is a man, like them,*[2] and also *rules as God over all things, blessed for ever.*[3] He was calling to me and saying *I am the way; I am truth and life.*[4] He it was who united with our flesh that food which I was too weak to take; for *the Word was made flesh*[5] so that your Wisdom, by which you created all things, might be milk to suckle us in infancy. For I was not humble enough to conceive of the humble Jesus Christ as my God, nor had I learnt what lesson his human weakness was meant to teach. The lesson is that your Word, the eternal Truth, which far surpasses even the higher parts of your creation, raises up to himself all who subject themselves to him. From the clay of which we are made he built for himself a lowly house in this world below, so that by this means he might cause those who were to be made subject to him to abandon themselves and come over to his side. He would cure them of the pride that swelled up in their hearts and would nurture love in its place, so that they should no longer stride ahead confident in themselves, but might realize their own weakness when at their feet they saw God himself, enfeebled by sharing this garment of our mortality. And at last, from weariness, they would cast themselves down upon his humanity, and when it rose they too would rise.

19

But my mind was filled with thoughts of another kind. I thought of Christ, my Lord, as no more than a man of extraordinary wisdom, whom none could equal. In particular, I saw his miraculous birth of a virgin mother, by which he showed us that worldly goods are to

[1] Rom. 1: 20.   [2] 1 Tim. 2: 5.   [3] Rom. 9: 5.   [4] John 14: 6.
[5] John 1: 14.

be despised for the sake of immortal life, as an act of the divine providence which looks after us, so that by it he merited his special authority as our Teacher. But I had not even an inkling of the meaning of the mystery of the Word made flesh. From what the Scriptures record of him, that is, that he ate and drank, that he slept and walked, that he was sometimes happy, sometimes sad, and that he preached his gospel, all I had learnt was that when your Word took human flesh, he must also have taken a human soul and a human mind. This much is known to all who know that your Word cannot suffer change, as by now I knew in so far as I was able to know it. In fact I had no doubt of it at all. For to move the limbs of the body at one moment, and at the next to hold them still; to feel some emotion and then not to feel it; at one instant to utter words which convey an intelligible meaning, and at another to remain silent – all these characteristics show that there is the possibility of change in the mind and in the soul. If they were falsely attributed to Christ in the records of his life, the whole of Scripture would be open to the charge of falsehood and mankind could no longer place any sure faith in it. So, granted that what the Scriptures say is true, I accepted that Christ was perfect man. I did not think of him as having only the body of a man or man's body and sensitive soul without his reasoning mind, but as a man complete. And I thought he was superior to other men, not because he was Truth in person, but because in him human nature had reached the highest point of excellence and he had a more perfect share of divine wisdom.

Alypius, on the other hand, thought that Catholics believed that God was clothed in the flesh in the sense that in Christ there was the Godhead and the flesh but no soul. He did not think that their teaching was that Christ had a human mind, and his approach to the Christian faith itself was delayed because he found it a convincing argument that the actions recorded of Christ could only have been performed by a creature endowed with vitality and the power of reason. Later on he realized that this was the error of the Apollinarian heretics and he then gladly accepted the Catholic faith. As for me, I must confess that it was not until later that I learned how true Catholic doctrine differs from the error of Photinus in interpreting the meaning of the incarnation. It is indeed true that the refutation of heretics gives greater prominence to the tenets of your Church and the principles of sound doctrine. *For parties there must needs be, so that those who are true metal may be distinguished from the rest.*[1]

20

By reading these books of the Platonists I had been prompted to look for truth as something incorporeal, and I *caught sight of your invisible nature, as it is known through your creatures.*[2] Though I was thwarted of my wish to know more, I was conscious of what it was that my mind was too clouded to see. I was certain both that you are and that you are infinite, though without extent in terms of space either limited or unlimited. I was sure that it is you who truly are, since you are always the same, varying in neither part nor motion. I knew too that all other things derive their being from you, and the one indisputable proof of this is the fact that they exist at all. I was quite certain of these truths, but I was too weak to enjoy you. I used to talk glibly as though I knew the meaning of it all, but unless I had looked for the way which leads to you in Christ our Saviour, instead of finding knowledge I should have found my end. For I had now begun to wish to be thought wise. I was full of self-esteem, which was a punishment of my own making. I ought to have deplored my state, but instead my *knowledge only bred self-conceit.*[3] For was I not without charity, which builds its edifice on the firm foundation of humility, that is, on Jesus Christ?[4] But how could I expect that the Platonist books would ever teach me charity? I believe that it was by your will that I came across those books before I studied the Scriptures, because you wished me always to remember the impression they had made on me, so that later on, when I had been chastened by your Holy Writ and my wounds had been touched by your healing hand, I should be able to see and understand the difference between presumption and confession, between those who see the goal that they must reach, but cannot see the road by which they are to reach it, and those who see the road to that blessed country which is meant to be no mere vision but our home. For if I had not come across these books until after I had been formed in the mould of your Holy Scriptures and had learnt to love you through familiarity with them, the Platonist teaching might have swept me from my foothold on

[1] I Cor. 11: 19.   [2] Rom. 1: 20.   [3] I Cor. 8: 1.   [4] See I Cor. 3: 11; 8: 1.

the solid ground of piety, and even if I had held firm to the spirit in which the Scriptures had imbued me for my salvation, I might have thought it possible for a man who read nothing but the Platonist books to derive the same spirit from them alone.

21

So I seized eagerly upon the venerable writings inspired by your Holy Spirit, especially those of the apostle Paul. At one time it had seemed to me that he sometimes contradicted himself and that the purport of his words did not agree with the evidence of the law and the prophets, but these difficulties now disappeared once and for all. I saw clearly that his sober discourse pointed to one meaning only, and I learned to *rejoice with awe in my heart*.[1] I began to read and discovered that whatever truth I had found in the Platonists was set down here as well, and with it there was praise for your grace bestowed. For Saint Paul teaches that he who sees ought not to boast as though what he sees, and even the power by which he sees, *had not come to him by gift*.[2] For, whatever powers he has, *did they not come to him by gift?*[2] By the gift of grace he is not only shown how to see you, who are always the same, but is also given the strength to hold you. By your grace, too, if he is far from you and cannot see you, he is enabled to walk upon the path that leads him closer to you, so that he may see you and hold you. For even if a man *inwardly applauds God's disposition*,[3] how is he to resist *that other disposition in his lower self, which raises war against the disposition of his conscience, so that he is handed over as a captive to that disposition towards sin, which his lower self contains?*[4] For *you have right on your side, O Lord, but we are sinners, that have wronged and forsaken you; all is amiss with us.*[5] *We are bowed down by your chastisement.*[6] In justice we have been delivered to the author of sin, the prince of death, because he has coaxed us to make our wills conform with his, for *he has never taken his stand upon your truth.*[7] What is man to do in his plight? *Who is to set him free from a nature thus doomed to death? Nothing else than the grace of God, through Jesus Christ our Lord*,[8] who was begotten by you to be co-eternal with yourself and whom you made *when first you went about your work*.[9] In

[1] Ps. 2: 11. [2] 1 Cor. 4: 7. [3] Rom. 7: 22. [4] Rom. 7: 23. [5] Dan. 3: 27–32.
[6] Ps. 31: 4 (32: 4). [7] John 8: 44. [8] Rom. 7: 24, 25.
[9] Prov. 8: 22.

him the prince of this world found no crime worthy of death:[1] yet he slew him, and thus *the decree made to our prejudice was cancelled.*[2]

None of this is contained in the Platonists' books. Their pages have not the mien of the true love of God. They make no mention of the tears of confession or of *the sacrifice that you will never disdain, a broken spirit, a heart that is humbled and contrite,*[3] nor do they speak of the salvation of your people, *the city adorned like a bride,*[4] *the foretaste of your Spirit,*[5] or the chalice of our redemption. In them no one sings *No rest has my soul but in God's hands; to him I look for deliverance. I have no other stronghold, no other deliverer but him; safe in his protection, I fear no deadly fall.*[6] In them no one listens to the voice which says *Come to me all you that labour.*[7] They disdain his teaching because *he is gentle and humble of heart. For you have hidden all this from the wise and revealed it to little children.*[7]

It is one thing to descry the land of peace from a wooded hilltop and, unable to find the way to it, struggle on through trackless wastes where traitors and runaways, captained by their prince, who is *lion and serpent*[8] in one, lie in wait to attack. It is another thing to follow the high road to that land of peace, the way that is defended by the care of the heavenly Commander. Here there are no deserters from heaven's army to prey upon the traveller, because they shun this road as a torment.

It was wonderful how these truths came home to me when I read *the least of your apostles*[9] and the thought of your works had set my heart trembling.

---

[1] See John 14: 30.   [2] Col. 2: 14.   [3] Ps. 50: 19 (51: 17).
[4] Apoc. (Rev.) 21: 2.   [5] II Cor. 1: 22.   [6] Ps. 61: 2, 3 (62: 1, 2).
[7] Matt. 11: 25, 28, 29.   [8] Ps. 90: 13 (91: 13).   [9] I Cor. 15: 9.

BOOK VIII

I

M<small>Y</small> God, let me be thankful as I remember and acknowledge all your mercies. Let my whole self be steeped in love of you and all my being cry *Lord, there is none like you!*[1] *You have broken the chains that bound me; I will sacrifice in your honour.*[2] I shall tell how it was that you broke them and, when they hear what I have to tell, all who adore you will exclaim, 'Blessed be the Lord in heaven and on earth. Great and wonderful is his name.'

The words of your Scriptures were planted firmly in my heart and on all sides you were there like a rampart to defend me. Of your eternal life I was certain, although I had only seen it like *a confused reflection in a mirror*,[3] and I had now been rid of all my doubts about an incorruptible substance from which all other substance takes its being. I did not ask for more certain proof of you, but only to be made more steadfast in you. But in my worldly life all was confusion. My heart had still to be *rid of the leaven which remained over*.[4] I should have been glad to follow the right road, to follow our Saviour himself, but still I could not make up my mind to venture along the narrow path.

By your inspiration it seemed to me a good plan to go and see Simplicianus who, as I could see for myself, was a good servant of yours. The light of your grace plainly shone in him and, besides, I had been told that from boyhood he had always led a most devout life. By now he was an old man and I thought that in all the long years he had spent to such good purpose in following your way he must have gained great experience and much knowledge, as indeed he had. I hoped that if I put my problems to him, he would draw upon his experience and his knowledge to show me how best a man in my state of mind might walk upon your way.

[1] Ps. 34: 10 (35: 10).   [2] Ps. 115: 7 (116: 7).   [3] 1 Cor. 13: 12.
[4] 1 Cor. 5: 7.

I saw that the Church was full, yet its members each followed a different path in the world. But my own life in the world was unhappy. It was a heavy burden to me, because the hope of honour and wealth was no longer, as before, a spur to my ambition, enabling me to bear so onerous a life devoted to their service. Such things now held no attractions for me in comparison with your sweetness and *my love of the house where you dwell, the shrine of your glory*.[1] But I was still held firm in the bonds of woman's love. Your apostle did not forbid me to marry, although he counselled a better state, wishing earnestly that all men should be as he was himself. But I was a weaker man and was tempted to choose an easier course, and this reason alone prevented me from reaching a decision upon my other problems. I was listless, exhausted by the canker of anxiety, because there were other reasons too why I found it irksome to be forced to adapt myself to living with a wife, as I was pledged to do. The voice of Truth had told me that there are some who have *made themselves eunuchs for love of the kingdom of heaven*.[2] But he also said Let only those *take this in whose hearts are large enough for it*.[3]

What folly it argues in man's nature, this ignorance of God! So much good seen, and he, who is existent Good, not known![3] But, in this sense, I was no longer the victim of such folly. I had overcome it, and from the evidence of all creation I had found you, our Creator, and your Word who is God with you, one God with you, by whom you created all things. But there are godless men of another kind, those who *have the knowledge of God, but do not honour him or give thanks to him as God*.[4] I had fallen into this error also, but *your right hand supported me*.[5] You rescued me and set me where I might recover the health of my soul. For you have told man that wisdom is *fearing the Lord*,[6] and you have warned him *Do not give yourself airs of wisdom*[7], for *they who claim to be so wise turn fools*.[8] I had already found the pearl of great value and I ought to have sold all that I had and bought it.[9] But I still held back.

[1] Ps. 25: 8 (26: 8).   [2] Matt. 19: 12.   [3] Wisdom, 13: 1.
[4] Rom. 1: 21.   [5] Ps. 17: 36 (18: 35).   [6] Job 28: 28.
[7] Prov. 3: 7.   [8] Rom. 1: 22.   [9] See Matt. 13: 46.

2

So I went to Simplicianus, the spiritual father of Ambrose who was now a bishop. Ambrose truly loved him like a father, for it was through him that he had received your grace. I told him how I had drifted from error to error, and when I mentioned that I had read some of the books of the Platonists translated into Latin by Victorinus, who had once been professor of rhetoric at Rome and, so I had been told, had died a Christian, Simplicianus said that he was glad that I had not stumbled upon the writings of other philosophers, which were full of fallacies and misrepresentations *drawn from worldly principles*.[1] In the Platonists, he said, God and his Word are constantly implied. Then, to encourage me to follow Christ's example of humility, which is *hidden from the wise and revealed to little children*,[2] he told me about Victorinus, whom he had known intimately when he was in Rome. I shall repeat the story here, because it shows the great glory of your grace and for your glory I must tell it.

Victorinus was an old man of great learning, with a profound knowledge of all the liberal sciences. He had studied a great many books of philosophy and published criticisms of them. He had been master to many distinguished members of the Senate, and to mark his outstanding ability as a teacher, he had even been awarded a statue in the Roman forum – a great honour in the eyes of the world. He had always been a worshipper of idols and had taken part in the sacrilegious rites which were then in vogue amongst most of the nobility of Rome. Rome, in fact, had become the suppliant of the gods whom she had once defeated, for her leaders now talked only of 'prodigies, monstrous deities of every sort, and Anubis who barked like a dog – all the gods who had once battled against Neptune, Venus, and Minerva.'[3] For many years Victorinus, now an old man, had never ceased to defend these practices with all the fire of his oratory, and yet he was not ashamed to be the child of Christ and to become an infant at your font, submitting his neck to the yoke of humility and bowing his head before the ignominy of the Cross.

O Lord, Lord, *who bade heaven stoop and came down to earth, at whose touch the mountains were wreathed in smoke*,[4] how did you find the way

[1] Col. 2: 8.   [2] Matt. 11: 25.   [3] Virgil, *Aeneid* VIII, 698–700.
[4] Ps. 143: 5 (144: 5).

to his heart? He read the Holy Scriptures, so Simplicianus told me, and made the most painstaking and careful study of all Christian literature. Privately as between friends, though never in public, he used to say to Simplicianus, 'I want you to know that I am now a Christian.' Simplicianus used to reply, 'I shall not believe it or count you as a Christian until I see you in the Church of Christ.' At this Victorinus would laugh and say, 'Is it then the walls of the church that make the Christian?'

He often repeated his claim to be a Christian, and each time Simplicianus gave him the same answer, only to receive the same rejoinder about the walls. He was afraid of offending his proud friends who worshipped heathen gods, and he thought that a storm of hostility would break upon him from the peak of their Babylonian dignity, as though it were from the cedars of Lebanon which the Lord had not yet brought down.[1] But later on, as a result of his attentive reading, he became resolute. He was seized by the fear that Christ might deny him before the holy angels if he was too faint-hearted to acknowledge Christ before men, and he felt himself guilty of a great crime in being ashamed of the sacraments instituted by your Word in his lowly state, whereas he was not ashamed of the impious rites devoted to those proud deities whom his own pride had led him to follow and accept. So he repudiated vanity and turned in shame to the truth. Simplicianus told me that quite unexpectedly and without warning he said, 'Let us go to the church. I want to be made a Christian.' So Simplicianus, unable to contain his joy, went with him to the church. He was instructed in the first mysteries of the faith and soon afterwards, to the wonder of Rome and the joy of the Church, he gave in his name to be reborn through baptism. *Ungodly men were ill content to see it. Vainly they gnashed their teeth in envy.*[2] But *happy was the man whose trust was there bestowed, who shunned the rites of strange gods, the lure of lies.*[3]

Eventually the time came for making his profession of faith. At Rome those who are about to enter into your grace usually make their profession in a set form of words which they learn by heart and recite from a raised platform in view of the faithful, but Simplicianus said that the priests offered to allow Victorinus to make his

[1] See Ps. 28: 5 (29: 5).   [2] Ps. 111: 10 (112: 10).   [3] Ps. 39: 5 (40: 4).

profession in private, as they often did for people who seemed likely to find the ceremony embarrassing. But Victorinus preferred to declare his salvation in full sight of the assembled faithful. For there was no salvation in the rhetoric which he taught, and yet he had professed it in public. If he was not afraid of uttering his own words before a crowd of madmen, why should he be frightened to name your Word before your meek flock? So when he mounted the platform to make his profession, all who knew him joyfully whispered his name to their neighbours. There can have been none who did not know him, and the hushed voices of the whole exultant congregation joined in the murmur 'Victorinus, Victorinus'. They were quick to let their joy be heard when they saw him, but just as quickly came a hush as they waited to hear him speak. He made his declaration of the true faith with splendid confidence, and all would gladly have seized him in their arms and clutched him to their hearts. But it was with the arms of love and joy that they seized him and made him their own.

3

O God, who are so good, what is it that makes men rejoice more for the salvation of a soul for which all had despaired, or one that is delivered from great danger, than for one for which hope has never been lost or one which has been in less peril? You too, merciful Father, *rejoice more over one sinner who repents than over ninety-nine souls that are justified and have no need of repentance.*[1] We also are overjoyed when we hear that the sheep that was lost is carried home on the happy shepherd's shoulders and that the coin is returned to your treasury, while the neighbours rejoice with the woman who found it.[2] The joy of Mass in your church moves us to tears when we hear the gospel which tells us how the younger son died and returned to life, and how he was lost and found again.[2] You rejoice in us and in your angels, who are sanctified by holy charity. For you are always the same, because all those things which are neither unchangeable nor endure for ever are for ever known to you and your knowledge of them is unchangeable.

What is it then that makes the soul rejoice more over things which it finds or regains than it would if it had always had them? There is

[1] Luke 15: 7.   [2] See Luke 15.

proof of this in worldly things as well and the evidence that pro‑ claims the truth of it is all around us. The victorious general marches home in triumph, but there would have been no victory if he had not fought, and the greater the danger in the battle, the greater the joy of the triumph. Sailors are tossed in a storm which threatens to wreck their ship. They are terror-stricken at the thought of impending death, but when the sky clears and the sea is calmed, their fear gives place to joy no less profound. One whom we love is ill. His pulse tells us that he is in danger and all who long for him to get well suffer in sympathy, but once he is on the road to recovery, even though he has not yet the strength to walk as he used to do, we are happier at this than we were before, when he was quite well and could walk without effort. Men even procure for themselves the pleasures of this life by means of pain, not unexpected pain which comes upon them uninvited, but pain which they deliberately induce for themselves. There is no pleasure in eating and drinking unless it is preceded by the discomfort of hunger and thirst. Drunkards eat salty things to make their throats dry and painful, so that they may enjoy the pleasure of quenching their thirst. It is customary, too, for girls who are engaged to be married to delay the wedding for fear that a husband who has not suffered the trials of a long courtship may think his bride too cheaply won.

If this is true of mean and reprehensible forms of pleasure, it is equally true of those which are legitimate and permissible. It can be seen in friendship of the purest and most honourable kind, and it was true of the younger son who died and returned to life, who was lost and found again. It is always the case that the greater the joy, the greater is the pain which precedes it. Why should this be, O Lord my God, when you are your own eternal joy, you are Joy itself and you are always surrounded by creatures which rejoice in you? Why is it that in this part of your creation which we know there is this ebb and flow of progress and retreat, of hurt and reconciliation? Is this the rhythm of our world? Is this what you prescribed when from the heights of heaven to the depths of earth, from the first beginnings to the end of time, from the angel to the worm, from the first movement to the last, you allotted a proper place and a proper time to good things of every kind and to all your just works? How can I hope to understand the height and the depth of you, from the greatest to the most lowly of your works? You never depart from us, yet it is hard for us to return to you.

<h1 style="text-align:center">4</h1>

Come, O Lord, and stir our hearts. Call us back to yourself. Kindle your fire in us and carry us away. Let us scent your fragrance and taste your sweetness. Let us love you and hasten to your side.

Are there not many who return to you from a deeper pit of darkness than Victorinus? They come to you and their darkness grows bright when they accept the light by which all who accept it *are empowered to become the children of God.*[1] But if they are less famous than Victorinus there is less rejoicing, even among those who know them. For when large numbers of people share their joy in common the happiness of each is greater, because each adds fuel to the other's flame. Moreover, when converts are well known, their example guides many others to salvation. Where they lead many are sure to follow, and this is why those who already have the faith are delighted at their conversion, because their joy is not reserved for the famous alone. It would be unthinkable that men of wealth and power should be more welcome in your Church than those who are poor and unknown. For *you have chosen what the world holds weak, so as to abash the strong; you have chosen what the world holds base and contemptible, nay you have chosen what is nothing, so as to bring to nothing what is now in being.*[2] It was through the apostle Paul that you spoke these words and he too, the least of the apostles, chose to change his name from Saul to Paul to mark the great victory when Sergius Paulus, the pro-consul, his pride laid low by the apostle's bold words, submitted to the gentle yoke of Christ and became a subject of the Great King.[3] For the firmer our enemy the devil holds a man in his power, and the greater the number of others whom he holds captive through this man, the greater the victory when he is won back. The devil has a firmer hold on men in high places because of their pride in their rank, and through them he keeps hold on many more because of the influence they wield. So the more your children prized the heart of Victorinus, which had been an impregnable stronghold of the devil, and his tongue, which Satan had used as a sharp and powerful

[1] John 1: 12.   [2] I Cor. 1: 27, 28.   [3] See Acts 13.

weapon to slay so many men, the more abundant, and rightly so, was their joy when they saw that our King had *made the strong man his prisoner*.[1] They saw his possessions taken from him and cleansed, so that he was *proved the object of his Lord's regard, hallowed, and service-able, and fit for all honourable employment*.[2]

5

When your servant Simplicianus told me the story of Victorinus, I began to glow with fervour to imitate him. This, of course, was why Simplicianus had told it to me. He went on to say that under the emperor Julian a law had been passed to prohibit Christians from teaching literature and rhetoric. Victorinus had obeyed the law, pre-ferring to give up his own school of words rather than desert your Word, by which you make *the lips of infants vocal with praise*.[3] In this he seemed to me not so much courageous as fortunate, because in this way he found the means of devoting himself entirely to you. I longed to do the same, but I was held fast, not in fetters clamped upon me by another, but by my own will, which had the strength of iron chains. The enemy held my will in his power and from it he had made a chain and shackled me. For my will was perverse and lust had grown from it, and when I gave in to lust habit was born, and when I did not resist the habit it became a necessity. These were the links which together formed what I have called my chain, and it held me fast in the duress of servitude. But the new will which had come to life in me and made me wish to serve you freely and enjoy you, my God, who are our only certain joy, was not yet strong enough to overcome the old, hardened as it was by the passage of time. So these two wills within me, one old, one new, one the servant of the flesh, the other of the spirit, were in conflict and be-tween them they tore my soul apart.

From my own experience I now understood what I had read – that *the impulses of nature and the impulses of the spirit are at war with one another*.[4] In this warfare I was on both sides, but I took the part of that which I approved in myself rather than the part of that which I disapproved. For my true self was no longer on the side of which I

---

[1] Matt. 12: 29. [2] II Tim. 2: 21. [3] Wisdom 10: 21.
[4] Gal. 5: 17.

disapproved, since to a great extent I was now its reluctant victim rather than its willing tool. Yet it was by my own doing that habit had become so potent an enemy, because it was by my own will that I had reached the state in which I no longer wished to stay. Who can justly complain when just punishment overtakes the sinner? I could no longer claim that I had no clear perception of the truth – the excuse which I used to make to myself for postponing my renunciation of the world and my entry into your service – for by now I was quite certain of it. But I was still bound to earth and refused to serve in your army. Instead of fearing, as I ought, to be held back by all that encumbered me, I was frightened to be free of it. In fact I bore the burden of the world as contentedly as one sometimes bears a heavy load of sleep. My thoughts, as I meditated upon you, were like the efforts of a man who tries to wake but cannot and sinks back into the depths of slumber. No one wants to sleep for ever, for everyone rightly agrees that it is better to be awake. Yet a man often staves off the effort to rouse himself when his body is leaden with inertia. He is glad to settle down once more, although it is against his better judgement and it is already time he were up and about. In the same way I was quite sure that it was better for me to give myself up to your love than to surrender to my own lust. But while I wanted to follow the first course and was convinced that it was right, I was still a slave to the pleasures of the second. I had no answer to make when you said *Awake, you who sleep, and arise from the dead, and Christ shall give you light.*[1] You used all means to prove the truth of your words, and now that I was convinced that they were true, the only answers I could give were the drowsy words of an idler – 'Soon', 'Presently', 'Let me wait a little longer'. But 'soon' was not soon and 'a little longer' grew much longer. It was in vain that *inwardly I applauded your disposition,* when that other *disposition in my lower self raised war against the disposition of my conscience and handed me over as a captive to that disposition towards sin, which my lower self contained.*[2] For the rule of sin is the force of habit, by which the mind is swept along and held fast even against its will, yet deservedly, because it fell into the habit of its own accord. *Pitiable creature that I was, who was to set me free from a nature thus doomed to death? Nothing else than the grace of God, through Jesus Christ our Lord.*[3]

[1] Eph. 5: 14.   [2] Rom. 7: 22, 23.   [3] Rom. 7: 24, 25.

6

O Lord, my Helper and my Redeemer, I shall now tell and confess to the glory of your name how you released me from the fetters of lust which held me so tightly shackled and from my slavery to the things of this world. I continued to lead my usual life, but I was growing more and more unsettled and day after day I poured out my heart to you. I went to your church whenever I had time from my work, which was a painful load upon my shoulders. Alypius was with me, now taking respite from his legal work after a third term of office as assessor. He was looking for clients who would pay him for his advice, just as my pupils paid me for skill in words, if it is possible to teach such an art. As a gesture of friendship to Alypius and me, Nebridius had consented to act as assistant to a great friend of ours named Verecundus, a Milanese, who was a teacher of grammar and had made most insistent demands upon our friendship for one of us to give him loyal help, for this he badly needed. It was not the desire of profit that had led Nebridius to accept the post, for if he had wished he could have earned more by teaching literature. But he was too good and kind a friend to refuse a request which appealed to his good nature. He did what was asked of him in an unobtrusive way, taking care not to attract the attention of important people, as the world reckons importance, in case contact with them should disturb his peace of mind. For he wanted to keep his mind free and enjoy as many hours of leisure as he could for the purpose of thinking and reading and listening to discussions on philosophy.

One day when for some reason that I cannot recall Nebridius was not with us, Alypius and I were visited at our house by a fellow-countryman of ours from Africa, a man named Ponticianus, who held a high position in the Emperor's household. He had some request to make of us and we sat down to talk. He happened to notice a book lying on a table used for games, which was near where we were sitting. He picked it up and opened it and was greatly surprised to find that it contained Paul's epistles, for he had supposed that it was one of the books which used to tax all my strength as a teacher. Then he smiled and looked at me and said how glad he was, and how surprised, to find this book, and no others, there before my eyes. He of course was a Christian and a faithful servant to you, our

God. Time and again he knelt before you in church repeating his prayers and lingering over them. When I told him that I studied Paul's writings with the greatest attention, he began to tell us the story of Antony, the Egyptian monk, whose name was held in high honour by your servants, although Alypius and I had never heard it until then. When Ponticianus realized this, he went into greater detail, wishing to instil some knowledge of this great man into our ignorant minds, for he was very surprised that we had not heard of him. For our part, we too were astonished to hear of the wonders you had worked so recently, almost in our own times, and witnessed by so many, in the true faith and in the Catholic Church. In fact all three of us were amazed, Alypius and I because the story we heard was so remarkable, and Ponticianus because we had not heard it before.

After this he went on to tell us of the groups of monks in the monasteries, of their way of life that savours of your sweetness, and of the fruitful wastes of the desert. All of this was new to us. There was a monastery at Milan also, outside the walls, full of good brethren under the care of Ambrose, but we knew nothing of this either. Ponticianus continued to talk and we listened in silence. Eventually he told us of the time when he and three of his companions were at Trêves. One afternoon, while the Emperor was watching the games in the circus, they went out to stroll in the gardens near the city walls. They became separated into two groups, Ponticianus and one of the others remaining together while the other two went off by themselves. As they wandered on, the second pair came to a house which was the home of some servants of yours, men poor in spirit, to whom the kingdom of heaven belongs.[1] In the house they found a book containing the life of Antony. One of them began to read it and was so fascinated and thrilled by the story that even before he had finished reading he conceived the idea of taking upon himself the same kind of life and abandoning his career in the world – both he and his friend were officials in the service of the State – in order to become your servant. All at once he was filled with the love of holiness. Angry with himself and full of remorse, he looked at his friend and said, 'What do we hope to gain by all the efforts we make? What are we looking for? What is our purpose in serving the State? Can we hope

[1] See Matt. 5: 3.

for anything better at Court than to be the Emperor's friends? Even so, surely our position would be precarious and exposed to much danger? We shall meet it at every turn, only to reach another danger which is greater still. And how long is it to be before we reach it? But if I wish, I can become the friend of God at this very moment.'

After saying this he turned back to the book, labouring under the pain of the new life that was taking birth in him. He read on and in his heart, where you alone could see, a change was taking place. His mind was being divested of the world, as could presently be seen. For while he was reading, his heart leaping and turning in his breast, a cry broke from him as he saw the better course and determined to take it. Your servant now, he said to his friend, 'I have torn myself free from all our ambitions and have decided to serve God. From this very moment, here and now, I shall start to serve him. If you will not follow my lead, do not stand in my way.' The other answered that he would stand by his comrade, for such service was glorious and the reward was great. So these two, now your servants, built their tower at the cost which had to be paid, that is, at the cost of giving up all they possessed and following you.[1]

At this moment Ponticianus and the man who had been walking with him in another part of the garden arrived at the house, looking for their friends. Now that they had found them they said that it was time to go home, as the daylight was beginning to fade. But the other two told them of the decision they had made and what they proposed to do. They explained what had made them decide to take this course and how they had agreed upon it, and they asked their friends, if they would not join them, at least not to put obstacles in their way. Ponticianus said that he and the other man did not change their old ways, but they were moved to tears for their own state of life. In all reverence they congratulated the others and commended themselves to their prayers. Then they went back to the palace, burdened with hearts that were bound to this earth; but the others remained in the house and their hearts were fixed upon heaven. Both these men were under a promise of marriage, but once the two women heard what had happened, they too dedicated their virginity to you.

[1] See Luke 14: 28–34.

7

This was what Ponticianus told us. But while he was speaking, O Lord, you were turning me around to look at myself. For I had placed myself behind my own back, refusing to see myself. You were setting me before my own eyes so that I could see how sordid I was, how deformed and squalid, how tainted with ulcers and sores. I saw it all and stood aghast, but there was no place where I could escape from myself. If I tried to turn my eyes away they fell on Ponticianus, still telling his tale, and in this way you brought me face to face with myself once more, forcing me upon my own sight so that I should see my wickedness and loathe it. I had known it all along, but I had always pretended that it was something different. I had turned a blind eye and forgotten it.

But now, the more my heart warmed to those two men as I heard how they had made the choice that was to save them by giving themselves up entirely to your care, the more bitterly I hated myself in comparison with them. Many years of my life had passed – twelve, unless I am wrong – since I had read Cicero's *Hortensius* at the age of nineteen and it had inspired me to study philosophy. But I still postponed my renunciation of this world's joys, which would have left me free to look for that other happiness, the very search for which, let alone its discovery, I ought to have prized above the discovery of all human treasures and kingdoms or the ability to enjoy all the pleasures of the body at a mere nod of the head. As a youth I had been woefully at fault, particularly in early adolesence. I had prayed to you for chastity and said 'Give me chastity and continence, but not yet.' For I was afraid that you would answer my prayer at once and cure me too soon of the disease of lust, which I wanted satisfied, not quelled. I had wandered on along the road of vice in the sacrilegious superstition of the Manichees, not because I thought that it was right, but because I preferred it to the Christian belief, which I did not explore as I ought but opposed out of malice.

I had pretended to myself that the reason why, day after day, I staved off the decision to renounce worldly ambition and follow you alone was that I could see no certain goal towards which I might steer my course. But the time had now come when I stood naked before my own eyes, while my conscience upbraided me. 'Am I to be silent? Did you not always say that you would not discard your load of vanity for the sake of a truth that was not proved? Now you know that the truth is proved, but the load is still on your shoulders. Yet here are others who have exchanged their load for wings, although they did not wear themselves out in the search for truth or spend ten years or more in making up their minds.'

All the time that Ponticianus was speaking my conscience gnawed away at me like this. I was overcome by burning shame, and when he had finished his tale and completed the business for which he had come, he went away and I was left to my own thoughts. I made all sorts of accusations against myself. I cudgelled my soul and belaboured it with reasons why it should follow me now that I was trying so hard to follow you. But it fought back. It would not obey and yet could offer no excuse. All its old arguments were exhausted and had been shown to be false. It remained silent and afraid, for as much as the loss of life itself it feared the stanching of the flow of habit, by which it was wasting away to death.

8

My inner self was a house divided against itself. In the heat of the fierce conflict which I had stirred up against my soul in our common abode, my heart, I turned upon Alypius. My looks betrayed the commotion in my mind as I exclaimed, 'What is the matter with us? What is the meaning of this story? These men have not had our schooling, yet they stand up and storm the gates of heaven while we, for all our learning, lie here grovelling in this world of flesh and blood! Is it because they have led the way that we are ashamed to follow? Is it not worse to hold back?'

I cannot remember the words I used. I said something to this effect and then my feelings proved too strong for me. I broke off and turned away, leaving him to gaze at me speechless and astonished. For my voice sounded strange and the expression of my face and eyes, my flushed cheeks, and the pitch of my voice told him more of the state of my mind than the actual words that I spoke.

There was a small garden attached to the house where we lodged. We were free to make use of it as well as the rest of the house because our host, the owner of the house, did not live there. I now found myself driven by the tumult in my breast to take refuge in this garden, where no one could interrupt that fierce struggle, in which I was my own contestant, until it came to its conclusion. What the conclusion was to be you knew, O Lord, but I did not. Meanwhile I was beside myself with madness that would bring me sanity. I was dying a death that would bring me life. I knew the evil that was in me, but the good that was soon to be born in me I did not know. So I went out into the garden and Alypius followed at my heels. His presence was no intrusion on my solitude, and how could he leave me in that state? We sat down as far as possible from the house. I was frantic, overcome by violent anger with myself for not accepting your will and entering into your covenant. Yet in my bones I knew that this was what I ought to do. In my heart of hearts I praised it to the skies. And to reach this goal I needed no chariot or ship. I need not even walk as far as I had come from the house to the place where we sat, for to make the journey, and to arrive safely, no more was required than an act of will. But it must be a resolute and whole-hearted act of the will, not some lame wish which I kept turning over and over in my mind, so that it had to wrestle with itself, part of it trying to rise, part falling to the ground.

During this agony of indecision I performed many bodily actions, things which a man cannot always do, even if he wills to do them. If he has lost his limbs, or is bound hand and foot, or if his body is weakened by illness or under some other handicap, there are things which he cannot do. I tore my hair and hammered my forehead with my fists; I locked my fingers and hugged my knees; and I did all this because I made an act of will to do it. But I might have had the will to do it and yet not have done it, if my limbs had been unable to move in compliance with my will. I performed all these actions, in which the will and the power to act are not the same. Yet I did not do that one thing which I should have been far, far better pleased to do than all the rest and could have done at once, as soon as I had the will to do it, because as soon as I had the will to do so, I should have willed it wholeheartedly. For in this case the power to act was the same as the will. To will it was to do it. Yet I did not do it. My body responded to the slightest wish of my mind by moving its limbs at the least hint from me, and it did so more readily than my mind obeyed itself by assenting to its own great desire, which could be accomplished simply by an act of will.

9

Why does this strange phenomenon occur? What causes it? O Lord in your mercy give me light to see, for it may be that the answer to my question lies in the secret punishment of man and in the penitence which casts a deep shadow on the sons of Adam. Why does this strange phenomenon occur? What causes it? The mind gives an order to the body and is at once obeyed, but when it gives an order to itself, it is resisted. The mind commands the hand to move and is so readily obeyed that the order can scarcely be distinguished from its execution. Yet the mind is mind and the hand is part of the body. But when the mind commands the mind to make an act of will, these two are one and the same and yet the order is not obeyed. Why does this happen? What is the cause of it? The mind orders itself to make an act of will, and it would not give this order unless it willed to do so; yet it does not carry out its own command. But it does not fully will to do this thing and therefore its orders are not fully given. It gives the order only in so far as it wills, and in so far as it does not will the order is not carried out. For the will commands that an act of will should be made, and it gives this command to itself, not to some other will. The reason, then, why the command is not obeyed is that it is not given with the full will. For if the will were full, it would not command itself to be full, since it would be so already. It is therefore no strange phenomenon partly to will to do something and partly to will not to do it. It is a disease of the mind, which does not wholly rise to the heights where it is lifted by the truth, because it is weighed down by habit. So there are two wills in us, because neither by itself is the whole will, and each possesses what the other lacks.

10

There are many abroad who talk of their own fantasies and lead men's minds astray.[1] They assert that because they have observed that there are two wills at odds with each other when we try to reach a decision,

[1] Titus 1: 10.

we must therefore have two minds of different natures, one good, the other evil. *Let them vanish at God's presence as the smoke vanishes.*[1] As long as they hold these evil beliefs they are evil themselves, but even they will be good if they see the truth and accept it, so that your apostle may say to them *Once you were all darkness; now, in the Lord you are all daylight.*[2] These people want to be light, not in the Lord, but in themselves, because they think that the nature of the soul is the same as God. In this way their darkness becomes denser still, because in their abominable arrogance they have separated themselves still further from you, who are *the true Light which enlightens every soul born into the world.*[3] I say to them 'Take care what you say, and blush for shame. Enter God's presence, and find there enlightenment; *here is no room for downcast looks.*'[4]

When I was trying to reach a decision about serving the Lord my God, as I had long intended to do, it was I who willed to take this course and again it was I who willed not to take it. It was I and I alone. But I neither willed to do it nor refused to do it with my full will. So I was at odds with myself. I was throwing myself into confusion. All this happened to me although I did not want it, but it did not prove that there was some second mind in me besides my own. It only meant that my mind was being punished. *My action did not come from me, but from the sinful principle that dwells in me.*[5] It was part of the punishment of a sin freely committed by Adam, my first father.

If there were as many different natures in us as there are conflicting wills, we should have a great many more natures than merely two. Suppose that someone is trying to decide whether to go to the theatre or to the Manichees' meeting-house. The Manichees will say, 'Clearly he has two natures, the good one bringing him here to us and the bad one leading him away. Otherwise, how can you explain this dilemma of two opposing wills?' I say that the will to attend their meetings is just as bad as the will to go off to the theatre, but in their opinion it can only be a good will that leads a man to come to them. Suppose then that one of us is wavering between two conflicting wills and cannot make up his mind whether to go to the theatre or to our church. Will not the Manichees be embarrassed to know what to say? Either they must admit – which they will not do – that it is a

[1] Ps. 67: 3 (68: 2).   [2] Eph. 5: 8.   [3] John 1: 9.   [4] Ps. 33: 6 (34: 5).
[5] Rom. 7: 17.

173

good will which brings a man to our church, just as in their opinion it is a good will which brings their own communicants and adherents to their church; or they must presume that there are two evil natures and two evil minds in conflict in one man. If they think this, they will disprove their own theory that there is one good and one evil will in man. The only alternative is for them to be converted to the truth and to cease to deny that when a man tries to make a decision, he has one soul which is torn between conflicting wills.

So let us hear no more of their assertion, when they observe two wills in conflict in one man, that there are two opposing minds in him, one good and the other bad, and that they are in conflict because they spring from two opposing substances and two opposing principles. For you, O God of truth, prove that they are utterly wrong. You demolish their arguments and confound them completely. It may be that both the wills are bad. For instance, a man may be trying to decide whether to commit murder by poison or by stabbing; whether he should swindle another man out of one part of his property or another, that is, if he cannot obtain both; whether he should spend his money extravagantly on pleasure or hoard it like a miser; or whether he should go to the games in the circus or to the theatre, when there is a performance at both places on the same day. In this last case there may be a third possibility, that he should go and rob another person's house, if he has the chance. There may even be a fourth choice open to him, because he may wonder whether to go and commit adultery, if the occasion arises at the same time. These possibilities may all occur at the same moment and all may seem equally desirable. The man cannot do all these things at once, and his mind is torn between four wills which cannot be reconciled – perhaps more than four, because there are a great many things that he might wish to do. But the Manichees do not claim that there are as many different substances in us as this.

It is just the same when the wills are good. If I question the Manichees whether it is good to find pleasure in reading Paul's Epistles or in the tranquil enjoyment of a Psalm or in a discussion of the Gospel, they will reply in each case that it is good. Supposing, then, that a man finds all these things equally attractive and the chance to do all of them occurs at the same time, is it not true that as long as he cannot make up his mind which of them he most wants to do his heart is torn between several different desires? All these different desires are good, yet they are in conflict with each other until he chooses a single course to which the will may apply itself as a single whole, so that it is no longer split into several different wills.

The same is true when the higher part of our nature aspires after eternal bliss while our lower self is held back by the love of temporal pleasure. It is the same soul that wills both, but it wills neither of them with the full force of the will. So it is wrenched in two and suffers great trials, because while truth teaches it to prefer one course, habit prevents it from relinquishing the other.

II

This was the nature of my sickness. I was in torment, reproaching myself more bitterly than ever as I twisted and turned in my chain. I hoped that my chain might be broken once and for all, because it was only a small thing that held me now. All the same it held me. And you, O Lord, never ceased to watch over my secret heart. In your stern mercy you lashed me with the twin scourge of fear and shame in case I should give way once more and the worn and slender remnant of my chain should not be broken but gain new strength and bind me all the faster. In my heart I kept saying 'Let it be now, let it be now!', and merely by saying this I was on the point of making the resolution. I was on the point of making it, but I did not succeed. Yet I did not fall back into my old state. I stood on the brink of resolution, waiting to take fresh breath. I tried again and came a little nearer to my goal, and then a little nearer still, so that I could almost reach out and grasp it. But I did not reach it. I could not reach out to it or grasp it, because I held back from the step by which I should die to death and become alive to life. My lower instincts, which had taken firm hold of me, were stronger than the higher, which were untried. And the closer I came to the moment which was to mark the great change in me, the more I shrank from it in horror. But it did not drive me back or turn me from my purpose: it merely left me hanging in suspense.

I was held back by mere trifles, the most paltry inanities, all my old attachments. They plucked at my garment of flesh and whispered, 'Are you going to dismiss us? From this moment we shall never be with you again, for ever and ever. From this moment you will never again be allowed to do this thing or that, for evermore.' What was it, my God, that they meant when they whispered 'this thing or that?' Things so sordid and so shameful that I beg you in your mercy to keep the soul of your servant free from them! These voices, as I heard them, seemed less than half as loud as they had been before. They no longer barred my way, blatantly contradictory, but their mutterings seemed to reach me from behind, as though they were stealthily plucking at my back, trying to make me turn my head when I wanted to go forward. Yet, in my state of indecision, they kept me from tearing myself away, from shaking myself free of them and leaping across the barrier to the other side, where you were calling me. Habit was too strong for me when it asked 'Do you think you can live without these things?'

But by now the voice of habit was very faint. I had turned my eyes elsewhere, and while I stood trembling at the barrier, on the other side I could see the chaste beauty of Continence in all her serene, unsullied joy, as she modestly beckoned me to cross over and to hesitate no more. She stretched out loving hands to welcome and embrace me, holding up a host of good examples to my sight. With her were countless boys and girls, great numbers of the young and people of all ages, staid widows and women still virgins in old age. And in their midst was Continence herself, not barren but a fruitful mother of children, of joys born of you, O Lord, her Spouse. She smiled at me to give me courage, as though she were saying, 'Can you not do what these men and these women do? Do you think they find the strength to do it in themselves and not in the Lord their God? It was the Lord their God who gave me to them. Why do you try to stand in your own strength and fail? Cast yourself upon God and have no fear. He will not shrink away and let you fall. Cast yourself upon him without fear, for he will welcome you and cure you of your ills.' I was overcome with shame, because I was still listening to the futile mutterings of my lower self and I was still hanging in suspense. And again Continence seemed to say, 'Close your ears to the unclean whispers of your body, so that it may be mortified. It tells you of things that delight you, but not such things as the law of the Lord your God has to tell.'[1]

[1] See Ps. 118: 85 (119: 85).

In this way I wrangled with myself, in my own heart, about my own self. And all the while Alypius stayed at my side, silently awaiting the outcome of this agitation that was new in me.

12

I probed the hidden depths of my soul and wrung its pitiful secrets from it, and when I mustered them all before the eyes of my heart, a great storm broke within me, bringing with it a great deluge of tears. I stood up and left Alypius so that I might weep and cry to my heart's content, for it occurred to me that tears were best shed in solitude. I moved away far enough to avoid being embarrassed even by his presence. He must have realized what my feelings were, for I suppose I had said something and he had known from the sound of my voice that I was ready to burst into tears. So I stood up and left him where we had been sitting, utterly bewildered. Somehow I flung myself down beneath a fig tree and gave way to the tears which now streamed from my eyes, the sacrifice that is acceptable to you.[1] I had much to say to you, my God, not in these very words but in this strain: *Lord, will you never be content?*[2] *Must we always taste your vengeance? Forget the long record of our sins.*[3] For I felt that I was still the captive of my sins, and in my misery I kept crying 'How long shall I go on saying "tomorrow, tomorrow"? Why not now? Why not make an end of my ugly sins at this moment?'

I was asking myself these questions, weeping all the while with the most bitter sorrow in my heart, when all at once I heard the sing-song voice of a child in a nearby house. Whether it was the voice of a boy or a girl I cannot say, but again and again it repeated the refrain 'Take it and read, take it and read'. At this I looked up, thinking hard whether there was any kind of game in which children used to chant words like these, but I could not remember ever hearing them before. I stemmed my flood of tears and stood up, telling myself that this could only be a divine command to open my book of Scripture and read the first passage on which my eyes should fall. For I had heard the story of Antony, and I remembered how he had happened to go into a church while the Gospel was being read and had taken it as a counsel addressed to himself when he heard the words *Go home*

[1] See Ps. 50: 19 (51: 17).   [2] Ps. 6: 4 (6: 3).   [3] Ps. 78: 5, 8 (79: 5, 8).

and sell all that belongs to you. Give it to the poor, and so the treasure you have shall be in heaven; then come back and follow me.[1] By this divine pronouncement he had at once been converted to you.

So I hurried back to the place where Alypius was sitting, for when I stood up to move away I had put down the book containing Paul's Epistles. I seized it and opened it, and in silence I read the first passage on which my eyes fell: *Not in revelling and drunkenness, not in lust and wantonness, not in quarrels and rivalries. Rather, arm yourselves with the Lord Jesus Christ; spend no more thought on nature and nature's appetites.*[2] I had no wish to read more and no need to do so. For in an instant, as I came to the end of the sentence, it was as though the light of confidence flooded into my heart and all the darkness of doubt was dispelled.

I marked the place with my finger or by some other sign and closed the book. My looks now were quite calm as I told Alypius what had happened to me. He too told me what he had been feeling, which of course I did not know. He asked to see what I had read. I showed it to him and he read on beyond the text which I had read. I did not know what followed, but it was this: *Find room among you for a man of over-delicate conscience.*[3] Alypius applied this to himself and told me so. This admonition was enough to give him strength, and without suffering the distress of hesitation he made his resolution and took this good purpose to himself. And it very well suited his moral character, which had long been far, far better than my own.

Then we went in and told my mother, who was overjoyed. And when we went on to describe how it had all happened, she was jubilant with triumph and glorified you, *who are powerful enough, and more than powerful enough, to carry out your purpose beyond all our hopes and dreams.*[4] For she saw that you had granted her far more than she used to ask in her tearful prayers and plaintive lamentations. You converted me to yourself, so that I no longer desired a wife or placed any hope in this world but stood firmly upon the rule of faith, where

[1] Matt. 19: 21.
[2] Rom. 13: 13, 14. Saint Augustine does not quote the whole passage, which begins '*Let us pass our time honourably, as by the light of day, not in revelling and drunkenness,*' etc.
[3] Rom. 14: 1.
[4] Eph. 3: 20.

you had shown me to her in a dream so many years before. And you *turned her sadness into rejoicing,*[1] into joy far fuller than her dearest wish, far sweeter and more chaste than any she had hoped to find in children begotten of my flesh.

[1] Ps. 29: 12 (30: 11).

BOOK IX

I

LORD, *I am your servant, born of your own handmaid. You have broken the chains that bound me; I will sacrifice in your honour.*[1] Let me praise you in my heart, let me praise you with my tongue. *Let this be the cry of my whole being: Lord, there is none like you.*[2] Let them say this and, in answer, I beg you to *whisper in my heart, I am here to save you.*[3]

Who am I? What kind of man am I? What evil have I not done? Or if there is evil that I have not done, what evil is there that I have not spoken? If there is any that I have not spoken, what evil is there that I have not willed to do? But you, O Lord, are good. You are merciful. You saw how deep I was sunk in death, and it was your power that drained dry the well of corruption in the depths of my heart. And all that you asked of me was to deny my own will and accept yours.

But, during all those years, where was my free will? What was the hidden, secret place from which it was summoned in a moment, so that I might bend my neck to your easy yoke and take your light burden on my shoulders, Christ Jesus, my Helper and my Redeemer? How sweet all at once it was for me to be rid of those fruitless joys which I had once feared to lose and was now glad to reject! You drove them from me, you who are the true, the sovereign joy. You drove them from me and took their place, you who are sweeter than all pleasure, though not to flesh and blood, you who outshine all light yet are hidden deeper than any secret in our hearts, you who surpass all honour though not in the eyes of men who see all honour in themselves. At last my mind was free from the gnawing anxieties of ambition and gain, from wallowing in filth and scratching the itching sore of lust. I began to talk to you freely, O Lord my God, my Light, my Wealth, and my Salvation.

[1] Ps. 115: 16, 17 (116: 16, 17).   [2] Ps. 34: 10 (35: 10).   [3] Ps. 34: 3 (35: 3).

Knowing that you were watching me I thought it best to retire quietly from the market where I sold the services of my tongue rather than make an abrupt and sensational departure. I intended that young pupils who gave no thought to your law or your peace, but only to lies and the insane warfare of the courts, should no longer buy from my lips any weapon to arm their madness. Luckily there were now only a few days left before the autumn holidays, and I decided to bear with this delay and withdraw at the proper time. Now that I had been redeemed by you I had no intention of offering myself for sale again. This plan was known to you, but no man knew of it except our closest friends. We had agreed that it should not be made generally known, although, as we climbed up from the valley of tears,[1] singing the song of ascent,[2] you had given us sharp arrows[3] and burning coals[3] to use against any cunning tongues[3] that might speak against us under the pretence of giving good advice and devour us with their love, just as men devour food for which they have a liking.

You had pierced our hearts with the arrows of your love, and we carried your words with us as though they were staked to our living bodies. Ranged before our minds, so that our thoughts were full of them, were the examples of your servants whose darkness you had made light and whose death you had changed to life. Their example fired us and banished our dull inertia, so that we turned no more to worldly things. It lighted in us so strong a flame that no cunning tongue[3] could puff it out with the breath of antagonism, but only fanned it to a fiercer heat. But for the sake of your name, which you have made holy throughout the world, there would certainly be others to applaud our decision and our plans. Because of this we thought it would seem like ostentation if instead of waiting for the holidays, which were now so close at hand, I were to resign at once from the profession which I practised openly and because of which I was a public figure. My action would attract the attention of everyone, and when they saw that I had chosen not to wait for the beginning of the holidays, although it was so close, many of them would say that it was because I wanted to win a fine reputation for myself.

[1] See Ps. 83: 7 (84: 6). [2] See Ps. 119–33 (120–34).
[3] See Ps. 119: 34 (120: 34).

And what good would it have done me to have my motives discussed and debated and *to have allowed that which was a good thing for me to be brought into disrepute?*[1]

Besides this, during the summer I had developed a weakness of the lungs, the result of too much study. I found breathing difficult and had pains in the chest which were symptomatic of lung-trouble. My voice was husky and I could not speak for long at a time. At first I had been worried, because I had nearly been obliged to give up the strain of teaching altogether or, at least, to take a rest from it in order to undergo treatment and regain my strength. But once the will to *wait quietly and have proof that you are God*[2] had begun to grow in me, and then had become a firm resolution – this you know, my God – I was even glad to have this genuine excuse with which I could appease indignant parents, who for the sake of their children would never have been willing to allow me my freedom. So, with this thought to cheer me, I managed to endure to the end of this period of waiting. It was a little less than three weeks, as far as I can remember, but I needed all my powers of endurance even to wait so short a time as this. I had lost the ambition to make money, which had always helped me to bear the strain of teaching, and if patience had not taken its place I should have been left without a prop to prevent me from being crushed beneath the burden. Some of your servants, my brothers in the faith, may say that it was sinful of me to allow myself to occupy the chair of lies even for one hour now that my heart was fully given to your service. I will not dispute it. But, O most merciful Lord, did you not forgive this sin and remit its guilt, as well as all my other horrible and deadly sins, in the holy water of baptism?

3

Vercundus was wearing himself out with worry over our new-found blessings. As he saw it, because of his own ties, which still bound him fast, he was deprived of our company. He was not yet a Christian, but it was his Christian wife who proved the strongest tie of all and he was kept, for the present, from taking the course which we had set ourselves, because he always said that he would not be a Christian except in the very way that was not open to him. All the

[1] Rom. 14: 16. [2] Ps. 45: 11 (46: 10).

same he kindly offered to allow us to stay in his country house for as long as we needed. You will surely repay him for his goodness, O Lord, when the just are given their reward, since you have already awarded him the lot of the just. For after our departure, when we were at Rome, he fell ill and died, but not before he had been received into the Church on his sick-bed. In this you had mercy not only on him but also on us, for the memory of the extreme kindness which he showed us as our friend would have tormented us with unbearable sorrow, if we had not known that he was one of your flock. We thank you for this, you who are our God. We are yours. We know it from the charges you lay upon us and the consolations you give. You are faithful to your promises, and for his country house at Cassiciacum, where we found rest in you, far from the world and its troubles, you are repaying Verecundus with the contentment of your paradise, where nothing ever fades away. For in your mountain, your fruitful mountain that is rich like butter,[1] you have forgiven him his sins upon earth.

But while Verecundus suffered these torments, Nebridius shared our joy. Before he was a Christian he, like us, had been caught in the pitfall of the most deadly error and had refused to believe in the reality of the Truth incarnate, the body of your Son. But he had now struggled free and although he had not yet received any of the sacraments of your Church, he was most persistent in his search for the truth. Not long after we had been converted and born again in your baptism you freed him from this life. By then he too had become a faithful Catholic. He served you in perfect chastity and continence at home in Africa with his family, for through him his whole household had been made Christian. Now he lives in Abraham's bosom, and whatever may be the meaning of that bosom, there, Nebridius lives, my very dear friend, taken by you to be your son, no longer simply one whom you had freed from bondage. There he lives. For what other place is there for a soul such as his? There he lives, in that very place about which he used to question me so much, poor ignorant man that I was. He no longer lays his ear to my lips, but with the lips of his spirit he drinks in wisdom at your fountain. He drinks till his thirst is slaked, and his happiness is never-ending. And I cannot believe that the draught intoxicates him so that he forgets me,

[1] See Ps. 67: 16 (68: 15).

for it is you, O Lord, whom he drinks in and you are mindful of your servants.

This was how matters stood with us. We consoled Verecundus in his sadness, not allowing our friendship with him to lapse because of our conversion and urging him to remain faithful to the married state which was his lot. As for Nebridius, we waited for him to follow our lead, and this he might well have done, for he was very close to doing so. In fact he was on the point of being converted when, at long last, my period of waiting came to an end. To me that time seemed to drag on day after day, because I was longing for respite and the freedom to give voice to the song that swelled up deep within me: *True to my heart's promise, I have eyes only for you; I long, Lord, for your presence.*[1]

4

The day came when my release from the profession of rhetoric was to become a reality, just as, in my mind, I was free from it already. The deed was done, and you rescued my tongue, as you had already rescued my heart. Praising you and full of joy I set out for the house in the country with all my friends and relations. Once we were there I began at last to serve you with my pen. The books I wrote are evidence of this, although the old air can still be sensed in them, as though I were still panting from my exertions in the school of pride. In them are recorded the discussions I held with my friends who were with me and my deliberations with myself when I was alone in your presence; and my correspondence with Nebridius, who was not with us, can still be read in my letters. But time could never suffice for me to set down on paper all the great blessings which you bestowed upon me, particularly at that time, since I must hurry on to tell of greater things.

For I remember the kind of man I was, O Lord, and it is a sweet task to confess how you tamed me by pricking my heart with your goad; how you *bridged every valley, levelled every mountain and hill* of my thoughts; how you *cut straight their windings, paved their rough paths*;[2] and how you also brought Alypius, whom in my heart I regarded as a brother, to submit to the name of your only-begotten Son, our Lord and Saviour Jesus Christ. At first he thought this

[1] Ps. 26: 8 (27: 8). [2] Is. 40: 4.

unworthy of mention in my books, because he wanted them to carry the scholarly fragrance of *the cedars of Lebanon, which the Lord has now broken*,[1] rather than that of the herbs with which the Church heals the bites of serpents.

How I cried out to you, my God, when I read the Psalms of David, those hymns of faith, those songs of a pious heart in which the spirit of pride can find no place! I was new to your true love. I was a catechumen living at leisure in that country house with Alypius, a catechumen like myself, and my mother, who never left us. She had the weak body of a woman but the strong faith of a man, the composure of her years, a mother's love for her son, and the devotion of a Christian. How I cried out to you when I read those Psalms! How they set me on fire with love of you! I was burning to echo them to all the world, if only I could, so that they might vanquish man's pride. And indeed they are sung throughout the world and just as none can hide away from the sun *none can escape your burning heat*[2]. The thought of the Manichees filled me with angry resentment and bitter sorrow, yet I pitied them too, because in their ignorance of the sacraments that heal us they raved against the very remedy that could have cured them of their madness. I wished that they could have been somewhere at hand, unknown to me, to watch my face and hear my voice as I read the fourth Psalm. They would have seen how deeply it moved me. *When I call on your name, listen to me, O God, and grant redress; still, in time of trouble, you have brought me relief; have pity on me now, and hear my prayer.*[3] How I wish that they could have heard me speak these words! And how I wish that I might have been unaware that they could hear, so that they need have no cause to think that my own words, which escaped from me as I recited the Psalm, were uttered for their benefit alone! And it is true enough that I would not have uttered them, or if I had, I should not have uttered them in the same way, if I had known that they were watching and listening. And if I had uttered them, the Manichees would not have understood them in the way that I spoke them. They would not have understood how this cry came from my inmost heart, when I was alone in your presence.

I quivered with fear, yet at the same time I was aglow with hope, rejoicing in your mercy, my Father. All these emotions were revealed

[1] Ps. 28: 5 (29: 5).   [2] Ps. 18: 7 (19: 6).   [3] P4: 2 (4: 1)

in the light of my eyes and the tremor of my voice, when I read the message of your Holy Spirit: *Great ones of the world, will your hearts always be hardened, will you never cease setting your heart on shadows, following a lie?*[1] For it was just this that I had done. But you, O Lord, had already raised your holy Son to glory. You had *raised him from the dead and bidden him sit on your right hand,*[2] so that from his place at your side he might send us the one whom he had promised, the Paraclete, *the truthgiving Spirit.*[3] He had already sent the Paraclete and I had not known it. He had already risen from the dead and ascended into heaven. He had already been raised to glory, and because of this he had sent the Paraclete. *The Spirit had not yet been given to men, because Jesus had not yet been raised to glory.*[4] But the words of the prophet are loud in our ears: *Will your hearts always be hardened, will you never cease setting your heart on shadows, following a lie? Be sure*[5] of this, that the Lord has raised his holy Son to glory. The words are loud in our ears – *Will your hearts always be hardened? Be sure* – and yet, for so long, I had not known their meaning. I had set my heart on shadows and followed a lie, and this was why I was frightened when I heard these words, because I remembered that I had been just such a man as those to whom they are spoken. For there had been shadows and lies in the phantasms which I had taken for the truth, and the memory of my past wrung many loud cries of sorrow from my lips. How I wish that my cries could have been heard by those who still set their hearts on shadows and followed lies! Perhaps they would have been made to feel the error of their ways and would have disgorged it like vomit. And you would have heard them when they cried out to you, for Christ, who pleads with you for us, truly died for us in the flesh.

I read on: *Tremble and sin no more,*[6] and this moved me deeply, my God, because by now I had learnt to tremble for my past, so that in future I might sin no more. And it was right that I should tremble, because it was not some other nature belonging to the tribe of darkness that had sinned in me, as the Manichees pretend. They do not tremble, but *they store up retribution for themselves against the day of retribution, when God will reveal the justice of his judgements.*[7]

[1] Ps. 4: 3 (4: 2).   [2] Eph. 1: 20.   [3] John 14: 17.   [4] John 7: 39.
[5] Ps. 4: 3 (4: 2)   [6] Ps. 4: 5 (4: 4).   [7] Rom. 2: 5.

The good which I now sought was not outside myself. I did not look for it in things which are seen with the eye of the flesh by the light of the sun. For those who try to find joy in things outside themselves easily vanish away into emptiness. They waste themselves on the temporal pleasures of the visible world. Their minds are starved and they nibble at empty shadows. How I wish that they would tire of going hungry and *cry out for a sight of better times*![1] This is the answer they would hear from us: *Already, Lord, the sunshine of your favour has been plainly shown to us.*[1] For we are not ourselves *the Light which enlightens every soul.*[2] We are enlightened by you, so that we who *once were all darkness* may now, *in the Lord, be all daylight.*[3] How I wish that they could see the eternal light within us! Now that I had glimpsed it myself I fretted and chafed because I could not make them see it. For if they had come to me and *cried out for a sight of better times,*[1] I should have seen that their hearts looked out through their eyes on the world outside, away from you. But it was in my inmost heart, where I had grown angry with myself, where I had been stung with remorse, where I had slain my old self and offered it in sacrifice, where I had first purposed to renew my life and had placed my hope in you, it was there that you had begun to make me love you and had *made me glad at heart.*[4] It was my eyes that read these words but my soul that knew their meaning. They brought a cry to my lips and I wished no more for the manifold riches of this earth, things on which I should lose time, only to be lost in time myself. For in eternity, which is one alone, I had other *corn and wine and oil.*[5]

When I read the next verse, a loud cry broke from my heart. *In peace and friendliness I will sleep; I will take my rest*[6] in the eternal God. O, the joy of these words! For, *when the saying of Scripture comes true, and death is swallowed up in victory,*[7] who shall withstand us? You truly are the eternal God, because in you there is no change and in you we find the rest that banishes all our labour. For there is no other besides you and we need not struggle for other things that are not what you are, and it was you, O Lord, who *bade me repose in confidence unprotected.*[8]

I read the Psalm and there was fire in my heart, but I could think of

[1] Ps. 4: 6, 7 (4: 5, 6).   [2] John 1: 9.   [3] Eph. 5: 8.   [4] Ps. 4: 7 (4: 6).
[5] Ps. 4: 8 (4: 7).   [6] Ps. 4: 9 (4: 8).   [7] 1 Cor. 15: 54.
[8] Ps. 4: 10 (4: 8).

no means of helping those deaf corpses, of whom I had myself been one. For I had been evil as the plague. Like a cur I had snarled blindly and bitterly against the Scriptures, which are sweet with the honey of heaven and radiant with your light. And now *I was sick at heart over the rebellion*[1] of those who hate them.

When shall I set down the record of those days of rest? One thing at least I shall not fail to tell, for I have not forgotten the sting of your lash nor how quickly your mercy came, and in how wonderful a way. During that vacation you let me suffer the agony of toothache, and when the pain became so great that I could not speak, my heart prompted me to ask all my friends who were with me to pray to you for me, since you are the God who gives health to the body as well as to the soul. I wrote down the message and gave it to them to read, and as soon as we knelt down to offer you this humble prayer, the pain vanished. What was that pain? How did it vanish? My Lord and my God, I confess that I was terrified, for nothing like this had ever happened to me in all my life. Deep within me I recognized the working of your will and I praised your name, rejoicing in my faith. But my faith would not let me feel at ease over my past sins, for they had not yet been forgiven in your baptism.

5

When the autumn vacation was over, I notified the people of Milan that they must find another vendor of words for their students, because I had chosen to be your servant and also because the difficulty I had in breathing and the pain in my lungs made me unfit for the duties of a professor. I wrote to your bishop, the saintly Ambrose, to tell him of my past errors and the purpose I now had in mind. I asked him to advise me which books of Scripture it would be best for me to study, so that I might be better prepared and more fitted to receive so great a grace. He told me to read the prophet Isaiah, presumably because the Gospel and the calling of the gentiles are foretold more clearly in that book than in any other. But I did not understand the first chapters and, on the assumption that the rest of the book would be equally difficult, I laid it aside to be taken up again later, when I should be more used to the style in which God's word is spoken.

[1] Ps. 138: 21 (139: 21).

6

When the time came for me to hand in my name for baptism, we left the country and went back to Milan. It was Alypius's wish to be reborn in you at the same time. He was already endued with the humility which fits a man for your sacraments, and he had subjected his body to such stern discipline that he would even walk barefoot on the icy soil of Italy, a thing which few would venture to do. With us we took the boy Adeodatus, my natural son born of my sin. You had given him every gift. Although he was barely fifteen, there were many learned and respected men who were not his equals in intelligence. I acknowledge that he had his gifts from you, O Lord my God, who are the Creator of all and have great power to reshape our deformities, for there was nothing of mine in that boy except my sin. It was you too, and none other, who had inspired us to bring him up as you would have him. These were your gifts and I acknowledge them.

There is a book of mine called *De magistro*, which consists of a dialogue between Adeodatus and myself. You know that all the ideas expressed by the second speaker in the discussion are his, although he was only sixteen when it took place, and I learned for myself that he had many other talents even more remarkable than this. His intelligence left me spell-bound. And who but you could work such wonders? But you took him from this world early in life, and now I remember him without apprehension, for there was nothing in his childhood or his youth or in any part of his life which need make me fear for him.

We made him our companion, in your grace no younger than ourselves. Together we were ready to begin our schooling in your ways. We were baptized, and all anxiety over the past melted away from us. The days were all too short, for I was lost in wonder and joy, meditating upon your far-reaching providence for the salvation of the human race. The tears flowed from me when I heard your hymns and canticles, for the sweet singing of your Church moved me deeply. The music surged in my ears, truth seeped into my heart, and my feelings of devotion overflowed, so that the tears streamed down. But they were tears of gladness.

7

It was not long before this that the Church at Milan had begun to seek comfort and spiritual strength in the practice of singing hymns, in which the faithful united fervently with heart and voice. It was only a year, or not much more, since Justina, the mother of the boy emperor Valentinian, had been persecuting your devoted servant Ambrose in the interests of the heresy into which the Arians had seduced her. In those days your faithful people used to keep watch in the church, ready to die with their bishop, your servant. My mother, your handmaid, was there with them, taking a leading part in that anxious time of vigilance and living a life of constant prayer. Although I was not yet fired by the warmth of your Spirit, these were stirring times for me as well, for the city was in a state of alarm and excitement. It was then that the practice of singing hymns and psalms was introduced, in keeping with the usage of the Eastern churches, to revive the flagging spirits of the people during their long and cheerless watch. Ever since then the custom has been retained, and the example of Milan has been followed in many other places, in fact in almost every church throughout the world.

It was at that time too that you revealed to your bishop Ambrose in a vision the place where the bodies of the martyrs Protasius and Gervasius were hidden. All these years you had preserved them incorrupt in your secret treasury, so that when the time came you could bring them to light to thwart the fury of a woman – a mere woman, but one who ruled an empire. For after the bodies had been discovered and dug up, they were carried to Ambrose's basilica with the honour that was due to them. On the way several persons who were tormented by evil spirits were cured, for even the devils acknowledged the holy relics. But this was not all. There was also a man who had been blind for many years, a well-known figure in the city. He asked why the crowd was running wild with joy, and when they told him the reason, he leaped to his feet and begged his guide to lead him where the bodies lay. When he reached the place, he asked to be allowed to touch the bier with his handkerchief, for it was the bier of your saints, *whose death is dear in your sight*.[1] No sooner had he done this and put the handkerchief to his eyes than his sight was restored.

[1] Ps. 115: 15 (116: 15).

The news spread. Your praises rang out loud and clear, and although this miracle did not convert the mind of your enemy, Justina, to sound beliefs, at least it restrained her from the madness of persecution.

Thanks be to you, my God! Why have you prompted my memory so that I should confess to you these great events which I had forgotten to mention? Yet even then, *when the fragrance of your perfumes allured, I did not hasten after you.*[1] So I wept all the more when I heard your hymns and holy songs, for it was as though, after I had so long sighed for your fragrance, I could at last breathe it in, at least in so far as human frailty can perceive it.

8

You, O God, who bring men of one mind to live together,[2] brought a young man from our own town, named Evodius, to join our company. He had been converted and baptized before us, while he was employed as a government officer, but he had given up the service of the State and entered upon yours. He remained with us and we intended to live together in the devout life which we proposed to lead. We discussed where we could most usefully serve you and together we set out to return to Africa. While we were at Ostia, at the mouth of the Tiber, my mother died.

There are many things which I do not set down in this book, since I am pressed for time. My God, I pray you to accept my confessions and also the gratitude I bear you for all the many things which I pass over in silence. But I will omit not a word that my mind can bring to birth concerning your servant, my mother. In the flesh she brought me to birth in this world: in her heart she brought me to birth in your eternal light. It is not of her gifts that I shall speak, but of the gifts you gave to her. For she was neither her own maker nor her own teacher. It was you who made her, and neither her father nor her mother knew what kind of woman their daughter would grow up to be. It was by Christ's teaching, by the guidance of your only Son, that she was brought up to honour and obey you in one of those good Christian families which form the body of your Church. Yet she always said that her good upbringing had been due not so much to

[1] Cant. 1: 3.   [2] See Ps. 67: 7 (68: 6).

the attentiveness of her mother as to the care of an aged servant, who had carried my grandfather on her back when he was a baby, as older girls do with small children. Her master and mistress, out of gratitude for her long service and respect for her great age and unexceptionable character, treated her as an honoured member of their Christian household. This was why they placed their daughters in her care. She was conscientious in attending to her duties, correcting the children when necessary with strictness, for the love of God, and teaching them to lead wise and sober lives. Except at the times when they ate their frugal meals at their parents' table she would not allow them to drink even water, however great their thirst, for fear that they might develop bad habits. She used to give them this very good advice: 'Now you drink water because you are not allowed to have wine. But when you are married and have charge of your own larders and cellars, you will not be satisfied with water, but the habit of drinking will be too strong for you.' By making rules of this sort and using her influence she was able to keep the natural greediness of childhood within bounds and teach the girls to control their thirst as they ought, so that they no longer wanted what it was not correct for them to have.

Yet in spite of this, as your servant my mother used to tell me herself, she developed a secret liking for wine. Her parents, believing her to be a good and obedient child, used to send her to draw wine from the cask, as was the custom. She used to dip the cup through the opening at the top of the barrel, and before pouring the wine into the flagon she would sip a few drops, barely touching it with her lips, but no more than this, because she found the taste disagreeable. She did this, not because she had any relish for the liquor and its effects, but simply from the exuberant high spirits of childhood, which find their outlet in playful escapades and are generally kept in check by the authority of older people. Each day she added a few more drops to her daily sip of wine. But *little things despise, and little by little you shall come to ruin*.[1] It soon became a habit, and she would drink her wine at a draught, almost by the cupful. Where then was that wise old woman? What use were her strict prohibitions? Could there have been any remedy for this secret disease except your healing power, O Lord, which always watches over us? Even when our fathers and mothers and those who have charge of us in childhood are

[1] Ecclus. 19: 1.

not with us, you are there, you who created us, you who call us to come to you, you who also use those who are placed over us to help us to save our souls. What did you do then, my God? How did you look after my mother and cure her disease? Was it not you who, from another soul, brought harsh words of rebuke, as though the sharp taunt were a surgeon's knife drawn from your secret store, with which you cut away the gangrene at one stroke? For my mother used to go to the cellar with a servant-girl. One day when they were alone, this girl quarrelled with her young mistress, as servants do, and intending it as a most bitter insult, called my mother a drunkard. The word struck home. My mother realized how despicable her fault had been and at once condemned it and renounced it. Our enemies can often correct our faults by their disparagement, just as the flattery of friends can corrupt us. But you, O Lord, reward them, not according to the ends which you achieve by using them, but according to the purpose which they have in mind. For the girl had lost her temper and wanted to provoke her young mistress, not to correct her. She did it when they were alone, either because the quarrel happened to take place at a time when no one else was present, or because she may have been afraid of being punished for not having mentioned the matter earlier. But you, O Lord, Ruler of all things in heaven and on earth, who make the deep rivers serve your purposes and govern the raging tide of time as it sweeps on, you even used the anger of one soul to cure the folly of another. Let this be a warning, so that none of us may ascribe it to our own doing if we find that others, whose ways we wish to see reformed, are corrected by the words we speak.

9

In this way my mother was brought up in modesty and temperance. It was you who taught her to obey her parents rather than they who taught her to obey you, and when she was old enough, they gave her in marriage to a man whom she served as her lord. She never ceased to try to gain him for you as a convert, for the virtues with which you had adorned her, and for which he respected, loved, and admired her, were like so many voices constantly speaking to him of you. He was unfaithful to her, but her patience was so great that his infidelity never became a cause of quarrelling between them. For she looked to you to show him mercy, hoping that chastity would come with faith. Though he was remarkably kind, he had a hot temper, but my mother knew better than to say or do anything to resist him when he was angry. If his anger was unreasonable, she used to wait until he was calm and composed and then took the opportunity of explaining what she had done. Many women, whose faces were disfigured by blows from husbands far sweeter-tempered than her own, used to gossip together and complain of the behaviour of their men-folk. My mother would meet this complaint with another – about the women's tongues. Her manner was light but her meaning serious when she told them that ever since they had heard the marriage deed read over to them, they ought to have regarded it as a contract which bound them to serve their husbands, and from that time onward they should remember their condition and not defy their masters. These women knew well enough how hot-tempered a husband my mother had to cope with. They used to remark how surprising it was that they had never heard, or seen any marks to show, that Patricius had beaten his wife or that there had been any domestic disagreement between them, even for one day. When they asked her, as friends, to tell them the reason, she used to explain the rule which I have mentioned. Those who accepted it found it a good one: the others continued to suffer humiliation and cruelty.

Her mother-in-law was at first prejudiced against her by the tale-bearing of malicious servants, but she won the older woman over by her dutiful attentions and her constant patience and gentleness. In the end her mother-in-law complained of her own accord to her son and asked him to punish the servants for their meddlesome talk, which was spoiling the peaceful domestic relations between herself and her daughter-in-law. Patricius, who was anxious to satisfy his mother as well as to preserve the good order of his home and the peace of his family, took the names of the offenders from his mother and had them whipped as she desired. She then warned them that anyone who told tales about her daughter-in-law, in the hope of pleasing her, could expect to receive the same reward. After this none of them dared to tell tales and the two women lived together in wonderful harmony and mutual goodwill.

There was another great gift which you had given to your good servant in whose womb you created me, O God, my Mercy.

Whenever she could, she used to act the part of the peacemaker between souls in conflict over some quarrel. When misunderstanding is rife and hatred raw and undigested, it often gives vent, in the presence of a friend, to spite against an absent enemy. But if one woman launched a bitter tirade against another in my mother's hearing, she never repeated to either what the other had said, except for such things as were likely to reconcile them. I should not regard this as especially virtuous, were it not for the fact that I know from bitter experience that a great many people, infected by this sin as though it were some horrible, widespread contagion, not only report to one disputant what the other has said, but even add words that were never spoken. And yet a man who loves his own kind ought not to be satisfied merely to refrain from exciting or increasing enmity between other men by the evil that he speaks: he should do his best to put an end to their quarrels by kind words. This was my mother's way, learned in the school of her heart, where you were her secret teacher.

In the end she won her husband for you as a convert in the very last days of his life on earth. After his conversion she no longer had to grieve over those faults which had tried her patience before he was a Christian. She was also the servant of your servants. Those of them who knew her praised you, honoured you, and loved you in her, for they could feel your presence in her heart and her holy conversation gave rich proof of it. *She had been faithful to one husband, had made due returns to those who gave her birth. Her own flesh and blood had had first claim on her piety, and she had a name for acts of charity.*[1] She had brought up her children and had been *in travail afresh*[2] each time she saw them go astray from you. Finally, O Lord, since by your gift you allow us to speak as your servants, she took good care of all of us when we had received the grace of your baptism and were living as companions before she fell asleep in you. She took good care of us, as though she had been the mother of us all, and served each one as though she had been his daughter.

10

Not long before the day on which she was to leave this life – you knew which day it was to be, O Lord, though we did not – my

[1] 1 Tim. 5: 4, 10. [2] Gal. 4: 19.

mother and I were alone, leaning from a window which overlooked
the garden in the courtyard of the house where we were staying at
Ostia. We were waiting there after our long and tiring journey, away
from the crowd, to refresh ourselves before our sea-voyage. I believe
that what I am going to tell happened through the secret working of
your providence. For we were talking alone together and our conversation was serene and joyful. *We had forgotten what we had left
behind and were intent on what lay before us.*[1] In the presence of Truth,
which is yourself, we were wondering what the eternal life of the
saints would be like, that life which *no eye has seen, no ear has heard, no
human heart conceived.*[2] But we laid the lips of our hearts to the
heavenly stream that flows from your fountain, *the source of all life*
which is *in you,*[3] so that as far as it was in our power to do so we might
be sprinkled with its waters and in some sense reach an understanding
of this great mystery.

Our conversation led us to the conclusion that no bodily pleasure,
however great it might be and whatever earthly light might shed
lustre upon it, was worthy of comparison, or even of mention, beside
the happiness of the life of the saints. As the flame of love burned
stronger in us and raised us higher towards the eternal God, our
thoughts ranged over the whole compass of material things in their
various degrees, up to the heavens themselves, from which the sun
and the moon and the stars shine down upon the earth. Higher still we
climbed, thinking and speaking all the while in wonder at all that you
have made. At length we came to our own souls and passed beyond
them to that place of everlasting plenty, where you feed Israel for
ever with the food of truth. There life is that Wisdom by which all
these things that we know are made, all things that ever have been
and all that are yet to be. But that Wisdom is not made: it is as it has
always been and as it will be for ever – or, rather, I should not say that
it *has been* or *will be,* for it simply *is,* because eternity is not in the past
or in the future. And while we spoke of the eternal Wisdom, longing
for it and straining for it with all the strength of our hearts, for one
fleeting instant we reached out and touched it. Then with a sigh,
leaving *our spiritual harvest*[4] bound to it, we returned to the sound of
our own speech, in which each word has a beginning and an ending –

[1] Philipp. 3: 13.   [2] 1 Cor. 2: 9.   [3] Ps. 35: 10 (36: 10).
[4] Rom. 8: 23.

far, far different from your Word, our Lord, who abides in himself for ever, yet never grows old and gives new life to all things.

And so our discussion went on. Suppose, we said, that the tumult of a man's flesh were to cease and all that his thoughts can conceive, of earth, of water, and of air, should no longer speak to him; suppose that the heavens and even his own soul were silent, no longer thinking of itself but passing beyond; suppose that his dreams and the visions of his imagination spoke no more and that every tongue and every sign and all that is transient grew silent – for all these things have the same message to tell, if only we can hear it, and their message is this: We did not make ourselves, but he who abides for ever made us. Suppose, we said, that after giving us this message and bidding us listen to him who made them, they fell silent and he alone should speak to us, not through them but in his own voice, so that we should hear him speaking, not by any tongue of the flesh or by an angel's voice, not in the sound of thunder or in some veiled parable, but in his own voice, the voice of the one whom we love in all these created things; suppose that we heard him himself, with none of these things between ourselves and him, just as in that brief moment my mother and I had reached out in thought and touched the eternal Wisdom which abides over all things; suppose that this state were to continue and all other visions of things inferior were to be removed, so that this single vision entranced and absorbed the one who beheld it and enveloped him in inward joys in such a way that for him life was eternally the same as that instant of understanding for which we had longed so much – would not this be what we are to understand by the words *Come and share the joy of your Lord?*[1] But when is it to be? Is it to be when *we all rise again, but not all of us will undergo the change?*[2]

This was the purport of our talk, though we did not speak in these precise words or exactly as I have reported them. Yet you know, O Lord, that as we talked that day, the world, for all its pleasures, seemed a paltry place compared with the life that we spoke of. And then my mother said, 'My son, for my part I find no further pleasure in this life. What I am still to do or why I am here in the world, I do not know, for I have no more to hope for on this earth. There was one reason, and one alone, why I wished to remain a little longer in this life, and that was to see you a Catholic Christian before I died.

[1] Matt. 25: 21. [2] I Cor. 15: 51.

God has granted my wish and more besides, for I now see you as his servant, spurning such happiness as the world can give. What is left for me to do in this world?'

I scarcely remember what answer I gave her. It was about five days after this, or not much more, that she took to her bed with a fever. One day during her illness she had a fainting fit and lost consciousness for a short time. We hurried to her bedside, but she soon regained consciousness and looked up at my brother and me as we stood beside her. With a puzzled look she asked 'Where was I?' Then watching us closely as we stood there speechless with grief, she said 'You will bury your mother here.' I said nothing, trying hard to hold back my tears, but my brother said something to the effect that he wished for her sake that she would die in her own country, not abroad. When she heard this, she looked at him anxiously and her eyes reproached him for his worldly thoughts. She turned to me and said, 'See how he talks!' and then, speaking to both of us, she went on, 'It does not matter where you bury my body. Do not let that worry you! All I ask of you is that, wherever you may be, you should remember me at the altar of the Lord.'

Although she hardly had the strength to speak, she managed to make us understand her wishes and then fell silent, for her illness was becoming worse and she was in great pain. But I was thinking of your gifts, O God. Unseen by us you plant them like seeds in the hearts of your faithful and they grow to bear wonderful fruits. This thought filled me with joy and I thanked you for your gifts, for I had always known, and well remembered now, my mother's great anxiety to be buried beside her husband's body in the grave which she had provided and prepared for herself. Because they had lived in the greatest harmony, she had always wanted this extra happiness. She had wanted it to be said of them that, after her journeyings across the sea, it had been granted to her that the earthly remains of husband and wife should be joined as one and covered by the same earth. How little the human mind can understand God's purpose! I did not know when it was that your good gifts had borne their full fruit and her heart had begun to renounce this vain desire, but I was both surprised and pleased to find that it was so. And yet, when we talked at the window and she asked, 'What is left for me to do in this world?', it was clear that she had no desire to die in her own country. Afterwards I also heard that one day during our stay at Ostia, when I was absent, she had talked in a motherly way to some of my friends and had spoken to them of the contempt of this life and the blessings of death. They were astonished to find such courage in a woman – it was your gift to her, O Lord – and asked whether she was not frightened at the thought of leaving her body so far from her own country. 'Nothing is far from God,' she replied, 'and I need have no fear that he will not know where to find me when he comes to raise me to life at the end of the world.'

And so on the ninth day of her illness, when she was fifty-six and I was thirty-three, her pious and devoted soul was set free from the body.

12

I closed her eyes, and a great wave of sorrow surged into my heart. It would have overflowed in tears if I had not made a strong effort of will and stemmed the flow, so that the tears dried in my eyes. What a terrible struggle it was to hold them back! As she breathed her last, the boy Adeodatus began to wail aloud and only ceased his cries when we all checked him. I, too, felt that I wanted to cry like a child, but a more mature voice within me, the voice of my heart, bade me keep my sobs in check, and I remained silent. For we did not think it right to mark my mother's death with weeping and moaning, because such lamentations are the usual accompaniment of death when it is thought of as a state of misery or as total extinction. But she had not died in misery nor had she wholly died. Of this we were certain, both because we knew what a holy life she had led and also because our faith was real and we had sure reasons not to doubt it.

What was it, then, that caused me such deep sorrow? It can only have been because the wound was fresh, the wound I had received when our life together, which had been so precious and so dear to me, was suddenly cut off. I found comfort in the memory that as I did what I could for my mother in the last stages of her illness, she had caressed me and said that I was a good son to her. With great emotion she told me that she could not remember ever having heard me speak a single hard or disrespectful word against her. And yet, O God who made us both, how could there be any comparison between the honour which I showed to her and the devoted service she had given me? It was because I was now bereft of all the comfort I had had from her that my soul was wounded and my life seemed shattered, for her life and mine had been as one.

When we had succeeded in quieting Adeodatus, Evodius took up a psaltery and began to sing the psalm *Of mercy and justice my song shall be; a psalm in thy honour, Lord,*[1] and the whole house sang the responses. On hearing what was happening many of our brothers in the faith and many pious women came to us, and while those whose duty it was made arrangements for the funeral, I remained in another room, where I could talk without irreverence, and conversed with friends on matters suitable to the occasion, for they did not think it right to leave me to myself. These words of truth were the salve with which I soothed my pain. You knew, O Lord, how I suffered, but my friends did not, and as they listened intently to my words, they thought that I had no sense of grief. But in your ears, where none of them could hear, I blamed myself for my tender feelings. I fought against the wave of sorrow and for a while it receded, but then it swept upon me again with full force. It did not bring me to tears and no sign of it showed in my face, but I knew well enough what I was stifling in my heart. It was misery to feel myself so weak a victim of these human emotions, although we cannot escape them, since they are the natural lot of mankind, and so I had the added sorrow of being grieved by my own feelings, so that I was tormented by a twofold agony.

When the body was carried out for burial, I went and returned without a tear. I did not weep even during the prayers which we recited while the sacrifice of our redemption was offered for my mother and her body rested by the grave before it was laid in the earth, as is the custom there. Yet all that day I was secretly weighed down with grief. With all my heart I begged you to heal my sorrow, but you did not grant my prayer. I believe that this was because you wished to impress upon my memory, if only by this one lesson, how firmly the mind is gripped in the bonds of habit, even when it is nourished on the word of truth. I thought I would go to the baths, because I had been told that the Latin name for them was derived

[1] Ps. 100: 1 (101: 1).

from the Greek βαλανεῖον, so called because bathing rids the mind of anxiety. And I acknowledge your mercy in this too, O Father of orphans,[1] for I went to the baths and came back in the same state as before. Water could not wash away the bitter grief from my heart. Then I went to sleep and woke up to find that the rest had brought me some relief from my sorrow. As I lay alone in bed, I remembered the verses of your servant Ambrose and realized the truth of them:

> Deus, Creator omnium,
> polique Rector, vestiens
> diem decoro lumine,
> noctem sopora gratia,
>
> Artus solutos ut quies
> reddat laboris usui,
> mentesque fessas allevet,
> luctusque solvat anxios.[2]

Then little by little, my old feelings about your handmaid came back to me. I thought of her devoted love for you and the tenderness and patience she had shown to me, like the holy woman that she was. Of all this I found myself suddenly deprived, and it was a comfort to me to weep for her and for myself and to offer my tears to you for her sake and for mine. The tears which I had been holding back streamed down, and I let them flow as freely as they would, making of them a pillow for my heart. On them it rested, for my weeping sounded in your ears alone, not in the ears of men who might have misconstrued it and despised it.

And now, O Lord, I make you my confession in this book. Let any

[1] See Ps. 67: 6 (68: 5).

[2] Maker of all things! God most high!
Great Ruler of the starry sky!
Who, robing day with beauteous light,
Hast clothed in soft repose the night,

That sleep may wearied limbs restore,
And fit for toil and use once more;
May gently soothe the careworn breast,
And lull our anxious griefs to rest.
— From Saint Ambrose's 'Evening Hymn',
trs. J. D. Chambers, 1854.

man read it who will. Let him understand it as he will. And if he finds that I sinned by weeping for my mother, even if only for a fraction of an hour, let him not mock at me. For this was the mother, now dead and hidden awhile from my sight, who had wept over me for many years so that I might live in your sight. Let him not mock at me but weep himself, if his charity is great. Let him weep for my sins to you, the Father of all the brothers of your Christ.

13

Now that my soul has recovered from that wound, in which perhaps I was guilty of too much worldly affection, tears of another sort stream from my eyes. They are tears which I offer to you, my God, for your handmaid. They flow from a spirit which trembles at the thought of the dangers which await every soul that *has died with Adam*.[1] For although she was alive in Christ even before her soul was parted from the body, and her faith and the good life she led resounded to the glory of your name, yet I cannot presume to say that from the time when she was reborn in baptism no word contrary to your commandments ever fell from her lips. Your Son, the Truth, has said: *Any man who says to his brother, You fool, must answer for it in hell fire*,[2] and however praiseworthy a man's life may be, it will go hard with him if you lay aside your mercy when you come to examine it. But you do not search out our faults ruthlessly, and because of this we hope and believe that one day we shall find a place with you. Yet if any man makes a list of his deserts, what would it be but a list of your gifts? If only men would know themselves for what they are! If only *they who boast would make their boast in the Lord*![3]

And so, my Glory and my Life, God of my heart, I will lay aside for a while all the good deeds which my mother did. For them I thank you, but now I pray to you for her sins. Hear me through your Son, who hung on the cross and now *sits at your right hand and pleads for us*,[4] for he is the true medicine of our wounds. I know that my mother always acted with mercy and that she forgave others with all her heart when they trespassed against her. Forgive her too, O Lord, if ever she trespassed against you in all the long years of her life after baptism.

[1] 1 Cor. 15: 22.   [2] Matt. 5: 22.   [3] II Cor. 10: 17.   [4] Rom. 8: 34.

Forgive her, I beseech you; *do not call her to account.*[1] *Let your mercy give your judgement an honourable welcome,*[2] for your words are true and you have promised mercy to the merciful. If they are merciful, it is by your gift; and *you will show pity on those whom you pity; you will show mercy where you are merciful.*[3]

I believe that you have already done what I ask of you, but, *Lord, accept these vows of mine.*[4] For on the day when she was so soon to be released from the flesh she had no care whether her body was to be buried in a rich shroud or embalmed with spices, nor did she wish to have a special monument or a grave in her own country. These were not the last wishes she passed on to us. All she wanted was that we should remember her at your altar, where she had been your servant day after day, without fail. For she knew that at your altar we receive the holy Victim, who *cancelled the decree made to our prejudice,*[5] and in whom we have triumphed over the enemy who reckons up our sins, trying to find some charge to bring against us, yet can find no fault in him in whom we conquer. Who shall restore to him his innocent blood? Who shall take us from him by repaying him the price for which he bought us? By the strong ties of faith your handmaid had bound her soul to this sacrament of our redemption. Let no one tear her away from your protection. Let not the devil, who is *lion and serpent*[6] in one, bar her way by force or by guile. For she will not answer that she has no debt to pay, for fear that her cunning accuser should prove her wrong and win her for himself. Her reply will be that her debt has been paid by Christ, to whom none can repay the price which he paid for us, though the debt was not his to pay.

Let her rest in peace with her husband. He was her first husband and she married no other after him. She served him, *yielding you a harvest,*[7] so that in the end she also won him for you. O my Lord, my God, inspire your servants my brothers – they are your sons and my masters, whom I serve with heart and voice and pen – inspire those of them who read this book to remember Monica, your servant, at your altar and with her Patricius, her husband, who died before her, by whose bodies you brought me into this life, though how it was I do

---

[1] Ps. 142: 2 (143: 2).   [2] James 2: 13.   [3] Rom. 9: 15.
[4] Ps. 118: 108 (119: 108).   [5] Col. 2: 14.   [6] Ps. 90: 13 (91: 13).
[7] Luke 8: 15.

not know. With pious hearts let them remember those who were not only my parents in this light that fails, but were also my brother and sister, subject to you, our Father, in our Catholic mother the Church, and will be my fellow citizens in the eternal Jerusalem for which your people sigh throughout their pilgrimage, from the time when they set out until the time when they return to you. So it shall be that the last request that my mother made to me shall be granted in the prayers of the many who read my confessions more fully than in mine alone.

BOOK X

1

Let me know you, for you are the God who knows me; *let me recognize you as you have recognized me.*[1] You are the power of my soul; come into it and make it fit for yourself, so that you may have it and hold it *without stain or wrinkle.*[2] This is my hope; this is why I speak as I do; this is the hope that brings me joy, when my joy is in what is to save me. As for the other things in life, the more we weep for them, the less they merit our tears, and the fewer tears we shed for them, the more we ought to weep for them. We know that *you are a lover of faithfulness,*[3] for *the man whose life is true comes to the light.*[4] I wish to act in truth, making my confession both in my heart before you and in this book before the many who will read it.

2

O Lord, the depths of man's conscience lie bare before your eyes. Could anything of mine remain hidden from you, even if I refused to confess it? I should only be shielding my eyes from seeing you, not hiding myself from you. But now that I have the evidence of my own misery to prove to me how displeasing I am to myself, you are my light and my joy. It is you whom I love and desire, so that I am ashamed of myself and cast myself aside and choose you instead, and I please neither you nor myself except in you.

So, O Lord, all that I am is laid bare before you. I have declared how it profits me to confess to you. And I make my confession, not in words and sounds made by the tongue alone, but with the voice of my soul and in my thoughts which cry aloud to you. Your ear can hear them. For when I am sinful, if I am displeased with myself, this is a confession that I make to you; and when I am good, if I do not claim the merit for myself, this too is confession. For you, O Lord,

[1] I Cor. 13: 12.   [2] Eph. 5: 27.   [3] Ps. 50: 8 (51: 6).   [4] John 3: 21.

207

give your benediction to the just,[1] but first *you make a just man of the sinner.*[2] And so my confession is made both silently in your sight, my God, and aloud as well, because even though my tongue utters no sound, my heart cries to you. For whatever good I may speak to men you have heard it before in my heart, and whatever good you hear in my heart, you have first spoken to me yourself.

3

Why, then, does it matter to me whether men should hear what I have to confess, as though it were they who were to cure all the evil that is in me? They are an inquisitive race, always anxious to pry into other men's lives, but never ready to correct their own. Why do they wish to hear from me what sort of man I am, though they will not listen to you when you tell them what they are? When they hear me speak about myself, how do they know whether I am telling the truth, since no one *knows a man's thoughts, except the man's own spirit that is within him*?[3] But if they listen to what you tell them about themselves, they cannot say 'The Lord is lying', for to heed what you tell them about themselves is simply to recognize themselves for what they are. And if a man recognizes his true self, can he possibly say 'This is false', unless he is himself a liar? But charity believes all things – all things, that is, which are spoken by those who are joined as one in charity – and for this reason I, too, O Lord, make my confession aloud in the hearing of men. For although I cannot prove to them that my confessions are true, at least I shall be believed by those whose ears are opened to me by charity.

Physician of my soul, make me see clearly how it profits me to do this. You have forgiven my past sins and drawn a veil over them, and in this way you have given me happiness in yourself, changing my life by faith and your sacrament. But when others read of those past sins of mine, or hear about them, their hearts are stirred so that they no longer lie listless in despair, crying 'I cannot'. Instead their hearts are roused by the love of your mercy and the joy of your grace, by which each one of us, weak though he be, is made strong, since by it he is made conscious of his own weakness. And the good are glad to hear of the past sins of others who are now free of them.

[1] Ps. 5: 13 (5: 12).   [2] Rom. 4: 5.   [3] 1 Cor. 2: 11.

They are glad, not because those sins are evil, but because what was evil is now evil no more.

What does it profit me, then, O Lord, to whom my conscience confesses daily, confident more in the hope of your mercy than in its own innocence, what does it profit me, I ask, also to make known to men in your sight, through this book, not what I once was, but what I am now? I know what profit I gain by confessing my past, and this I have declared. But many people who know me, and others who do not know me but have heard of me or read my books, wish to hear what I am now, at this moment, as I set down my confessions. They cannot lay their ears to my heart, and yet it is in my heart that I am whatever I am. So they wish to listen as I confess what I am in my heart, into which they cannot pry by eye or ear or mind. They wish to hear and they are ready to believe; but can they really know me? Charity, which makes them good, tells them that I do not lie about myself when I confess what I am, and it is this charity in them that believes me.

4

But what good do they hope will be done if they listen to what I say? Is it that they wish to join with me in thanking you, when they hear how close I have come to you by your grace, and to pray for me, when they hear how far I am set apart from you by the burden of my sins? If this is what they wish, I shall tell them what I am. For no small good is gained, O Lord my God, if many offer you thanks for me and many pray to you for me. Let all who are truly my brothers love in me what they know from your teaching to be worthy of their love, and let them sorrow to find in me what they know from your teaching to be occasion for remorse. This is what I wish my true brothers to feel in their hearts. I do not speak of strangers or of *alien foes, who make treacherous promises, and lift their hands in perjury.*[1] But my true brothers are those who rejoice for me in their hearts when they find good in me, and grieve for me when they find sin. They are my true brothers, because whether they see good in me or evil, they love me still. To such as these I shall reveal what I am. Let them breathe a sigh of joy for what is good in me and a sigh of grief for what is bad. The good I do is done by you in me and by your grace:

[1] Ps. 143: 8 (144: 8).

the evil is my fault; it is the punishment you send me. Let my brothers draw their breath in joy for the one and sigh with grief for the other. Let hymns of thanksgiving and cries of sorrow rise together from their hearts, as though they were vessels burning with incense before you. And I pray you, O Lord, to be pleased with the incense that rises in your holy temple and, for your name's sake, to *have mercy on me, as you are ever rich in mercy*.[1] Do not relinquish what you have begun, but make perfect what is still imperfect in me.

So, if I go on to confess, not what I was, but what I am, the good that comes of it is this. There is joy in my heart when I confess to you, yet there is fear as well; there is sorrow, and yet hope. But I confess not only to you but also to the believers among men, all who share my joy and all who, like me, are doomed to die; all who are my fellows in your kingdom and all who accompany me on this pilgrimage, whether they have gone before or are still to come or are with me as I make my way through life. They are your servants and my brothers. You have chosen them to be your sons. You have named them as the masters whom I am to serve if I wish to live with you and in your grace. This is your bidding, but it would hold less meaning for me if it were made known to me in words alone and I had not the example of Christ, who has shown me the way by his deeds as well. I do your bidding in word and deed alike. I do it beneath the protection of your wings, for the peril would be too great if it were not that my soul has submitted to you and sought the shelter of your wings and that my weakness is known to you. I am no more than a child, but my Father lives for ever and I have a Protector great enough to save me. For he who begot me and he who watches over me are one and the same, and for me there is no good but you, the Almighty, who are with me even before I am with you. So to such as you command me to serve I will reveal, not what I have been, but what I have become and what I am. But, since I do not *scrutinize my own conduct*,[2] let my words be understood as they are meant.

5

It is you, O Lord, who judge me. For though no one *can know a man's thoughts, except the man's own spirit that is within him*,[3] there are some

---

[1] Ps. 50: 3 (51: 1). [2] 1 Cor. 4: 3. [3] 1 Cor. 2: 11.

things in man which even his own spirit within him does not know. But you, O Lord, know all there is to know of him, because you made him. Yet though, in your sight, I despise myself and consider myself as mere dust and ashes, there is one thing that I know about you which I do not know about myself. I know that it is impossible for you to suffer harm, whereas I do not know which temptations I can resist and which I cannot. This much I know, although *at present I am looking at a confused reflection in a mirror, not yet face to face*,[1] and therefore, as long as I am away from you, during my pilgrimage, I am more aware of myself than of you. But my hope lies in the knowledge that *you do not play us false; you will not allow us to be tempted beyond our powers. With the temptation itself, you will ordain the issue of it, and enable us to hold our own.*[2]

I shall therefore confess both what I know of myself and what I do not know. For even what I know about myself I only know because your light shines upon me; and what I do not know about myself I shall continue not to know until I see you face to face and *my dusk is noonday*.[3]

6

My love of you, O Lord, is not some vague feeling: it is positive and certain. Your word struck into my heart and from that moment I loved you. Besides this, all about me, heaven and earth and all that they contain proclaim that I should love you, and their message never ceases to sound in the ears of all mankind, so that there is no excuse for any not to love you. But, more than all this, *you will show pity on those whom you pity; you will show mercy where you are merciful;*[4] for if it were not for your mercy, heaven and earth would cry your praises to deaf ears.

But what do I love when I love my God? Not material beauty or beauty of a temporal order; not the brilliance of earthly light, so welcome to our eyes; not the sweet melody of harmony and song; not the fragrance of flowers, perfumes, and spices; not manna or honey; not limbs such as the body delights to embrace. It is not these that I love when I love my God. And yet, when I love him, it is true that I love a light of a certain kind, a voice, a perfume, a food, an embrace; but they are of the kind that I love in my inner self, when

[1] 1 Cor. 13: 12.　[2] 1 Cor. 10: 13　[3] Is. 58: 10.　[4] Rom. 9: 15.

my soul is bathed in light that is not bound by space; when it listens to sound that never dies away; when it breathes fragrance that is not borne away on the wind; when it tastes food that is never consumed by the eating; when it clings to an embrace from which it is not severed by fulfilment of desire. This is what I love when I love my God.

But what is my God? I put my question to the earth. It answered, 'I am not God', and all things on earth declared the same. I asked the sea and the chasms of the deep and the living things that creep in them, but they answered, 'We are not your God. Seek what is above us.' I spoke to the winds that blow, and the whole air and all that lives in it replied, 'Anaximenes[1] is wrong. I am not God.' I asked the sky, the sun, the moon, and the stars, but they told me, 'Neither are we the God whom you seek.' I spoke to all the things that are about me, all that can be admitted by the door of the senses, and I said, 'Since you are not my God, tell me about him. Tell me something of my God.' Clear and loud they answered, 'God is he who made us.' I asked these questions simply by gazing at these things, and their beauty was all the answer they gave.

Then I turned to myself and asked, 'Who are you?' 'A man,' I replied. But it is clear that I have both body and soul, the one the outer, the other the inner part of me. Which of these two ought I to have asked to help me find my God? With my bodily powers I had already tried to find him in earth and sky, as far as the sight of my eyes could reach, like an envoy sent upon a search. But my inner self is the better of the two, for it was to the inner part of me that my bodily senses brought their messages. They delivered to their arbiter and judge the replies which they carried back from the sky and the earth and all that they contain, those replies which stated 'We are not God' and 'God is he who made us'. The inner part of man knows these things through the agency of the outer part. I, the inner man, know these things; I, the soul, know them through the senses of my body. I asked the whole mass of the universe about my God, and it replied, 'I am not God. God is he who made me.'

Surely everyone whose senses are not impaired is aware of the universe around him? Why, then, does it not give the same message

[1] Anaximenes of Miletus, the philosopher, who lived in the sixth century B.C. His teaching was that air is the first cause of all things.

to us all? The animals, both great and small, are aware of it, but they cannot inquire into its meaning because they are not guided by reason, which can sift the evidence relayed to them by their senses. Man, on the other hand, can question nature. He is able to *catch sight of God's invisible nature through his creatures*,[1] but his love of these material things is too great. He becomes their slave, and slaves cannot be judges. Nor will the world supply an answer to those who question it, unless they also have the faculty to judge it. It does not answer in different language – that is, it does not change its aspect – according to whether a man merely looks at it or subjects it to inquiry while he looks. If it did, its appearance would be different in each case. Its aspect is the same in both cases, but to the man who merely looks it says nothing, while to the other it gives an answer. It would be nearer the truth to say that it gives an answer to all, but it is only understood by those who compare the message it gives them through their senses with the truth that is in themselves. For truth says to me, 'Your God is not heaven or earth or any kind of bodily thing.' We can tell this from the very nature of such things, for those who have eyes to see know that their bulk is less in the part than in the whole. And I know that my soul is the better part of me, because it animates the whole of my body. It gives it life, and this is something that no body can give to another body. But God is even more. He is the Life of the life of my soul.

7

What, then, do I love when I love God? Who is this Being who is so far above my soul? If I am to reach him, it must be through my soul. But I must go beyond the power by which I am joined to my body and by which I fill its frame with life. This is not the power by which I can find my God, for if it were, *the horse and the mule, senseless creatures*,[2] could find him too, because they also have this same power which gives life to their bodies. But there is another faculty in me besides this. By it I not only give life to my body but also give it the power of perceiving things by its senses. God gave me this faculty when he ordered my eyes not to hear but to see and my ears not to see but to hear. And to each of the other senses he assigned its own place and its own function. I, the soul, who am one alone, exercise

[1] Rom. 1: 20. [2] Ps. 31: 9 (32: 9).

all these different functions by means of my senses. But I must go beyond this faculty as well, for horses and mules also have it, since they too feel by means of their bodies.

8

So I must also go beyond this natural faculty of mine, as I rise by stages towards the God who made me. The next stage is memory, which is like a great field or a spacious palace, a storehouse for countless images of all kinds which are conveyed to it by the senses. In it are stored away all the thoughts by which we enlarge upon or diminish or modify in any way the perceptions at which we arrive through the senses, and it also contains anything else that has been entrusted to it for safe keeping, until such time as these things are swallowed up and buried in forgetfulness. When I use my memory, I ask it to produce whatever it is that I wish to remember. Some things it produces immediately; some are forthcoming only after a delay, as though they were being brought out from some inner hiding place; others come spilling from the memory, thrusting themselves upon us when what we want is something quite different, as much as to say 'Perhaps we are what you want to remember?' These I brush aside from the picture which memory presents to me, allowing my mind to pick what it chooses, until finally that which I wish to see stands out clearly and emerges into sight from its hiding place. Some memories present themselves easily and in the correct order just as I require them. They come and give place in their turn to others that follow upon them, and as their place is taken they return to their place of storage, ready to emerge again when I want them. This is what happens when I recite something by heart.

In the memory everything is preserved separately, according to its category. Each is admitted through its own special entrance. For example, light, colour, and shape are admitted through the eyes; sound of all kinds through the ears; all sorts of smell through the nostrils; and every kind of taste through the mouth. The sense of touch, which is common to all parts of the body, enables us to distinguish between hard and soft, hot and cold, rough and smooth, heavy and light, and it can be applied to things which are inside the body as well as to those which are outside it. All these sensations are retained in the great storehouse of the memory, which in some indescribable way secretes them in its folds. They can be brought out and called back again when they are needed, but each enters the memory through its own gateway and is retained in it. The things which we sense do not enter the memory themselves, but their images are there ready to present themselves to our thoughts when we recall them.

We may know by which of the senses these images were recorded and laid up in the memory, but who can tell how the images themselves are formed? Even when I am in darkness and in silence I can, if I wish, picture colours in my memory. I can distinguish between black and white and any other colours that I wish. And while I reflect upon them, sounds do not break in and confuse the images of colour, which reached me through the eye. Yet my memory holds sounds as well, though it stores them separately. If I wish, I can summon them too. They come forward at once, so that I can sing as much as I want, even though my tongue does not move and my throat utters no sound. And when I recall into my mind this rich reserve of sound, which entered my memory through my ears, the images of colour, which are also there in my memory, do not interfere or intrude. In the same way I can recall at will all the other things which my other senses brought into my memory and deposited in it. I can distinguish the scent of lilies from that of violets, even though there is no scent at all in my nostrils, and simply by using my memory I recognize that I like honey better than wine and smooth things better than rough ones, although at that moment I neither taste nor touch anything.

All this goes on inside me, in the vast cloisters of my memory. In it are the sky, the earth, and the sea, ready at my summons, together with everything that I have ever perceived in them by my senses, except the things which I have forgotten. In it I meet myself as well. I remember myself and what I have done, when and where I did it, and the state of my mind at the time. In my memory, too, are all the events that I remember, whether they are things that have happened to me or things that I have heard from others. From the same source I can picture to myself all kinds of different images based either upon my own experience or upon what I find credible because it tallies with my own experience. I can fit them into the general picture of the past; from them I can make a surmise of actions and events and hopes for the future; and I can contemplate them all over again as if they were actually present. If I say to myself in the vast cache of my mind, where all those images of great things are stored, 'I shall do this or that', the picture of this or that particular thing comes into my mind at once. Or I may say to myself 'If only this or that would happen!' or 'God forbid that this or that should be!' No sooner do I say this than the images of all the things of which I speak spring forward from the same great treasure-house of the memory. And, in fact, I could not even mention them at all if the images were lacking.

The power of the memory is prodigious, my God. It is a vast, immeasurable sanctuary. Who can plumb its depths? And yet it is a faculty of my soul. Although it is part of my nature, I cannot understand all that I am. This means, then, that the mind is too narrow to contain itself entirely. But where is that part of it which it does not itself contain? Is it somewhere outside itself and not within it? How, then, can it be part of it, if it is not contained in it?

I am lost in wonder when I consider this problem. It bewilders me. Yet men go out and gaze in astonishment at high mountains, the huge waves of the sea, the broad reaches of rivers, the ocean that encircles the world, or the stars in their courses. But they pay no attention to themselves. They do not marvel at the thought that while I have been mentioning all these things, I have not been looking at them with my eyes, and that I could not even speak of mountains or waves, rivers or stars, which are things that I have seen, or of the ocean, which I know only on the evidence of others, unless I could see them in my mind's eye, in my memory, and with the same vast spaces between them that would be there if I were looking at them in the world outside myself. When I saw them with the sight of my eyes, I did not draw them bodily into myself. They are not inside me themselves, but only their images. And I know which of my senses imprinted each image on my mind.

9

But these are not the only treasures stored in the vast capacity of my memory. It also contains all that I have ever learnt of the liberal sciences, except what I have forgotten. This knowledge it keeps apart from the rest, in an inner place – though it is wrong to speak of it as a place – and in their case it does not retain mere images but the facts themselves. For any knowledge I may have of grammar, or of the art of debating, or of the different categories of questions, remains in my memory, but not as though I merely retained an image of it, leaving the facts outside myself, or as though it had sounded in my ear and then passed away. It is not like a voice which is imprinted on the mind through the ears, leaving a trace by which it can be recalled, as if its sound were still to be heard even after it has become silent. Nor is it like an odour which, even though it does not last and is carried away on the wind, affects the sense of smell and through it conveys to the memory an impression of itself, by which it can be remembered and reproduced. It is not like food, which certainly loses its taste once it reaches the belly, and yet can be said to retain its taste in the memory. Again, it is unlike anything which the body feels by the sense of touch and can still be sensed in the memory even after contact with it is lost. In these cases the things themselves do not penetrate into the memory. It is simply that the memory captures their images with astonishing speed and stores them away in its wonderful system of compartments, ready to produce them again in just as wonderful a way when we remember them.

10

When I am told that it is possible to ask three kinds of question – whether a thing is, what it is, and of what sort it is – I retain images of the sounds of which these words are composed. I know that these sounds have passed through the air and now are no more. But the facts which they represent have not reached me through any of my bodily senses. I could not see them at all except in my mind, and it is not their images that I store in my memory but the facts themselves. But they must themselves tell me, if they can, by what means they entered my mind. For I can run through all the organs of sense, which are the body's gateways to the mind, but I cannot find any by which these facts could have entered. My eyes tell me 'If they have colour, we reported them'. My ears say 'If they have sound, it was we who gave notice of them'. My nose says 'If they have any smell, it was through me that they passed into the mind'. The sense of taste says

'If they have no taste, do not put your question to me'. The sense of touch says 'If it is not a body, I did not touch it, and if I did not touch it, I had no message to transmit'.

How, then, did these facts get into my memory? Where did they come from? I do not know. When I learned them, I did not believe them with another man's mind. It was my own mind which recognized them and admitted that they were true. I entrusted them to my own mind as though it were a place of storage from which I could produce them at will. Therefore they must have been in my mind even before I learned them, though not present to my memory. Then whereabouts in my mind were they? How was it that I recognized them when they were mentioned and agreed that they were true? It must have been that they were already in my memory, hidden away in its deeper recesses, in so remote a part of it that I might not have been able to think of them at all, if some other person had not brought them to the fore by teaching me about them.

11

From this we can conclude that learning these facts, which do not reach our minds as images by means of the senses but are recognized by us in our minds, without images, as they actually are, is simply a process of thought by which we gather together things which, although they are muddled and confused, are already contained in the memory. When we give them our attention, we see to it that these facts, which have been lying scattered and unheeded, are placed ready to hand, so that they are easily forthcoming once we have grown used to them. My memory holds a great number of facts of this sort, things which I have already discovered and, as I have said, placed ready to hand. This is what is meant by saying that we have learnt them and know them. If, for a short space of time, I cease to give them my attention, they sink back and recede again into the more remote cells of my memory, so that I have to think them out again, like a fresh set of facts, if I am to know them. I have to shepherd them out again from their old lairs, because there is no other place where they can have gone. In other words, once they have been dispersed, I have to collect them again, and this is the derivation of the word *cogitare*, which means *to think* or *to collect one's thoughts*. For in Latin the word *cogo*, meaning *I assemble* or *I collect*, is related to *cogito*, which means *I think*, in the same way as *ago* is related to *agito* or *facio* to *factito*. But the word *cogito* is restricted to the function of the mind. It is correctly used only of what is assembled in the mind, not what is assembled elsewhere.

12

The memory also contains the innumerable principles and laws of numbers and dimensions. None of these can have been conveyed to it by means of the bodily senses, because they cannot be seen, heard, smelled, tasted, or touched. I have heard the sounds of the words by which their meaning is expressed when they are discussed, but the words are one thing and the principles another. The words may sometimes be spoken in Latin and at other times in Greek, but the principles are neither Greek nor Latin. They are not language at all. I have seen lines drawn by architects, and they are sometimes as fine as the thread spun by spiders. But these principles are different. They are not images of things which the eye of my body has reported to me. We know them simply by recognizing them inside ourselves without reference to any material object. With all the senses of my body I have become aware of numbers as they are used in counting things. But the principle of number, by which we count, is not the same. It is not an image of the things we count, but something which is there in its own right. If anyone is blind to it, he may laugh at my words: I shall pity him for his ridicule.

13

I carry all these facts in my memory, and I also remember how I learned them. I have also heard, and remember, many false arguments put forward to dispute them. Even if the arguments are false, the fact that I remember them is not false. I also remember distinguishing between the true facts and the false theories advanced against them, and there is a difference between seeing myself make this distinction now and remembering that I have made it often in the past, every time that I have given the matter any thought. So I not only remember that I have often understood these facts in the past, but I also commit to memory the fact that I understand them and distinguish the truth from the falsehood at the present moment. By this means I ensure that later on I shall remember that I understood them at this time. And I remember that I have remembered, just as later on, if I remember that I have been able to remember these facts now, it will be by the power of my memory that I shall remember doing so.

14

My memory also contains my feelings, not in the same way as they are present to the mind when it experiences them, but in a quite different way that is in keeping with the special powers of the memory. For even when I am unhappy I can remember times when I was cheerful, and when I am cheerful I can remember past unhappiness. I can recall past fears and yet not feel afraid, and when I remember that I once wanted something, I can do so without wishing to have it now. Sometimes memory induces the opposite feeling, for I can be glad to remember sorrow that is over and done with and sorry to remember happiness that has come to an end. There would be nothing remarkable in this if memory recalled only our bodily sensations, for the mind is one thing and the body another, and it would not be strange if I were glad to remember some bygone bodily pain. But the mind and the memory are one and the same. We even call the memory the mind, for when we tell another person to remember something, we say 'See that you bear this in mind', and when we forget something, we say 'It was not in my mind' or 'It slipped out of my mind'. This being so, how can it be that, when I am glad to remember sorrow that is past – that is, when there is joy in my mind and sadness in my memory – how can it be that my mind is happy because of the joy that is in it and yet my memory is not sad by of the sadness that is in it? No one could pretend that the memory does not belong to the mind. We might say that the memory is a sort of stomach for the mind, and that joy or sadness are like sweet or bitter food. When this food is committed to the memory, it is as though it had passed into the stomach where it can remain but also loses its taste. Of course it is absurd to suppose that the memory is like the stomach, but there is some similarity none the less.

But when I say that the mind can experience four kinds of emotion – desire, joy, fear, and sorrow – I call them to mind from my memory, and if I enlarge upon this by analysing and defining each of these emotions according to the different forms which each can take, I draw upon my memory and produce from it whatever I am going to say. Yet while I remember these feelings by drawing them from my memory, they do not produce any emotional effect in me. Before I recalled them and thought about them, they must have been present in my memory, because it was from there that I was able to summon them by the act of remembering. Perhaps these emotions are brought forward from the memory by the act of remembering in the same way as cattle bring up food from the stomach when they chew the cud. But if this is so, when a man discusses them – that is, when he recalls them to mind – why does he not experience the pleasure of joy or the pain of sorrow in his mind, just as the animal tastes the food in its mouth? Perhaps the simile is unjustified, because the two processes are not alike in all points. For if we had to experience sorrow or fear every time that we mentioned these emotions, no one would be willing to speak of them. Yet we could not speak of them at all unless we could find in our memory not only the sounds of their names, which we retain as images imprinted on the memory by the senses of the body, but also the ideas of the emotions themselves. But we did not admit these ideas through any of the body's gateways to the mind. They were either committed to the memory by the mind itself, as a result of its own experience of emotion, or else the memory retained them even though they were not entrusted to it by the mind.

15

Whether this process takes place by means of images or not, it is not easy to say. I can mention a stone or the sun when these things are not actually present to my senses, but their images are present in my memory. I can speak of physical pain, but as long as I do not feel it, the pain itself is not present to me. Yet if an image of pain were not present in my memory, I should not know how to describe it nor could I distinguish it from pleasure when I spoke of it. I can talk of physical health when I am in good health. The condition of which I speak is present to me. But unless an image of it were also present in my memory, I could not possibly remember what the sound of the word meant, nor could sick people know what was meant when health was mentioned, unless an image of it were retained by the power of memory even when health itself is absent from the body. I can speak of the numbers which we use in counting, but it is the numbers themselves, not their images, which are present in my memory. I speak of the sun's image, and this too is in my memory, but it is the image itself, not the image of an image, that I recall. It is the sun's image that presents itself to my mind when I perform the act of remembering. I can speak of memory and I recognize what I speak of. But where else do I recognize it except in my memory itself? Can it be that the memory is not present to itself in its own right but only by means of an image of itself?

16

I can mention forgetfulness and recognize what the word means, but how can I recognize the thing itself unless I remember it? I am not speaking of the sound of the word but of the thing which it signifies. If I had forgotten the thing itself, I should be utterly unable to recognize what the sound implied. When I remember memory, my memory is present to itself by its own power; but when I remember forgetfulness, two things are present, memory, by which I remember it, and forgetfulness, which is what I remember. Yet what is forgetfulness but absence of memory? When it is present, I cannot remember. Then how can it be present in such a way that I can remember it? If it is true that what we remember we retain in our memory, and if it is also true that unless we remembered forgetfulness, we could not possibly recognize the meaning of the word when we heard it, then it is true that forgetfulness is retained in the memory. It follows that the very thing which by its presence causes us to forget must be present if we are to remember it. Are we to understand from this that, when we remember it, it is not itself present in the memory, but is only there by means of its image? For if forgetfulness were itself present, would not its effect be to make us forget, not to remember?

Who is to carry the research beyond this point? Who can understand the truth of the matter? O Lord, I am working hard in this field, and the field of my labours is my own self. I have become a problem to myself, like land which a farmer works only with difficulty and at the cost of much sweat. For I am not now investigating the tracts of the heavens, or measuring the distance of the stars, or trying to discover how the earth hangs in space. I am investigating myself, my memory, my mind. There is nothing strange in the fact that whatever is not myself is far from me. But what could be nearer to me than myself? Yet I do not understand the power of memory that is in myself, although without it I could not even speak of myself. What am I to say, when I am quite certain that I can remember forgetfulness? Am I to say that what I remember is not in my memory? Or am I to say that the reason why forgetfulness is in my memory is to prevent me from forgetting? Both suggestions are utterly absurd. There is the third possibility, that I should say that when I remember forgetfulness, it is its image that is retained in my memory, not the thing itself. But how can I say this when, if the image of any thing is imprinted on the memory, the thing itself must first be present in order that the memory may receive the impression of its image? It is by this means that I remember Carthage and all the other places where I have been. By the same method I remember the faces of persons whom I have seen and everything that the other senses have reported to me. By it I remember the health and sickness of my own body. My memory captured images of these things when they were present, and the images remained so that I could see them and think about them by remembering them even when the things themselves were absent. Therefore, if forgetfulness is retained in the memory, not by itself, but by means of its image, it must have been present at some time in order that the memory could capture its image. But when it was present, how did it inscribe its image on the memory when its mere presence is enough to delete what is already noted there? Yet, however it may be, and in whatever inexplicable and incomprehensible way it happens, I am certain that I remember forgetfulness, even though forgetfulness obliterates all that we remember.

17

The power of the memory is great, O Lord. It is awe-inspiring in its profound and incalculable complexity. Yet it is my mind: it is my self. What, then, am I, my God? What is my nature? A life that is ever varying, full of change, and of immense power. The wide plains of my memory and its innumerable caverns and hollows are full beyond compute of countless things of all kinds. Material things are there by means of their images; knowledge is there of itself; emotions are there in the form of ideas or impressions of some kind, for the memory retains them even while the mind does not experience them, although whatever is in the memory must also be in the mind. My mind has the freedom of them all. I can glide from one to the other. I can probe deep into them and never find the end of them. This is the power of memory! This is the great force of life in living man, mortal though he is!

My God, my true Life, what, then, am I to do? I shall go beyond this force that is in me, this force which we call memory, so that I may come to you, my Sweetness and my Light. What have you to say to me? You are always there above me, and as I rise up towards you in my mind, I shall go beyond even this force which is in me, this force which we call memory, longing to reach out to you by the only possible means and to cling to you in the only way in which it is possible to cling to you. For beasts and birds also have memory: otherwise they could never find their lairs or nests or the many other things which are part of their habitual life. In fact they could have no habits at all if it were not for their memory. So I must go beyond memory too, if I am to reach the God who made me different from the beasts that walk on the earth and wiser than the birds that fly in the air. I must pass beyond memory to find you, my true Good, my sure Sweetness. But where will the search lead me? Where am I to find you? If I find you beyond my memory, it means that I have no memory of you. How, then, am I to find you, if I have no memory of you?

18

The woman who had lost a coin searched for it by the light of a lantern,[1] but she would never have found it unless she had remembered it. Otherwise, when it was found, how would she have known whether it was the one she was looking for? I remember that I have often lost things and found them again after a search, and I know

[1] See Luke 15.

this because, when I was looking for them, people would ask me 'Is this it?' or 'Is that it?' and I always answered 'No', until they showed me the one thing I wanted. Whatever it was, unless I had remembered it, I should never have found it, even when it was shown to me, because I should not have recognized it. It is always the same when we look for something that we have lost and then find it. If a thing vanishes from sight but not from the memory – and this may happen with any visible object – its image is retained within us and we look for it until it comes to light again. Once it has been found it is recognized by means of the image within us. We do not say that we have found what was lost unless we recognize it, and we cannot recognize it unless we remember it. It was only lost to sight, not to the memory.

19

When, therefore, the memory loses something – and this is what happens whenever we forget something and try to remember it – where are we to look for it except in the memory itself? And if the memory offers us something else instead, as may happen, we reject what it offers until the one thing which we want is presented. When it is presented to us we say 'This is it', but we could not say this unless we recognized it, and we could not recognize it unless we remembered it. True enough, we had forgotten it. Or could it be that it had not entirely escaped our memory, but part of it remained, giving a clue to the remainder, because the memory, realizing that something was missing and feeling crippled by the loss of something to which it had grown accustomed, kept demanding that the missing part should be restored? Something of this sort happens when we see or think of a person whom we know, but cannot remember his name and try to recall it. If any other name but his occurs to us, we do not apply it to him, because we do not normally associate that name with him. So we reject all names until we think of the one which corresponds accurately with our normal mental picture of the man. But how can we think of his name unless we bring it out from the memory? For even if we recognize it because someone else prompts us, it is still by our own memory that we do so, because we do not accept it as a fresh piece of knowledge but agree that it is the right name, since we can now remember it. If the name were completely obliterated from our minds, we could not remember it even if we were prompted. For we do not entirely forget what we remember that we have forgotten. If we had completely forgotten it, we should not even be able to look for what was lost.

20

How, then, do I look for you, O Lord? For when I look for you, who are my God, I am looking for a life of blessed happiness. I shall look for you, so that my soul may live. For it is my soul that gives life to my body, and it is you who give life to my soul. How, then, am I to search for this blessed life? For I do not possess it until I can rightly say, 'This is all that I want. Happiness is here.' Am I to seek it in memory, as though I had forgotten it but still remembered that I had forgotten it? Or am I to seek it through the desire to get to know it as if it were something unknown to me, either because I have never known it or because I have forgotten it so completely that I do not even remember having forgotten it? Surely happiness is what everyone wants, so much so that there can be none who do not want it. But if they desire it so much, where did they learn what it was? If they have learnt to love it, where did they see it? Certainly happiness is in us, though how it comes to be there I cannot tell. Some people are happy in the sense that they have actually achieved a state of happiness. Others are happy only in the hope of achieving it. They possess happiness in a lesser degree than those who have achieved it, but even so they are better off than those who are happy neither in the achievement of this blessed state nor in the expectation of it. Yet even these others must possess happiness in a certain sense, otherwise they would not long for it as they do; and there can be no doubt that they do long for it. By some means or other they have learnt what it is. In some sense they have knowledge of it, and the problem before me is to discover whether or not this knowledge is in the memory. If it is, it means that at some time in the past we have been happy. It may be that we were all once happy individually, or it may be that we were all happy in Adam, the first sinner, in whom we all died and from whom we are all descended in a heritage of misery. But this is not the question which is now before me. The problem is whether happiness is in the memory. For we should not love happiness unless we knew what it was. We have heard it named and we all admit that it is our ambition to achieve it, for we do not take pleasure simply in the sound of the word. When a Greek hears it named in Latin, he derives no pleasure from it because he does not know what has been said. But we get pleasure from it, just as he would if he heard it spoken in Greek. This is because happiness is neither Greek nor Latin, but we are all eager to achieve it, whether we speak Greek or Latin or any other language. It must, then, be known to all, and there can be no doubt that if it were possible to put the question in a common language and ask all men whether they wished to be happy, all would reply that they did. But this could only happen if happiness itself, that is, the state which the word signifies, were to be found somewhere in their memories.

21

But is it to be found in the memory in the same way as Carthage, which I have seen, is present in my memory? This cannot be the case, because happiness cannot be seen by the eye, since it is not a material object. Is it in the memory in the same way as we remember numbers? Again this cannot be the case, because once we have the knowledge of numbers we cease trying to acquire it; but even though we have knowledge of happiness, and love it for that reason, we continue to wish to achieve it, so that we may be happy. Is it then in the memory in the same way as the art of public speaking is there? Here again the answer is no. People recognize what is meant by the word 'eloquence' even though they have not mastered the art themselves, and many of them would like to be eloquent. This shows that they have knowledge of what it is. But by means of their bodily senses they have been made aware of eloquence in others. It has given them pleasure and they desire the gift for themselves. Of course they would get no pleasure from it unless they had some deeper knowledge of it, and they would not wish to have it for themselves unless they enjoyed it. But in the case of happiness there is no bodily sense by which we can experience it in others.

Perhaps it is in the memory in the same way as we remember joy. Even when I am sad I can remember joy, just as I can visualize happiness when I am unhappy. Yet I have never been aware of joy through any of the bodily senses. I have not seen or heard it, smelled, tasted or touched it. It is something that I have experienced in my mind on occasions of joy, and the knowledge of it has remained firmly in my memory, so that I can always recall it, sometimes with disgust and sometimes with longing, according to the differences between the things which I remember having enjoyed. For I have at times taken great joy in shameful things, and when I remember them now, I loathe and detest them. At other times I have enjoyed good and honourable things and I remember them with longing, although they may now be beyond my reach, so that the remembrance of past joy makes me sad.

Where and when, therefore, did I experience a state of blessed happiness, so that I am enabled to remember it and love it and long for it? I am not alone in this desire, nor are there only a few who share it with me: without exception we all long for happiness. Unless we had some sure knowledge of it, we should not desire it with such certainty. But if two men were asked whether they wanted to serve in the army, one might reply that he did and the other that he did not. If, on the other hand, they were asked whether they wanted to be happy, they would both reply at once and without hesitation that they did. The only reason why one of them should wish to serve in the army and the other not to serve would be that they wanted to be happy. Is it that different persons find joy in different things? All agree that they want to be happy, just as, if they were asked, they would all agree that they desired joy. In fact they think that joy is the same as happiness. They may all search for it in different ways, but all try their hardest to reach the same goal, that is, joy. No one can say that he has no experience of joy, and this is why he finds it in his memory and recognizes it when he hears the phrase 'a state of happiness'.

22

O Lord, far be it from the heart of your servant who confesses to you, far be it from me to think that whatever joy I feel makes me truly happy. For there is a joy that is not given to those who do not love you, but only to those who love you for your own sake. You yourself are their joy. Happiness is to rejoice in you and for you and because of you. This is true happiness and there is no other. Those who think that there is another kind of happiness look for joy else-

where, but theirs is not true joy. Yet their minds are set upon something akin to joy.

23

We cannot therefore be certain that all men desire true happiness,
because there are some who do not look for joy in you; and since
to rejoice in you is the only true happiness, we must conclude that
they do not desire true happiness. It may be that all men do desire to
be happy, but because *the impulses of nature and the impulses of the
spirit are at war with one another*, so that *they cannot do all that their will
approves*,[1] they fall back upon what they are able to do and find contentment in this way. For their will to do what they cannot do is not
strong enough to enable them to do it. If I ask them whether they
prefer truth or falsehood as the foundation of their joy, they all reply
that they would choose truth, and they say this as unhesitatingly as
they say that they wish to be happy. True happiness is to rejoice in
the truth, for to rejoice in the truth is to rejoice in you, O God, who are
the Truth, you, my God, my true Light, to whom I look for salvation. This is the happiness that all desire. All desire this, the only true
state of happiness. All desire to rejoice in truth. I have known many
men who wished to deceive, but none who wished to be deceived.
Where did they learn the meaning of happiness unless it was where
they learned the meaning of truth? For they love truth, since they do
not like to be deceived, and when they love happiness – which is the
same as to rejoice in truth – they must love truth also. But they could
not love it unless they had some knowledge of it in their memory.
Why, then, do they not take joy in it? Why are they not happy? It is
because they attend far more closely to other things whose power to
make them unhappy is greater than the power of their dim memory
of truth to make them happy. There is still a faint glow of light in
man.[2] Let him walk on, for fear that darkness may engulf him.

But why does truth engender hatred? Why does your servant meet
with hostility when he preaches the truth, although men love happiness, which is simply the enjoyment of truth? It can only be that
man's love of truth is such that when he loves something which is
not the truth, he pretends to himself that what he loves is the truth,
and because he hates to be proved wrong, he will not allow himself

[1] Gal. 5: 17. [2] See John 12: 35.

to be convinced that he is deceiving himself. So he hates the real truth for the sake of what he takes to his heart in its place. Men love the truth when it bathes them in its light: they hate it when it proves them wrong. Because they hate to be deceived themselves, but are glad if they can deceive others, they love the truth when it is revealed to them but hate it when it reveals that they are wrong. They reap their just reward, for those who do not wish to stand condemned by the truth find themselves unmasked against their will and also find that truth is denied to them. This is precisely the behaviour of the human mind. In its blind inertia, in its abject shame, it loves to lie concealed, yet it wishes that nothing should be concealed from it. Its reward is just the opposite of its desire, for it cannot conceal itself from the truth, but truth remains hidden from it. Yet even in this wretched state it would still rather find joy in truth than in falsehood. One day, then, it shall be happy, if it learns to ignore all that distracts it and to rejoice in truth, the sole Truth by which all else is true.

24

See how I have explored the vast field of my memory in search of you, O Lord! And I have not found you outside it. For I have discovered nothing about you except what I have remembered since the time when I first learned about you. Ever since then I have not forgotten you. For I found my God, who is Truth itself, where I found truth, and ever since I learned the truth I have not forgotten it. So, since the time when I first learned of you, you have always been present in my memory, and it is there that I find you whenever I am reminded of you and find delight in you. This is my holy joy, which in your mercy you have given me, heedful of my poverty.

25

But in which part of my memory are you present, O Lord? What cell have you constructed for yourself in my memory? What sanctuary have you built there for yourself? That you should be present in it is a great honour, but I must now ask myself in what part of it you are present. When I remind myself of you I go beyond those functions of the memory which I share with the beasts, for I did not find you amongst the images of material things. I went on to search for you in the part of my memory where the emotions of my mind are stored, but here too I did not find you. I passed on to the seat of the mind itself – for this too is in the memory, since the mind can remember itself – but you were not there. For you are not the image of a material body, nor are you an emotion such as is felt by living men when they are glad or sorry, when they have sensations of desire or fear, when they remember or forget, or when they experience any other feeling. In the same way you are not the mind itself, for you are the Lord God of the mind. All these things are subject to change, but you remain supreme over all things, immutable. And yet you have deigned to be present in my memory ever since I first learned of you. Why do I ask what place is set aside in my memory as your dwelling, as if there were distinctions of place in the memory? Truly you do dwell in it, because I remember you ever since I first came to learn of you, and it is there that I find you when I am reminded of you.

26

Where, then, did I find you so that I could learn of you? For you were not in my memory before I learned of you. Where else, then, did I find you, to learn of you, unless it was in yourself, above me? Whether we approach you or depart from you, you are not confined in any place. You are Truth, and you are everywhere present where all seek counsel of you. You reply to all at once, though the counsel each seeks is different. The answer you give is clear, but not all hear it clearly. All ask you whatever they wish to ask, but the answer they receive is not always what they want to hear. The man who serves you best is the one who is less intent on hearing from you what he wills to hear than on shaping his will according to what he hears from you.

27

I have learnt to love you late, Beauty at once so ancient and so new! I have learnt to love you late! You were within me, and I was in the world outside myself. I searched for you outside myself and, disfigured as I was, I fell upon the lovely things of your creation. You were with me, but I was not with you. The beautiful things of this world kept me far from you and yet, if they had not been in you, they would have had no being at all. You called me; you cried aloud to me; you broke my barrier of deafness. You shone upon me; your radiance enveloped me; you put my blindness to flight. You shed your fragrance about me; I drew breath and now I gasp for your sweet odour. I tasted you, and now I hunger and thirst for you. You touched me, and I am inflamed with love of your peace.

28

When at last I cling to you with all my being, for me there will be no more sorrow, no more toil. Then at last I shall be alive with true life, for my life will be wholly filled by you. You raise up and sustain all whose lives you fill, but my life is not yet filled by you and I am a burden to myself. The pleasures I find in the world, which should be cause for tears, are at strife with its sorrows, in which I should rejoice, and I cannot tell to which the victory will fall. Have pity on me, O Lord, in my misery! My sorrows are evil and they are at strife with joys that are good, and I cannot tell which will gain the victory. Have pity on me, O Lord, in my misery! I do not hide my wounds from you. I am sick, and you are the physician. You are merciful: I have need of your mercy. Is not our life on earth a period of trial? For who would wish for hardship and difficulty? You command us to endure these troubles, not to love them. No one loves what he endures, even though he may be glad to endure it. For though he may rejoice in his power of endurance, he would prefer that there should be nothing for him to endure. When I am in trouble I long for good fortune, but when I have good fortune I fear to lose it. Is there any middle state between prosperity and adversity, some state in which human life is not a trial? In prosperity as the world knows it there is twofold cause for grief, for there is grief in the fear of adversity and grief in joy that does not last. And in what the world knows as adversity the causes of grief are threefold, for not only is it hard to bear, but it also causes us to long for prosperous times and to fear that our powers of endurance may break. Is not man's life on earth a long, unbroken period of trial?

29

There can be no hope for me except in your great mercy. Give me the grace to do as you command, and command me to do what you will! You command us to control our bodily desires. And, as we are told, when I knew that no man can *be master of himself, except of God's bounty, I was wise enough already to know whence the gift came.*[1] Truly it is by continence that we are made as one and regain that unity of self which we lost by falling apart in the search for a variety of pleasures. For a man loves you so much the less if, besides you, he also loves something else which he does not love for your sake. O Love ever burning, never quenched! O Charity, my God, set me on fire with your love! You command me to be continent. Give me the grace to do as you command, and command me to do what you will!

30

It is truly your command that I should be continent and restrain myself from *gratification of corrupt nature, gratification of the eye, the empty pomp of living.*[2] You commanded me not to commit fornication, and though you did not forbid me to marry, you counselled me to take a better course. You gave me the grace and I did your bidding, even before I became a minister of your sacrament. But in my memory, of which I have said much, the images of things imprinted upon it by my former habits still linger on. When I am awake they obtrude themselves upon me, though with little strength. But when I dream, they not only give me pleasure but are very much like acquiescence in the act. The power which these illusory images have over my soul and my body is so great that what is no more than a vision can influence me in sleep in a way that the reality cannot do when I am awake. Surely it cannot be that when I am asleep I am not myself, O Lord my God? And yet the moment when I pass from wakefulness to sleep, or return again from sleep to wakefulness, marks a great difference in me. During sleep where is my reason which, when I am awake, resists such suggestions and remains firm and undismayed even in face of the realities themselves? Is it sealed off when I close my eyes? Does it fall asleep with the senses of the

[1] Wisdom 8: 21. [2] 1 John 2: 16.

body? And why is it that even in sleep I often resist the attractions of these images, for I remember my chaste resolutions and abide by them and give no consent to temptations of this sort? Yet the difference between waking and sleeping is so great that even when, during sleep, it happens otherwise, I return to a clear conscience when I wake and realize that, because of this difference, I was not responsible for the act, although I am sorry that by some means or other it happened to me.

The power of your hand, O God Almighty, is indeed great enough to cure all the diseases of my soul. By granting me more abundant grace you can even quench the fire of sensuality which provokes me in my sleep. More and more, O Lord, you will increase your gifts in me, so that my soul may follow me to you, freed from the concupiscence which binds it, and rebel no more against itself. By your grace it will no longer commit in sleep these shameful, unclean acts inspired by sensual images, which lead to the pollution of the body: it will not so much as consent to them. For to you, the Almighty, who are *powerful enough to carry out your purpose beyond all our hopes and dreams*,[1] it is no great task to prescribe that no temptations of this kind, even such slight temptations as can be checked by the least act of will, should arouse pleasure in me, even in sleep, provided that my dispositions are chaste. This you can do for me at any time of life, even in the prime of manhood. But now I make this confession to my good Lord, declaring how I am still troubled by this kind of evil. *With awe in my heart I rejoice*[2] in your gifts, yet I grieve for my deficiencies, trusting that you will perfect your mercies in me until I reach the fullness of peace, which I shall enjoy with you in soul and body, when *death is swallowed up in victory*.[3]

31

There is another evil which we meet with day by day. If only it were the only one! For we repair the daily wastage of our bodies by eating and drinking, until the time comes when you *will bring both food and our animal nature to an end*.[4] When that time comes, your wonderful fullness will spell the end of our need, and you will *clothe this corruptible nature of ours with incorruptible life*.[5] But for the

[1] Eph. 3: 20. [2] Ps. 2: 11. [3] 1 Cor. 15: 54. [4] 1 Cor. 6: 13. [5] 1 Cor. 15: 53.

present I find pleasure in this need, though I fight against it, for fear of becoming its captive. Every day I wage war upon it by fasting. Time and again I force my body to obey me, but the pain which this causes me is cancelled by the pleasure of eating and drinking. For of course hunger and thirst are painful. Like a fever they parch and kill unless they are relieved by the remedies of food and drink. And since, to console us, we have your gifts – for you have given us earth and water and sky to serve us in our weakness – the remedies are there for us to find and we think of this hardship as a source of delight.

Because you have taught me to understand this, I look upon food as a medicine. But the snare of concupiscence awaits me in the very process of passing from the discomfort of hunger to the contentment which comes when it is satisfied. For the process itself is a pleasure and there is no other means of satisfying hunger except the one which we are obliged to take. And although the purpose of eating and drinking is to preserve health, in its train there follows an ominous kind of enjoyment, which often tries to outstrip it, so that it is really for the sake of pleasure that I do what I claim to do and mean to do for the sake of my health. Moreover, health and enjoyment have not the same requirements, for what is sufficient for health is not enough for enjoyment, and it is often hard to tell whether the body, which must be cared for, requires further nourishment, or whether we are being deceived by the allurements of greed demanding to be gratified. My unhappy soul welcomes this uncertainty, using it to vindicate and excuse itself. It is glad that the proper requirements of health are in doubt, so that under the pretence of caring for health it may disguise the pursuit of pleasure.

Every day I try my hardest to resist these temptations. I call for your helping hand and tell you of my difficulties, because this is a problem which I have not yet resolved. I hear the voice of my God who commands us: *Do not let your hearts grow dull with revelry and drunkenness.*[1] Drunkenness is far from me. By your grace may you prevent it from coming near! But there have been times when over-eating has stolen upon your servant. By your mercy may you keep it far from me! For no man *can be master of himself, except of God's bounty.*[2]

---

[1] Luke 21: 34.   [2] Wisdom 8: 21.

You grant us many gifts when we pray for them. And even before we pray for them, all the good things that we have ever received have come from you. That we should later recognize that they came from you is also your gift. I have never been a drunkard myself, but I have known drunkards made sober by you. Therefore, just as it is by your doing that men who were once drunkards are not so for ever, it is also by your doing that those who were never drunkards are not drunkards now. And in the same way it is also by your doing that men of both sorts know that it was you who did this for them.

I have also heard these other words of yours: *Do not follow the counsel of appetite. Turn your back on your own liking.*[1] By your gift I have also heard and found great comfort in the words: *We gain nothing by eating, lose nothing by abstaining.*[2] This means that eating will not bring me plenty nor abstinence reduce me to misery. I have heard these words too: *I have learned to be content with my circumstances as they are. I know what it is to have abundant means and what it is to live in want. Nothing is beyond my powers, thanks to the strength God gives me.*[3] Here speaks a true soldier of the heavenly army, not mere dust like the rest of us! But remember, O Lord, that we are dust. Remember that you made man from dust, and that he was lost and found again. My heart goes out to Paul for the words that he wrote by your inspiration: *Nothing is beyond my powers, thanks to the strength God gives me.*[3] But he too was dust and could not do all things by his own power. Give me strength, O Lord, so that I may do all things. Give me the grace to do as you command, and command me to do what you will! Paul acknowledges your gifts and the boast that he makes is made in the Lord.[4] I have also heard another of your servants begging for your gifts in these words: *Let the itch of gluttony pass me by.*[5] All this makes it clear, O holy God, that when your commands are obeyed, it is from you that we receive the power to obey them.

Good Father, you have taught me that nothing can be *unclean for those who have clean hearts,*[6] yet it goes ill with the man who eats to the hurt of his own conscience.[7] You have taught me that *all is good that God has made, nothing is to be rejected; only we must be thankful to him when we partake of it;*[8] that *it is not what we eat that gives us our standing in God's sight;*[9] that *no one must be allowed to take us to task over what we*

---

[1] Ecclus. 18: 30. [2] 1 Cor. 8: 8. [3] Philipp. 4: 11–13. [4] See 11 Cor. 10: 17.
[5] Ecclus. 23: 6. [6] Tit. 1: 15. [7] Rom. 14: 20. [8] 1 Tim. 4: 4. [9] 1 Cor. 8: 8.

eat or drink;[1] and that no man, *over his meat,* should *mock at him who does not eat it,* nor, *while he abstains, pass judgement on him who eats it.*[2] For these lessons which I have learnt all praise and all thanks be to you, my God, my Master, to you who knock at the door of my ears and shed your light over my heart! Deliver me from all temptation. It is the uncleanness of gluttony that I fear, not unclean meat. For I know that Noe was allowed to eat all kinds of meat that were suitable as food; that Elias was fed on meat; and that John the Baptist, remarkable ascetic though he was, was not polluted by the flesh of living creatures, the locusts which were granted him as food. On the other hand I know that Esau was defrauded by his greed for a dish of lentils; that David reproached himself for longing for a drink of water; and that Christ our King was tempted not by meat but by bread. And the Israelites in the desert deserved rebuke, not because they wanted meat, but because in their greed for food they sulked and grumbled against the Lord.

In the midst of these temptations I struggle daily against greed for food and drink. This is not an evil which I can decide once and for all to repudiate and never to embrace again, as I was able to do in the case of fornication. I must therefore hold back my appetite with neither too firm nor too slack a rein. But is there anyone, O Lord, who is never enticed a little beyond the strict limit of need? If there is such a one, he is a great man. Let him praise your name. But I am not such a man: I am a poor sinner. Yet I too praise your name, and Christ, who conquered the world, pleads with you for my sins. He numbers me among the weak members of his Body, for *your eyes looked upon me, when I was yet unformed; all human lives are already written in your record.*[3]

32

The sense of smell does not trouble me greatly with its attractions. I do not miss sweet scents when they are absent, but neither do I refuse them where I find them. I am even ready to do without them altogether. This, at least, is my own opinion of myself, but I may be wrong. For the powers of my inner self are veiled in darkness which I must deplore. When my mind speculates upon its own capabilities, it realizes that it cannot safely trust its own judgement, because its

[1] Col. 2: 16. [2] Rom. 14: 3. [3] Ps. 138: 16 (139: 16).

inner workings are generally so obscure that they are only revealed in the light of experience; and, besides this, during this life, which may be called a perpetual trial, no one should be confident that although he has been able to pass from a worse state to a better, he may not also pass from a better state to a worse. Our only hope, our only confidence, the only firm promise that we have is your mercy.

33

I used to be much more fascinated by the pleasures of sound than the pleasures of smell. I was enthralled by them, but you broke my bonds and set me free. I admit that I still find some enjoyment in the music of hymns, which are alive with your praises, when I hear them sung by well-trained, melodious voices. But I do not enjoy it so much that I cannot tear myself away. I can leave it when I wish. But if I am not to turn a deaf ear to music, which is the setting for the words which give it life, I must allow it a position of some honour in my heart, and I find it difficult to assign it to its proper place. For sometimes I feel that I treat it with more honour than it deserves. I realize that when they are sung these sacred words stir my mind to greater religious fervour and kindle in me a more ardent flame of piety than they would if they were not sung; and I also know that there are particular modes in song and in the voice, corresponding to my various emotions and able to stimulate them because of some mysterious relationship between the two. But I ought not to allow my mind to be paralysed by the gratification of my senses, which often leads it astray. For the senses are not content to take second place. Simply because I allow them their due, as adjuncts to reason, they attempt to take precedence and forge ahead of it, with the result that I sometimes sin in this way but am not aware of it until later.

Sometimes, too, from over-anxiety to avoid this particular trap I make the mistake of being too strict. When this happens, I have no wish but to exclude from my ears, and from the ears of the Church as well, all the melody of those lovely chants to which the Psalms of David are habitually sung; and it seems safer to me to follow the precepts which I remember often having heard ascribed to Athanasius, bishop of Alexandria, who used to oblige the lectors to recite the psalms with such slight modulation of the voice that they seemed to be speaking rather than chanting. But when I remember the tears that I shed on hearing the songs of the Church in the early days, soon after I had recovered my faith, and when I realize that nowadays it is not the singing that moves me but the meaning of the words when they are sung in a clear voice to the most appropriate tune, I again acknowledge the great value of this practice. So I waver between the danger that lies in gratifying the senses and the benefits which, as I know from experience, can accrue from singing. Without committing myself to an irrevocable opinion, I am inclined to approve of the custom of singing in church, in order that by indulging the ears weaker spirits may be inspired with feelings of devotion. Yet when I find the singing itself more moving than the truth which it conveys, I confess that this is a grievous sin, and at those times I would prefer not to hear the singer.

This, then, is my present state. Let those of my readers whose hearts are filled with charity, from which good actions spring, weep with me and weep for me. Those who feel no charity in themselves will not be moved by my words. But I beg you, O Lord my God, to look upon me and listen to me. Have pity on me and heal me, for you see that I have become a problem to myself, and this is the ailment from which I suffer.

34

Finally I must confess how I am tempted through the eye. Let the ears of your Church, the ears of my devout brothers in Christ, listen to my words, so that I may bring to an end my discussion of the body's temptations to pleasure, which still provoke me as *I sigh, longing for the shelter of that home which heaven will give me*.[1]

The eyes delight in beautiful shapes of different sorts and bright and attractive colours. I would not have these things take possession of my soul. Let God possess it, he who made them all. He made them all *very good*,[2] but it is he who is my Good, not they. All day and every day, while I am awake, they are there before my eyes. They allow me no respite such as I am granted in moments of silence when there is no singing and sometimes no sound at all to be heard. For light, the queen of colours, pervades all that I see, wherever I am throughout the day, and by the ever-changing pattern of its rays it entices me

[1] II Cor. 5: 2. [2] Gen. 1: 31.

even when I am occupied with something else and take no special note of it. It wins so firm a hold on me that, if I am suddenly deprived of it, I long to have it back, and if I am left for long without it, I grow dispirited.

But the true Light is the Light which Tobias saw when, though his eyes were blind, he taught his son the path he should follow in life, and himself led the way, charity guiding his steps so that he did not stray. It is the Light which Isaac saw when the sight of his eyes was dimmed and clouded by old age and it was granted to him, not to bless his sons in full knowledge as to which was which, but to know them by blessing them. It is the Light which Jacob saw when, though his eyes were blinded by old age, a Light shone in his heart and cast its beams over the tribes of Israel yet to come, as he foresaw them in the persons of his sons. It is the Light which he saw when he laid his hands on his grandchildren, the sons of Joseph, not in the way that their father, who saw only the outward act, tried to make him do it, but mystically crossed, in the way that he discerned by the Light that shone within him. This is the true Light. It is one alone and all who see and love it are one.

But in our life in the world this earthly light, of which I was speaking, is a seasoning, sweet and tempting, but dangerous for those whose love for it is blind. Yet those who have learnt to praise you for this as well as for your other gifts, *O God, Maker of all things*,[1] sing you a hymn of praise for it: they are not beguiled by it in their dreams. For myself, I wish to be as they are. I resist the allurements of the eye for fear that as I walk upon your path, my feet may be caught in a trap. Instead, I raise the eyes of my spirit to you, so that you may *save my feet from the snare*.[2] Time and again you save them, for I fail to escape the trap. You never cease to free me, although again and again I find myself caught in the snares that are laid all about me. For you are *the guardian of Israel, one who is never weary, never sleeps*.[3]

By every kind of art and the skill of their hands men make innumerable things – clothes, shoes, pottery, and other useful objects, besides pictures and various works which are the fruit of their imagination. They make them on a far more lavish scale than is required to satisfy their own modest needs or to express their devotion, and all

---

[1] Saint Ambrose's 'Evening Hymn'; see Book IX, chapter 12.
[2] Ps. 24: 15 (25: 15). [3] Ps. 120: 4 (121: 4).

these things are additional temptations to the eye, made by men who love the worldly things they make themselves but forget their own Maker and destroy what he made in them. But, O my God, my Glory, for these things too I offer you a hymn of thanksgiving. I make a sacrifice of praise to him who sanctifies me, for the beauty which flows through men's minds into their skilful hands comes from that Beauty which is above their souls and for which my soul sighs all day and night. And it is from this same supreme Beauty that men who make things of beauty and love it in its outward forms derive the principle by which they judge it: but they do not accept the same principle to guide them in the use they make of it. Yet it is there, and they do not see it. If only they could see it, they would not depart from it. They would preserve their strength for you,[1] not squander it on luxuries that make them weary.

Though I say this and see that it is true, my feet are still caught in the toils of this world's beauty. But you will free me, O Lord; I know that you will free me. For *ever I keep your mercies in mind.*[2] I am caught and need your mercy, and by your mercy you will save me from the snare. Sometimes, if I have not fallen deep into the trap, I shall feel nothing when you rescue me; but at other times, when I am fast ensnared, I shall suffer the pain of it.

35

I must now speak of a different kind of temptation, more dangerous than these because it is more complicated. For in addition to our bodily appetites, which make us long to gratify all our senses and our pleasures and lead to our ruin if we stay away from you by becoming their slaves, the mind is also subject to a certain propensity to use the sense of the body, not for self-indulgence of a physical kind, but for the satisfaction of its own inquisitiveness. This futile curiosity masquerades under the name of science and learning, and since it derives from our thirst for knowledge and sight is the principal sense by which knowledge is acquired, in the Scriptures it is called *gratification of the eye.*[3] For although, correctly speaking, to see is the proper function of the eyes, we use the word of the other senses too, when we employ them to acquire knowledge. We do not say 'Hear how it

---

[1] See Ps. 58: 10 (59: 9).   [2] Ps. 25: 3 (26: 3).   [3] 1 John 2: 16.

glows', 'Smell how bright it is', 'Taste how it shines', or 'Feel how it glitters', because these are all things which we say that we see. Yet we not only say 'See how it shines' when we are speaking of something which only the eyes can perceive, but we also say 'See how loud it is', 'See how it smells', 'See how it tastes', and 'See how hard it is'. So, as I said, sense-experience in general is called the lust of the eyes because, although the function of sight belongs primarily to the eyes, we apply it to the other organs of sense as well, by analogy, when they are used to discover any item of knowledge.

We can easily distinguish between the motives of pleasure and curiosity. When the senses demand pleasure, they look for objects of visual beauty, harmonious sounds, fragrant perfumes, and things that are pleasant to the taste or soft to the touch. But when their motive is curiosity, they may look for just the reverse of these things, simply to put it to the proof, not for the sake of an unpleasant experience, but from a relish for investigation and discovery. What pleasure can there be in the sight of a mangled corpse, which can only horrify? Yet people will flock to see one lying on the ground, simply for the sensation of sorrow and horror that it gives them. They are even afraid that it may bring them nightmares, as though it were something that they had been forced to look at while they were awake or something to which they had been attracted by rumours of its beauty. The same is true of the other senses, although it would be tedious to give further examples. It is to satisfy this unhealthy curiosity that freaks and prodigies are put on show in the theatre, and for the same reason men are led to investigate the secrets of nature, which are irrelevant to our lives, although such knowledge is of no value to them and they wish to gain it merely for the sake of knowing. It is curiosity, too, which causes men to turn to sorcery in the effort to obtain knowledge for the same perverted purpose. And it even invades our religion, for we put God to the test when we demand signs and wonders from him, not in the hope of salvation, but simply for the love of the experience.

In this immense forest, so full of snares and dangers, I have pared away many sins and thrust them from my heart, for you have given me the grace to do this, O God, my Saviour. But as long as my daily life is passed in the midst of the clamour raised by so many temptations of this sort, when can I presume to say that nothing of this kind can hold my attention or tempt me into idle speculation? It is true that the theatres no longer attract me; the study of astrology does not interest me; I have never dealt in necromancy; and I detest all sacrilegious rites. But how often has not the enemy used his wiles upon me to suggest that I should ask for some sign from you, O Lord my God, to whom I owe my humble, undivided service? I beseech you, by Christ our King and by Jerusalem the chaste, our only homeland, that just as I now withhold my consent from these suggestions, I may always continue to ward them off and keep them still farther from me. But when I pray to you for the salvation of another, the purpose and intention of my prayer is far different. For you do what you will and you grant me, as you always will, the grace to follow you gladly.

Yet who can tell how many times each day our curiosity is tempted by the most trivial and insignificant matters? Who can tell how often we give way? So often it happens that, when others tell foolish tales, at first we bear with them for fear of offending the weak, and then little by little we begin to listen willingly. I no longer go to watch a dog chasing a hare at the games in the circus. But if I should happen to see the same thing in the country as I pass by, the chase might easily hold my attention and distract me from whatever serious thoughts occupied my mind. It might not actually compel me to turn my horse from the path, but such would be the inclination of my heart; and unless you made me realize my weakness and quickly reminded me, either to turn my eyes from the sight and raise my thoughts to you in contemplation, or to despise it utterly and continue on my way, I should simply stop and gloat. What excuse can I make for myself when often, as I sit at home, I cannot turn my eyes from the sight of a lizard catching flies or a spider entangling them as they fly into her web? Does it make any difference that these are only small animals? It is true that the sight of them inspires me to praise you for the wonders of your creation and the order in which you have disposed all things, but I am not intent upon your praises when I first begin to watch. It is one thing to rise quickly from a fall, another not to fall at all.

My life is full of such faults, and my only hope is in your boundless mercy. For when our hearts become repositories piled high with such worthless stock as this, it is the cause of interruption and distraction from our prayers. And although, in your presence, the voices of our hearts are raised to your ear, all kinds of trivial thoughts break in and cut us off from the great act of prayer.

36

Must I not consider this too as one of the faults which I ought to despise? Can anything restore me to hope except your mercy? That you are merciful I know, for you have begun to change me. You know how great a change you have worked in me, for first of all you have cured me of the desire to assert my claim to liberty, so that you may also pardon me all my other sins, *heal all my mortal ills, rescue my life from deadly peril, crown me with the blessings of your mercy, content all my desire for good.*[1] You know how great a change you have worked in me, for you have curbed my pride by teaching me to fear you and you have tamed my neck to your yoke. And now that I bear your yoke, I find its burden light, for this was your promise and you have kept your word. In truth, though I did not know it, it was light even in the days when I was afraid to bend my neck to it.

But, O Lord, you who alone rule without pride since you are the only true Lord and no other lord rules over you, there is a third kind of temptation which, I fear, has not passed from me. Can it ever pass from me in all this life? It is the desire to be feared or loved by other men, simply for the pleasure that it gives me, though in such pleasure there is no true joy. It means only a life of misery and despicable vainglory. It is for this reason more than any other that men neither love you nor fear you in purity of heart. It is for this reason that *you thwart the proud and keep your grace for the humble.*[2] This is why, with a voice of thunder, you condemn the ambitions of this world, so that *the very foundations of the hills quail and quake.*[3] This is why the enemy of our true happiness persists in his attacks upon me, for he knows that when men hold certain offices in human society, it is necessary that they should be loved and feared by other men. He sets his traps about me, baiting them with tributes of applause, in the hope that in my eagerness to listen I may be caught off my guard. He wants me to divorce my joy from the truth and place it in man's duplicity. He wants me to enjoy being loved and

[1] Ps. 102: 3-5 (103: 3-5). [2] 1 Pet. 5: 5. [3] Ps. 17: 8 (18: 7).

feared by others, not for your sake, but in your place, so that in this way he may make me like himself and keep me to share with him, not the true fellowship of charity, but the bonds of common punishment. For he determined to set his throne in the north,[1] where, chilled and benighted, men might serve him as he imitates you in his perverse, distorted way.

But we, O Lord, are your *little flock*.[2] Keep us as your own. Spread your wings and let us shelter beneath them. Let us glory in you alone. If we are loved or feared by others, let it be for your sake. No man who seeks the praise of other men can be defended by men when you call him to account. Men cannot save him when you condemn. But it happens too, not that praise is given to the man who is *proud of his wicked end achieved*[3] or that the evildoer wins applause, but that a man is praised for some gift which you have given him. And if he takes greater joy in the praise which he receives than in the possession of the gift for which men praise him, then the price he pays for their applause is the loss of your favour and he, the receiver of praise, is worse off than the giver. For the one finds pleasure in God's gift in man, while the other finds less pleasure in God's gift than in the gift of men.

37

Day after day without ceasing these temptations put us to the test, O Lord. The human tongue is a furnace in which the temper of our souls is daily tried. And in this matter too you command us to be continent. Give me the grace to do as you command, and command me to do what you will! You know how I have cried to you from the depths of my heart, and how I have wept floods of tears because of this difficulty. For I cannot easily deduce how far I am cured of this disease, and I have great fear of offending you unawares by sins to which I am blind, though to your eyes they are manifest. In other kinds of temptation I have some means of examining myself, but in this I have almost none. For I can see what progress I have made in the ability to restrain my mind from giving in to sensual pleasures or idle curiosity. It becomes plain when I do without these things, either voluntarily or for lack of the occasion, because I then ask myself how much, or how little, it troubles me to be without

[1] The allusion is to Is. 14: 13, 14. [2] Luke 12: 32. [3] Ps. 9: 24 (10: 3).

them. The same is true of wealth, which men grasp because they want the means of satisfying one or another of these three kinds of temptation, or perhaps two or even all three of them. If the soul, when it has riches, cannot tell whether it despises them, it can put itself to the proof by discarding them. But if we are to do without praise in order to test our powers, are we to live such outrageously wicked and abandoned lives that all who know us will detest us? Is it possible to imagine a more insane proposal than this? If praise is normally associated with a good life and good works, and rightly so, we ought neither to cease living good lives nor to abandon the rightful consequence. But I cannot tell whether or not I have the forbearance to do without anything, unless it is taken away from me.

What, then, is my attitude to temptation of this kind? What am I to confess to you, O Lord? I can only say that I am gratified by praise, but less by praise than by the truth. For if I were asked whether I would prefer to be commended by all my fellow men for wild delusions and errors on all counts, or to be stigmatized by them for constancy and assurance in the truth, it is clear which I would choose. But I wish that words of praise from other men did not increase the joy I feel for any good qualities that I may have. Yet I confess that it does increase my joy. What is more, their censure detracts from it. And when I am worried by this wretched failing, an excuse occurs to me, though how good an excuse it is only you know, O God: it leaves me in doubt. For you have commanded us not only to be continent, but also to be just; that is, to withhold our love from certain things and to bestow it on others. You want us not only to love you, but also to love our neighbour. For this reason I tell myself that when I am gratified by the praise of a man who well understands what it is that he praises, the true reason for my pleasure is that my neighbour has made good progress and shows promise for the future. Similarly, when I hear him cast a slur upon something which he does not understand or something which in fact is good, I am sorry that he should have this failing. I am sometimes sorry, too, to hear my own praises, either when others commend me for qualities which I am not glad to possess, or when they value in me, more highly than their due, qualities which may be good, but are of little importance. But here again I cannot tell whether this feeling comes from reluctance to allow the man who praises me to disagree with me about my own qualities, not because I am concerned for his welfare, but because the good qualities which please me in myself please me still more when they please others as well. For in a certain sense it is no compliment to me when my own opinion of myself is not upheld, in other words either when qualities which displease me are commended, or when those which please me least are most applauded.

Am I not right, then, to say that I am in doubt about this problem? My God, in the light of your truth I see that if my feelings are stirred by the praise which I receive, it should not be for my own sake but for the good of my neighbour. But whether this is so with me I do not know, for in this matter I know less about myself than I know of you. I beg you, my God, to reveal me to my own eyes, so that I may confess to my brothers in Christ what wounds I find in myself, for they will pray for me. Let me examine myself again, more closely. If it is the good of my neighbour that touches my heart when I hear my own praises, why am I less aggrieved when blame is unjustly laid at another's door than when it is laid at mine? Why do insults sting me more when they are offered to me than when I hear them offered to others with equal injustice? Can I plead ignorance in this case too? Or is the truth of the matter that I deceive myself and that in heart and tongue alike I am guilty of falsehood in your presence? O Lord, keep such folly far from me, for fear that my lips should sin, *sleeking my head with the oil of their flattery*.[1]

38

I am poor and needy and I am better only when in sorrow of heart I detest myself and seek your mercy, until what is faulty in me is repaired and made whole and finally I come to that state of peace which the eye of the proud cannot see. Yet in what others say about us and in what they know of our deeds there is grave danger of temptation. For our love of praise leads us to court the good opinion of others and hoard it for our personal glorification. And even when I reproach myself for it, the love of praise tempts me. There is temptation in the very process of self-reproach, for often, by priding himself on his contempt for vainglory, a man is guilty of even emptier pride; and for this reason his contempt of vainglory is an empty

[1] Ps. 140: 5 (141: 5).

boast, because he cannot really hold it in contempt as long as he prides himself on doing so.

39

Deep in our inner selves there is another evil, the outcome of the same kind of temptation. This is self-complacency, the vanity of those who are pleased with themselves, although they either fail to please others or have no wish to do so and even actively displease them. But though they are pleasing to themselves, they are gravely displeasing to you, because they congratulate themselves not only upon qualities which are not good, as though they were good, but also upon good qualities received from you, as though they were their own gifts to themselves; or else they recognize them as yours, but claim them for their own merits; or, again, they know that they have received them by your grace alone, but still they grudge your grace to others and will not rejoice in it with them.

You see how my heart trembles and strains in the midst of all these perils and others of a like kind. It is not as though I do not suffer wounds, but I feel rather that you heal them over and over again.

40

You have walked everywhere at my side, O Truth, teaching me what to seek and what to avoid, whenever I laid before you the things that I was able to see in this world below and asked you to counsel me. As far as my senses enabled me to do so, I surveyed the world about me and explored both the life which my body has from me and the senses themselves. Next I probed the depths of my memory, so vast in its ramifications and filled in so wonderful a way with riches beyond number. I scrutinized all these things and stood back in awe, for without you I could see none of them, and I found that none of them was you. Nor was I myself the truth, I who found them, I who explored them all and tried to distinguish and appraise each according to its worth. Some of them were conveyed to me by means of my physical senses, and I subjected them to question. Others, which closely concerned my own self, I encountered in my feelings. I enumerated the various means by which their messages were brought to me and distinguished between them. And in the great treasury of my memory there were yet other things that I examined. Some of them I returned to the keeping of my memory, others I picked out for study. But when I was doing all this, I was not myself the truth; that is, the power by which I did it was not the truth; for you, the Truth, are the unfailing Light from which I sought counsel upon all these things, asking whether they were, what they were, and how they were to be valued. But I heard you teaching me and I heard the commands you gave.

Often I do this. I find pleasure in it, and whenever I can relax from my necessary duties, I take refuge in this pleasure. But in all the regions where I thread my way, seeking your guidance, only in you do I find a safe haven for my mind, a gathering-place for my scattered parts, where no portion of me can depart from you. And sometimes you allow me to experience a feeling quite unlike my normal state, an inward sense of delight which, if it were to reach perfection in me, would be something not encountered in this life, though what it is I cannot tell. But my heavy burden of distress drags me down again to earth. Again I become a prey to my habits, which hold me fast. My tears flow, but still I am held fast. Such is the price we pay for the burden of custom! In this state I am fit to stay, unwilling though I am; in that other state, where I wish to stay, I am not fit to be. I have double cause for sorrow.

41

I have now considered the sorry state to which my sins have brought me, according to the three different forms which temptation may take, and I have invoked your helping hand to save me. For in my wounded heart I saw your splendour and it dazzled me. I asked: Who can come close to such glory? *Your watchful care has lost sight of me.*[1] You are the Truth which presides over all things. But in my selfish longing I did not wish to lose you. Together with you I wanted to possess a lie, much as a man will not utter so glaring a falsehood that it blinds his own eyes to the truth. And in this way I lost you, because you do not deign to be possessed together with a lie.

[1] Ps. 30: 23 (31: 22).

42

Whom could I find to reconcile me to you? Ought I to have sought the help of the angels? But if I had sought their help, what prayers should I have uttered? What rites should I have used? Many men, so I have heard, for lack of strength to return to you by themselves, have tried to do so by this means, but they ended by craving for strange visions, and their only reward was delusion. For they tried to find you in all the conceit and arrogance of their learning. They thrust out their chests in pride, when they should have beaten their breasts in mourning. And because they resembled them at heart, they attracted to their side the fallen angels, *the princes of the lower air*,[1] their companions and associates in pride. But these allies tricked them, using magic craft, for while they sought a mediator who would cleanse them of their impurities, it was no mediator that they found. It was the devil, *passing for an angel of light*,[2] and it was a potent lure for their proud flesh that he was not a creature of flesh and blood. For they were mortal men and sinners; but you, O Lord, to whom they wanted to be reconciled, are immortal and without sin. But a mediator between God and man must have something in common with God and something in common with man. For if in both these points he were like men, he would be far from God; and if in both of them he were like God, he would be far from men. In neither case could he be a mediator. But since, by the hidden pronouncements of your justice, you have given the devil licence to make a mockery of pride, he poses as a mediator. For in one point he is like man: he is sinful. And in the other he pretends to be like God: because he is not clothed with a mortal body of flesh and blood, he tries to represent himself as immortal. But since *sin offers death for wages*,[3] in common with men he has this reason to be condemned to die.

43

But there is a true Mediator, whom in your secret mercy you have shown to men. You sent him so that by his example they too might learn humility. He is *the Mediator between God and men, Jesus Christ, who is a man*,[4] and he appeared on earth between men, who are sinful

[1] Eph 2: 2. [2] II Cor. 11: 14. [3] Rom. 6: 23. [4] I Tim. 2: 5.

and mortal, and God, who is immortal and just. Like men he was mortal: like God, he was just. And because the reward of the just is life and peace, he came so that by his own justness, which is his in union with God, he might make null the death of the wicked whom he justified, by choosing to share their death. He was made known to holy men in ancient times, so that they might be saved through faith in his passion to come, just as we are saved through faith in the passion he suffered long ago. For as man, he is our Mediator; but as the Word of God, he is not an intermediary between God and man because he is equal with God, and God with God, and together with him one God.

How great was your love for us, good Father, for *you did not even spare your own son, but gave him up*[1] to save us sinners! How great was your love for us, when it was for us that Christ, who *did not see, in the rank of Godhead, a prize to be coveted, accepted an obedience which brought him to death, death on a cross*![2] He who alone was free among the dead[3], for he was free to lay down his life and free to take it up again,[4] was for us both Victor and Victim in your sight, and it was because he was the Victim that he was also the Victor. In your sight he was for us both Priest and Sacrifice, and it was because he was the Sacrifice that he was also the Priest. By being your Son, yet serving you, he freed us from servitude and made us your sons. Rightly do I place in him my firm hope that you will cure all my ills through him who *sits at your right hand and pleads for us*:[5] otherwise I should despair. For my ills are many and great, many and great indeed; but your medicine is greater still. We might have thought that your Word was far distant from union with man, and so we might have despaired of ourselves, if he had not been *made flesh and come to dwell among us.*[6]

Terrified by my sins and the dead weight of my misery, I had turned my problems over in my mind and was half determined to seek refuge in the desert. But you forbade me to do this and gave me strength by saying: *Christ died for us all, so that being alive should no longer mean living with our own life, but with his life who died for us.*[7] Lord, I cast all my troubles on you and from now on *I shall contemplate the wonders of your law.*[8] You know how weak I am and how

[1] Rom. 8: 32. [2] Philipp. 2: 6–8. [3] See Ps. 87: 6 (88: 5).
[4] See John 10: 18. [5] Rom. 8: 34. [6] John 1: 14. [7] II Cor. 5: 15.
[8] Ps. 118: 18 (119: 18).

inadequate is my knowledge: teach me and heal my frailty. Your only Son, *in whom the whole treasury of wisdom and knowledge is stored up*,[1] has redeemed me with his blood. *Save me from the scorn of my enemies*,[2] for the price of my redemption is always in my thoughts. I eat it and drink it and minister it to others; and as one of the poor I long to be filled with it, to be one of those who *eat and have their fill*. And *those who look for the Lord will cry out in praise of him*.[3]

[1] Col. 2: 3.   [2] Ps. 118: 122 (119: 122).   [3] Ps. 21: 27 (22: 26).

BOOK XI

1

O LORD, since you are outside time in eternity, are you unaware of the things that I tell you? Or do you see in time the things that occur in it? If you see them, why do I lay this lengthy record before you? Certainly it is not through me that you first hear of these things. But by setting them down I fire my own heart and the hearts of my readers with love of you, so that we all may ask: *Can any praise be worthy of the Lord's majesty?*[1] I have said before, and I shall say again, that I write this book for love of your love.

When we pray we ask for what we need, yet the Truth himself has told us: *Your heavenly Father knows well what your needs are before you ask him.*[2] So by confessing our own miserable state and acknowledging your mercy towards us we open our hearts to you, so that you may free us wholly, as you have already begun to do. Then we shall no longer be miserable in ourselves, but will find our true happiness in you. For you have called us to be poor in spirit, to be patient and to mourn, to hunger and thirst for holiness, to be merciful and clean of heart, and to be peacemakers.

To the best of my power and the best of my will I have laid this long account before you, because you first willed that I should confess to you, O Lord my God. *For you are gracious, your mercy endures for ever.*[3]

2

But if my pen is my spokesman, when shall I be able to tell of all the means you used to make of me a preacher of your word and a minister of your sacrament to your people? When shall I be able to tell how you urged me, how you filled me with fear, how you consoled and guided me? Every particle of sand in the glass of time is precious to me, even if I were able to set my facts in order and give an

[1] Ps. 144: 3 (145: 3).   [2] Matt. 6: 8.   [3] Ps. 117: 1 (118: 2).

account of them. I have long been burning with desire to *contemplate your law*[1] and to confess to you both what I know of it and where my knowledge fails; how far the first gleams of your light have illumined me and how dense my darkness still remains and must remain, until my weakness is swallowed up in your strength. And I do not wish to allow my time to slip away by undertaking any other task when I am free from the necessity of caring for my bodily needs, of studying, and of giving to others the service which I render them, whether it is my duty to give it or not.

O Lord my God, listen to my prayer. In your mercy grant what I desire, for it is not for myself alone that I so ardently desire it: I wish also that it may serve the love I bear to others. You see in my heart that this is true. Let me offer you in sacrifice the service of my thoughts and my tongue, but first give me what I may offer to you. For *I am needy and poor*, but you who care for us, yet are free from care for yourself, *have enough and to spare for all those who call upon you.*[2] Circumcise the lips of my mind and my mouth. Purify them of all rash speech and falsehood. Let your Scriptures be my chaste delight. Let me not deceive myself in them nor deceive others about them. Hear me, O Lord. Have mercy on me, O Lord my God, Light of the blind and Strength of the weak, Light, too, of those who see and Strength of the strong. Listen to my soul as it cries from the depths. For if you are not there to hear us even in our deepest plight, what is to become of us? To whom shall we cry?

Yours is the day, yours the night.[3] No moment of time passes except by your will. Grant me some part of it for my meditations on the secrets of your law. Do not close your door to those who knock: do not close the book of your law to me. For it was not to no purpose that you willed that the hidden mysteries of all its many pages should be written down, nor is this forest without its deer, which repair to it and there refresh themselves, roaming at will and browsing upon its pastures, and lying there to chew the cud.[4] O Lord, perfect your work in me. Open to me the pages of your book. Your voice is my joy, a greater joy than any profusion of worldly pleasures. Give me what I love, for truly I love it and this love, too, was your gift. Do

[1] Ps. 118: 18 (119: 18).   [2] Rom. 10: 12.   [3] Ps. 73: 16 (74: 16).
[4] The allusion is to Ps. 28: 9 (29: 9). The deer penetrating the forest are to be taken figuratively as those who are gifted to understand the Scriptures.

not abandon what you have given me. Do not scorn what you have planted when it is parched with thirst for you. Let me acknowledge as yours whatever I find in your books. *Let me listen to the sound of your praises.*[1] Let me drink you in and *contemplate the wonders of your law*[2] from the very beginning, when you made heaven and earth, to the coming of your kingdom, when we shall be for ever with you in your holy city.

O Lord, have mercy on me and grant what I desire. For, as I believe, this longing of mine does not come from a desire for earthly things, for gold and silver, precious stones and fine garments, worldly honours and power, sensual pleasures or the things which are needed for my body and for my pilgrimage through life. If we *make it our first care to find the kingdom of God, and his approval, all these things shall be ours without the asking.*[3]

Listen, my God, as I tell you the cause of my longing. The wicked have told me of things that delight them, but not such things as your law has to tell.[4] This is the reason for my longing. Take heed of it, Father. Examine it. Let it find approval in your eyes. And may it be pleasing to you, as I stand before your mercy, that I should find grace in your sight, so that the hidden meaning of your words may be revealed to me. Open your door to my knocking. This I beg of you through our Lord Jesus Christ, your Son, the Man of your right hand, the Son of Man, whom you have established for yourself[5] as mediator between yourself and us. He was the one whom you sent to find us when we were not looking for you, and you sent him to find us so that we should look for you. He is your Word, by which you have made all things, myself among them. He is your only Son, through whom you have called your faithful people, and myself among them, to make them your sons by adoption. Through him I beseech you, for *he sits at your right hand and pleads for us.*[6] In him *the whole treasury of wisdom and knowledge is stored up,*[7] and these are the treasures that I seek in your books. He told us himself – and he is the Truth – that he is one *of whom Moses wrote.*[8]

[1] Ps. 25: 7 (26: 7).   [2] Ps. 118: 18 (119: 18).   [3] Matt. 6: 33.
[4] See Ps. 118: 85 (119: 85).   [5] See Ps. 79: 18 (80: 17). [6] Rom. 8: 34.
[7] Col. 2: 3.   [8] John 5: 46.

3

Let me hear and understand the meaning of the words: In the Beginning you made heaven and earth.[1] Moses wrote these words. He wrote them and passed on into your presence, leaving this world where you spoke to him. He is no longer here and I cannot see him face to face. But if he were here, I would lay hold of him and in your name I would beg and beseech him to explain those words to me. I would be all ears to catch the sounds that fell from his lips. If he spoke in Hebrew, his words would strike my ear in vain and none of their meaning would reach my mind. If he spoke in Latin, I should know what he said. But how should I know whether what he said was true? If I knew this too, it could not be from him that I got such knowledge. But deep inside me, in my most intimate thought, Truth, which is neither Hebrew nor Greek nor Latin nor any foreign speech, would speak to me, though not in syllables formed by lips and tongue. It would whisper, 'He speaks the truth.' And at once I should be assured. In all confidence I would say to this man, your servant, 'What you tell me is true.'

Since, then, I cannot question Moses, whose words were true because you, the Truth, filled him with yourself, I beseech you, my God, to forgive my sins and grant me the grace to understand those words, as you granted him, your servant, the grace to speak them.

4

Earth and the heavens are before our eyes. The very fact that they are there proclaims that they were created, for they are subject to change and variation; whereas if anything exists that was not created, there is nothing in it that was not there before; and the meaning of change and variation is that something is there which was not there before. Earth and the heavens also proclaim that they did not create themselves. 'We exist', they tell us, 'because we were made. And this is proof that we did not make ourselves. For to make ourselves, we should have had to exist before our existence began.' And the fact that they plainly do exist is the voice which proclaims this truth.

It was you, then, O Lord, who made them, you who are beautiful,

[1] See Gen. 1: 1. '*God, at the beginning of time, created heaven and earth*' (Knox).

for they too are beautiful; you who are good, for they too are good; you who ARE, for they too are, But they are not beautiful and good as you are beautiful and good, nor do they have their being as you, their Creator, have your being. In comparison with you they have neither beauty nor goodness nor being at all. This we know, and thanks be to you for this knowledge. But our knowledge, compared with yours, is ignorance.

5

But by what means did you make heaven and earth? What tool did you use for this vast work? You did not work as a human craftsman does, making one thing out of something else as his mind directs. His mind can impose upon his material whatever form it perceives within itself by its inner eye. But how could his mind do this unless it was because you had made it? It imposes this form upon a substance which already exists and already has being, such as clay or stone, wood or gold, or any other material of this sort. But how could these materials have come to be unless you had given them their being? It was you who made the craftsman's body and the mind which controls his limbs. It was you who made the material from which he makes his goods. It was you who made the intelligence by which he masters his craft and visualizes whatever he is to make. It was you who made his physical senses, which are the channels through which his mental picture of the thing he is making is transmitted to the material. They then relay the finished product to his mind, so that by referring it to the truth, which presides there as arbiter, it may decide whether it is well or badly made.

All these things proclaim your glory as their Creator, O God. But how do you create them? How did you make heaven and earth? Clearly it was not in heaven or on earth that you made them. Nor was it in the air or beneath the sea, because these are part of the domain of heaven and earth. Nor was it in the universe that you made the universe, because until the universe was made there was no place where it could be made. Nor did you have in your hand any matter from which you could make heaven and earth, for where could you have obtained matter which you had not yet created, in order to use it as material for making something else? Does anything exist by any other cause than that you exist?

It must therefore be that *you spoke and they were made.*[1] In your Word alone you created them.

6

But how did you speak? Did you speak as you did when your voice was heard in the clouds saying: *This is my beloved Son?*[2] At that time your voice sounded and then ceased. It was speech with a beginning and an end. Each syllable could be heard and then died away, the second following after the first and the third after the second, and so on in sequence until the last syllable followed all the rest and then gave place to silence. From this it is abundantly clear that your speech was expressed through the motion of some created thing, because it was motion subject to the laws of time, although it served your eternal will. These words, which you had caused to sound in time, were reported by the bodily ear of the hearer to the mind, which has intelligence and inward hearing responsive to your eternal Word. The mind compared these words, which it heard sounding in time, with your Word, which is silent and eternal, and said, 'God's eternal Word is far, far different from these words which sound in time. They are far beneath me; in fact, they are not at all, because they die away and are lost. But the Word of my God is above me and endures for ever.'

If, therefore, in order that heaven and earth should come into being, you spoke in words which sounded and then died away, and if this was the way in which you created heaven and earth, then there must have been some material thing created before heaven and earth, something which, by its motion in time, could lend itself as a mouthpiece through which those words could be spoken in time. But there was no material thing before heaven and earth; or, if there was, you must certainly have created it by an utterance outside time, so that you could use it as the mouthpiece for your decree, uttered in time, that heaven and earth should be made. For whatever you might have used to produce the voice by which the decree was uttered, it would not have existed at all unless it had been made by you. But to create a material thing which could be used to give voice to the decree, what Word did you speak?

[1] Ps. 32: 9 (33: 9).   [2] Matt. 3: 17.

7

It is in this way, then, that you mean us to understand your Word, who is God with you, God with God, your Word uttered eternally in whom all things are uttered eternally. For your Word is not speech in which each part comes to an end when it has been spoken, giving place to the next, so that finally the whole may be uttered. In your Word all is uttered at one and the same time, yet eternally. If it were not so, your Word would be subject to time and change, and therefore would be neither truly eternal nor truly immortal.

This I know, my God, and I thank you for the knowledge. I know it, O Lord my God. I confess it to you. And whoever is not ungrateful for the certainty of your truth knows it and praises you for it as I do. For we know, O Lord, that the extent to which something once was, but no longer is, is the measure of its death; and the extent to which something once was not, but now is, is the measure of its beginning. Your Word, then, in no degree either gives place to anything or takes the place of anything, because it is truly immortal and eternal. Therefore it is by a Word co-eternal with yourself that you say all that you say; you say all at one and the same time, yet you say all eternally; and it is by this Word that all things are made which you say are to be made. You create them by your Word alone and in no other way. Yet the things which you create by your Word do not all come into being at one and the same time, nor are they eternal.

8

Why is this so, O Lord my God? In some degree I see why it is, but I do not know how to put it into words except by saying that whatever begins to be, or ceases to be, does so at the moment when the eternal reason knows that it should begin to be or cease to be, although in the eternal reason there is no beginning and no ending. The eternal reason is your Word, who is also the Beginning, because he also speaks to us.[1] So he tells us in the Gospel by word of mouth. Your Word, the Beginning, made himself audible to the bodily ears of men, so that they should believe in him and, by looking for him within themselves, should find him in the eternal Truth, where the

[1] See John 8: 25.

one good Master teaches all who listen to him. It is there that I hear your voice, O Lord, telling me that only a master who really teaches us really speaks to us: if he does not teach us, even though he may be speaking, it is not to us that he speaks. But who is our teacher except the Truth which never changes? Even when we learn from created things, which are subject to change, we are led to the Truth which does not change. And there we truly learn, as *we stand by and listen to him and rejoice at hearing the bridegroom's voice,*[1] restoring ourselves to him who gave us our being. He is therefore the Beginning, the abiding Principle, for unless he remained when we wandered in error, there would be none to whom we could return and restore ourselves. But when we return from error, we return by knowing the Truth; and in order that we may know the Truth, he teaches us, because he is the Beginning and he also speaks to us.[2]

9

He is the Beginning, O God, in which you made heaven and earth. In this wonderful way you spoke and created them in your Word, in your Son, who is your Strength, your Wisdom, and your Truth.

Who can understand this mystery or explain it to others? What is that light whose gentle beams now and again strike through to my heart, causing me to shudder in awe yet firing me with their warmth? I shudder to feel how different I am from it: yet in so far as I am like it, I am aglow with its fire. It is the light of Wisdom, Wisdom itself, which at times shines upon me, parting my clouds. But when I weakly fall away from its light, those clouds envelop me again in the dense mantle of darkness which I bear for my punishment. For *my strength ebbs away for very misery,*[3] so that I cannot sustain my blessings. And so I shall remain until you, O Lord, who *have pardoned all my sins,* also *heal all my mortal ills.* For you will *rescue my life from deadly peril, crown me with the blessings of your mercy, content all my desire for good, restore my youth as the eagle's plumage is restored.*[4] *Our salvation is founded upon the hope of something,*[5] and in endurance we await the fulfilment of your promises. Let those who are able listen to your voice speaking to their hearts. Trusting in your inspired words, I shall

---

[1] John 3: 29. [2] See John 8: 25. [3] Ps. 30: 11 (31: 10).
[4] Ps. 102: 3–5 (103: 3–5). [5] Rom. 8: 24.

cry out: *What diversity, Lord, in your creatures! What wisdom has designed them all!*[1] The Beginning is Wisdom and Wisdom is the Beginning in which you made heaven and earth.

10

Those who ask 'What was God doing before he made heaven and earth?' are still steeped in error which they should have discarded. 'If he was at rest', they say, 'and doing nothing, why did he not continue to do nothing for ever more, just as he had always done in the past? If the will to create something which he had never created before was new in him – if it was some new motion stirring in him – how can we say that his is true eternity, when a new will, which had never been there before, could arise in it? For the will of God is not a created thing. It is there before any creation takes place, because nothing could be created unless the will of its Creator preceded its creation. The will of God, then, is part of his substance. Yet if something began to be in God's substance, something which had not existed beforehand, we could not rightly say that his substance was eternal. But if God's will that there should be a creation was there from all eternity, why is it that what he has created is not also eternal?'

11

People who speak in this way have not learnt to understand you, Wisdom of God, Light of our minds. They do not yet understand how the things are made which come to be in you and through you. Try as they may to savour the taste of eternity, their thoughts still twist and turn upon the ebb and flow of things in past and future time. But if only their minds could be seized and held steady, they would be still for a while and, for that short moment, they would glimpse the splendour of eternity which is for ever still. They would contrast it with time, which is never still, and see that it is not comparable. They would see that time derives its length only from a great number of movements constantly following one another into the past, because they cannot all continue at once. But in eternity nothing moves into the past: all is present. Time, on the other hand, is

[1] Ps. 103: 24 (104: 24).

never all present at once. The past is always driven on by the future, the future always follows on the heels of the past, and both the past and the future have their beginning and their end in the eternal present. If only men's minds could be seized and held still! They would see how eternity, in which there is neither past nor future, determines both past and future time. Could mine be the hand strong enough to seize the minds of men? Could any words of mine have power to achieve so great a task?

12

My answer to those who ask 'What was God doing before he made heaven and earth?' is not 'He was preparing Hell for people who pry into mysteries'. This frivolous retort has been made before now, so we are told, in order to evade the point of the question. But it is one thing to make fun of the questioner and another to find the answer. So I shall refrain from giving this reply. For in matters of which I am ignorant I would rather admit the fact than gain credit by giving the wrong answer and making a laughing-stock of a man who asks a serious question.

Instead of this I will say that you, my God, are the Creator of all creation, and if we mean the whole of creation when we speak of heaven and earth, I unreservedly say that before he made heaven and earth, God made nothing. For if he did make anything, could it have been anything but a creature of his own creation? I only wish I knew everything that I could profit by knowing with as much certainty as I know that no creature was made before any creation took place.

13

A fickle-minded man, whose thoughts were all astray because of his conception of time past, might wonder why you, who are God almighty, Creator of all, Sustainer of all, and Maker of heaven and earth, should have been idle and allowed countless ages to elapse before you finally undertook the vast work of creation. My advice to such people is to shake off their dreams and think carefully, because their wonder is based on a misconception.

How could those countless ages have elapsed when you, the

Creator, in whom all ages have their origin, had not yet created them? What time could there have been that was not created by you? How could time elapse if it never was?

You are the Maker of all time. If, then, there was any time before you made heaven and earth, how can anyone say that you were idle? You must have made that time, for time could not elapse before you made it.

But if there was no time before heaven and earth were created, how can anyone ask what you were doing 'then'? If there was no time, there was no 'then'.

Furthermore, although you are before time, it is not in time that you precede it. If this were so, you would not be before all time. It is in eternity, which is supreme over time because it is a never-ending present, that you are at once before all past time and after all future time. For what is now the future, once it comes, will become the past, whereas *you are unchanging, your years can never fail*.[1] Your years neither go nor come, but our years pass and others come after them, so that they all may come in their turn. Your years are completely present to you all at once, because they are at a permanent standstill. They do not move on, forced to give way before the advance of others, because they never pass at all. But our years will all be complete only when they have all moved into the past. Your years are one day, yet your day does not come daily but is always today, because your today does not give place to any tomorrow nor does it take the place of any yesterday. Your today is eternity. And this is how the Son, to whom you said *I have begotten you this day*,[2] was begotten co-eternal with yourself. You made all time; you are before all time; and the 'time', if such we may call it, when there was no time was not time at all.

14

It is therefore true to say that when you had not made anything, there was no time, because time itself was of your making. And no time is co-eternal with you, because you never change; whereas, if time never changed, it would not be time.

What, then, is time? There can be no quick and easy answer, for it is no simple matter even to understand what it is, let alone find words

[1] Ps. 101: 28 (102: 27).   [2] Ps. 2: 7.

to explain it. Yet, in our conversation, no word is more familiarly used or more easily recognized than 'time'. We certainly understand what is meant by the word both when we use it ourselves and when we hear it used by others.

What, then, is time? I know well enough what it is, provided that nobody asks me; but if I am asked what it is and try to explain, I am baffled. All the same I can confidently say that I know that if nothing passed, there would be no past time; if nothing were going to happen, there would be no future time; and if nothing *were*, there would be no present time.

Of these three divisions of time, then, how can two, the past and the future, *be*, when the past no longer is and the future is not yet? As for the present, if it were always present and never moved on to become the past, it would not be time but eternity. If, therefore, the present is time only by reason of the fact that it moves on to become the past, how can we say that even the present *is*, when the reason why it *is* is that it is *not to be*? In other words, we cannot rightly say that time *is*, except by reason of its impending state of *not being*.

15

Yet we speak of a 'long time' and a 'short time', though only when we mean the past or the future. For example, we say that a hundred years is a long time ago or a long time ahead. A short time ago or a short time ahead we might put at ten days. But how can anything which does not exist be either long or short? For the past is no more and the future is not yet. Surely, then, instead of saying 'It is a long time' we ought to say of the past 'It was a long time' and of the future 'It will be a long time'.

My Lord, my Light, does not your truth make us look foolish in this case too? For if we speak of a long time in the past, do we mean that it was long when it was already past or before it became the past and was still the present? It could only be long when it was there to be long: once it was past it no longer was, and if it no longer was, it could not be long.

So we must not say that the past was long, because we shall not be able to find anything in it that could be long, for the simple reason that once it becomes the past it ceases to be. Instead we must say that the time of which we are speaking was long when it was the present, because it could have been long only while it was the present. It had not yet become the past – which would have meant that it no longer existed – and therefore something existed which could be long. But as soon as it became the past it ceased to be long, because it ceased to be at all.

Now let us see if our human wits can tell us whether present time can be long, for we are gifted with the ability to feel and measure intervals of time. What is the answer to be?

Is the present century a long time? Before we answer this we must see whether a hundred years can possibly be present. If we are in the first year of the hundred, that year is present but the other ninety-nine are future. Therefore they are not yet. If we are in the second year, one year has already passed, one is present, and the rest are future. In the same way, whichever of the hundred years that go to make the century we choose to regard as present, those which went before it will be past and those which come after it will be future. This proves that a hundred years cannot be present.

Let us see, then, whether at least the one year in which we are is present. If we are in the first month, the other eleven are future. If we are in the second month, the first has passed and the rest are still to come. So we cannot even say that the whole of the current year is present, and if the whole of it is not present, the year is not present. For a year is made up of twelve months. Any one of them, the current one, is present, but the others are either past or future. It is not even true that the current month is present, but only one of its days. If it is the first day, the remainder are future. If it is the last day, the rest are past. If it is any day in the middle of the month, it falls between past and future days.

Now we can see that the present, which we found was the only one of the three divisions of time that could possibly be said to be long, has been whittled down to the space of scarcely one day. But here again we must look into the matter more closely, because not even the whole of one day is present. It is made up of hours of darkness and hours of daylight, twenty-four of them. In relation to the first hour the others are future; in relation to the last the others are past; and any intermediate hour comes between the hours which precede it and those which follow it. Even that one hour consists of minutes which are continually passing. The minutes which have gone by are past, and any part of the hour which remains is future. In fact the only time that can be called present is an instant, if we can conceive of such, that cannot be divided even into the most minute fractions, and a point of time as small as this passes so rapidly from the future to the past that its duration is without length. For if its duration were prolonged, it could be divided into past and future. When it is present it has no duration.

This being so, when does a time come which we can call long? Not the future, surely; for we do not say of the future that it *is* long, because it does not yet exist in order to be long. We say that it *will* be long. But when will it be long? Not while it is still future, because it does not yet exist and therefore cannot be long. If it is to be long when it passes out of the future, which is not yet in being, and comes into being by becoming the present, this would satisfy the condition that something must exist to be capable of being long. But, as we have already seen quite clearly, the present cannot possibly have duration.

16

Nevertheless, O Lord, we are aware of periods of time. We compare them one with another and say that some are longer and others shorter. We even calculate how much longer or shorter one period is than another, and the result of our calculations tells us that it is twice or three times the length of the one which we take as the unit of measurement, or that the two are of equal duration. If we measure them by our own awareness of time, we must do so while it is passing, for no one can measure it either when it is past and no longer exists, or when it is future and does not yet exist – that is, unless he is bold enough to claim that what does not exist can be measured. The conclusion is that we can be aware of time and measure it only while it is passing. Once it has passed it no longer is, and therefore cannot be measured.

17

These are tentative theories, Father, not downright assertions. O God, be my Judge and my Guide.

As a boy I learned that there were three divisions of time, past, present, and future, and later on I taught the same lesson to other boys. But there might be people who would maintain that there are not three divisions of time but only one, the present, because the other two do not exist. Another view might be that past and future do exist, but that time emerges from some secret refuge when it passes from the future to the present, and goes back into hiding when it moves from the present to the past. Otherwise, how do prophets see the future, if there is not yet a future to be seen? It is impossible to see what does not exist. In the same way people who describe the past could not describe it correctly unless they saw it in their minds, and if the past did not exist it would be impossible for them to see it at all. Therefore both the past and the future do exist.

18

O Lord, my Hope, allow me to explore further. Do not let me grow confused and lose track of my purpose.

If the future and the past do exist, I want to know where they are. I may not yet be capable of such knowledge, but at least I know that wherever they are, they are not there as future or past, but as present. For if, wherever they are, they are future, they do not yet exist; if past, they no longer exist. So wherever they are and whatever they are, it is only by being present that they *are*.

When we describe the past correctly, it is not past facts which are drawn out of our memories but only words based on our memory-pictures of those facts, because when they happened they left an impression on our minds, by means of our sense-perception. My own childhood, which no longer exists, is in past time, which also no longer exists. But when I remember those days and describe them, it is in the present that I picture them to myself, because their picture is still present in my memory.

Whether some similar process enables the future to be seen, some process by which events which have not yet occurred become present to us by means of already existing images of them, I confess, my God, that I do not know. But at least I know that we generally think about what we are going to do before we do it, and this preliminary thought is in the present, whereas the action which we premeditate does not yet exist because it is future. Once we have set to work and started to put our plans into action, that action exists, because it is now not future but present.

By whatever mysterious means it may be that the future is foreseen, it is only possible to see something which exists; and whatever exists is not future but present. So when we speak of foreseeing the future, we do not see things which are not yet in being, that is, things which are future, but it may be that we see their causes or signs, which are already in being. In this way they are not future but present to the eye of the beholder, and by means of them the mind can form a concept of things which are still future and thus is able to predict them. These concepts already exist, and by seeing them present in their minds people are able to foretell the actual facts which they represent.

Let me give one example of the many from which I could choose. Suppose that I am watching the break of day. I predict that the sun is about to rise. What I see is present, but what I foretell is future. I do not mean that the sun is future, for it already exists, but that its rise is future, because it has not yet happened. But I could not foretell the sunrise unless I had a picture of it in my mind, just as I have at this moment while I am speaking about it. Yet the dawn, which I see in the sky, is not the sunrise, although it precedes it; nor is the picture which I have in my mind the sunrise. But both the dawn and my mental picture are seen in the present, and it is from them that I am able to predict the sunrise, which is future. The future, then, is not yet; it is not at all; and if it is not at all, it cannot possibly be seen. But it can be foretold from things which are present, because they exist now and can therefore be seen.

19

In what way, then, do you, Ruler of all that you have created, reveal the future to the souls of men? You have revealed it to your prophets. But how do you reveal the future to us when, for us, the future does not exist? Is it that you only reveal present signs of things that are to come? For it is utterly impossible that things which do not exist should be revealed. The means by which you do this is far beyond our understanding. I have not the strength to comprehend this mystery, and by my own power I never shall. But in your strength I shall understand it, when you grant me the grace to see, sweet Light of the eyes of my soul.

20

From what we have said it is abundantly clear that neither the future nor the past exist, and therefore it is not strictly correct to say that there are three times, past, present, and future. It might be correct to say that there are three times, a present of past things, a present of present things, and a present of future things. Some such different times do exist in the mind, but nowhere else that I can see. The present of past things is the memory; the present of present things is direct perception; and the present of future things is expectation. If we may speak in these terms, I can see three times and I admit that they do exist.

By all means, then, let us speak of three times, past, present, and future. Incorrect though it is, let us comply with usage. I shall not object or argue, nor shall I rebuke anyone who speaks in these terms, provided that he understands what he is saying and does not imagine that the future or the past exists now. Our use of words is generally inaccurate and seldom completely correct, but our meaning is recognized none the less.

21

I said just now that we measure time as it passes. This enables us to say that a given space of time is twice as long as whatever period we take as the unit of measurement, or that the two are of equal duration, and we apply the same principle to any other space of time that we are able to measure.

As I said, we measure time while it is passing. If I am asked how I know this, my answer is that I know it because we do measure time. We could not measure a thing which did not exist, and time does not exist when it is past or future. How, then, do we measure present time, when present time has no duration? It must be measured while it is in process of passing. It cannot be measured after it has passed, because nothing then exists to be measured.

But while we are measuring it, where is it coming from, what is it passing through, and where is it going? It can only be coming from the future, passing through the present, and going into the past. In other words, it is coming out of what does not yet exist, passing through what has no duration, and moving into what no longer exists.

But how can we measure time except in relation to some measure-able period? We cannot use the terms 'as long', 'twice as long', 'three times as long', and so on, when we speak of time, except in relation to a given period. But to what period do we relate time when we measure it as it is passing? To the future, from which it comes? No: because we cannot measure what does not exist. To the present, through which it is passing? No: because we cannot measure what has no duration. To the past, then, towards which it is going? No again: because we cannot measure what no longer exists.

22

My mind is burning to solve this intricate puzzle. O Lord my God, good Father, it is a problem at once so familiar and so mysterious. I long to find the answer. Through Christ I beseech you, do not keep it hidden away but make it clear to me. Let your mercy give me light. To whom am I to put my questions? To whom can I confess my ignorance with greater profit than to you? For my burning desire to study your Scriptures is not displeasing to you. Grant me what I love, for it was your gift that I should love it. Grant me this, Father, for *you know well enough how to give your children what is good for them.*[1] Grant me this, for *I have set myself to read the riddle, but it will prove a hard search*[2] until you reveal it to me. Through Christ I beseech you, in the name of him who is the Holy of Holies, let no man stand in my way. *I trust, and trusting find words to utter.*[3] This is my hope and for this I live, that I may *gaze at the beauty of the Lord.*[4] *You have measured my years with a brief span;*[5] they pass away; but how they pass, I do not know.

'Time' and 'times' are words forever on our lips. 'How long did he speak?' we ask. 'How long did he take to do that?' 'How long it is since I have seen it!' 'This syllable is twice the length of that.' We use these words and hear others using them. They understand what we mean and we understand them. No words could be plainer or more commonly used. Yet their true meaning is concealed from us. We have still to find it out.

[1] Matt. 7: 11.   [2] Ps. 72: 16 (73: 16).   [3] Ps. 115: 10 (116: 10).
[4] Ps. 26: 4 (27: 4).   [5] Ps. 38: 6 (39: 5).

23

I once heard a learned man say that time is nothing but the movement of the sun and the moon and the stars, but I did not agree. Would it not be more likely that time was the movement, not only of heavenly bodies, but of all other bodies as well? If all the lights of the sky ceased to move but the potter's wheel continued to turn, would there not still be time by which we could measure its rotations? Should we no longer be able to say that it turned with a regular rhythm, or that its speed varied, or that some turns took more and others less time? When we said this, should we not be speaking in time? And would not our words consist of syllables of unequal length, simply because more time is required for the pronunciation of some than of others?

O God, grant that men should recognize in some small thing like this potter's wheel the principles which are common to all things, great and small alike. There are stars and other lights in the sky, set there to be *portents, and be the measures of time, to mark out the day and the year*.[1] This much is plain. But if I cannot claim that a turn of that little wooden wheel is one day, neither can the learned assert that it is not time at all.

My problem is to discover the fundamental nature of time and what power it has. It is by time that we measure the movement of bodies. For example, we say that one movement takes twice the time that another takes. By the word 'day' we mean not only the length of time that the sun remains in the sky above the earth, which determines the difference between night and day, but also the time of its complete circuit from sunrise to sunrise. It is this period that we mean when we say that a given number of days has gone by, because the nights are not counted separately but are reckoned as included in the days. Since, then, a day is completed by the movement of the sun through its total orbit, from the time when it rises in the east until it again reaches the east, my question is whether a day is that movement itself, the time needed for its completion, or a combination of both.

If a day were the movement of the sun through a whole circuit, there would still be a day even if the sun completed its course in a space of time as short as one hour. If, on the other hand, a day were the length of time which the sun actually takes to complete its

[1] Gen. 1: 14.

circuit, it would not be a day if the period between one sunrise and the next were as short as one hour. In this case the sun would have to circle the earth twenty-four times to make one day. If, according to the third hypothesis, the movement of the sun and the time it takes to complete its circuit together constituted a day, there would be a day neither if the sun travelled through its complete orbit in the space of one hour, nor if it stood still while as much time passed as the sun regularly takes to circle the earth between one morning and the next.

But for the present I shall not inquire what it is that we call a day. I shall confine myself to asking what time is, for it is by time that we measure the course of the sun. If it travelled around the earth in a space of time equal to twelve hours, we should say that it had completed its course in half the usual time. By comparing the two times we should say that, if twelve hours were taken as a single period, twenty-four hours was a double period, and this calculation would hold good whether the sun completed its circuit from the east round to the east again in the single or the double period on different occasions.

I cannot therefore accept the suggestion that time is constituted by the movement of heavenly bodies, because although the sun once stood still in answer to a man's prayer,[1] so that he could fight on until victory was his, the sun indeed stood still but time continued to pass. The battle went on for as long as was necessary and was then over. I see time, therefore, as an extension of some sort. But do I really see this or only seem to see it? You will make it clear to me, my Light and my Truth.

24

It is not your will that I should agree to the proposition that time is constituted by the movement of a material body. For no body moves except in time. I hear your voice which tells me this. But it is not your voice which tells me that the movement of a body itself constitutes time. For when a body moves, it is by time that I measure how long its motion lasts, from the time when it begins to move until its movement ceases. If I do not see when its movement begins, and if its movement continues after I have ceased to watch, so that I do not

[1] See Jos. 10: 13.

see when it ends, I am not able to measure it, except perhaps from the time when I begin to watch until the time when I cease watching. If I watch it for any length of time, I can only say that its movement lasts a long time. I cannot say how long that time is, because we can only say how long time is when we compare it with a given standard. For example, we say that one period is as long, or twice as long, as another, and so on. But if we can mark the points in space between which a moving body travels or, in the case of a body rotating upon its own axis, the distance through which its parts are moving, we can say how much time is needed for the body to complete its movement between the two points or for its parts to complete their revolution.

It is clear, then, that the movement of a body is not the same as the means by which we measure the duration of its movement. This being so, it must be obvious which of the two ought more properly to be called time. The same body may move at different speeds, and sometimes it is at rest, and we measure not only its motion but also its rest by means of time. We say that it was at rest for the same length of time as it was in motion, or that it stood still for twice or three times as long as it moved, and so on, whether we make an exact calculation or a rough estimate – 'more or less', as the saying goes.

Time, therefore, is not the movement of a body.

25

I confess to you, Lord, that I still do not know what time is. Yet I confess too that I do know that I am saying this in time, that I have been talking about time for a long time, and that this long time would not be a long time if it were not for the fact that time has been passing all the while. How can I know this, when I do not know what time is? Is it that I do know what time is, but do not know how to put what I know into words? I am in a sorry state, for I do not even know what I do not know!

My God, I am in your presence. You see that I do not lie, for I say only what is in my heart. *It is you, Lord, that keep the lamp of my hopes still burning; shine on the darkness about me.*[1]

[1] Ps. 17: 29 (18: 28).

Does my soul speak the truth to you when I say that I can measure time? I do indeed measure it, but I do not know what I measure. By means of time I measure the movement of bodies. Does this not mean that I measure time itself? Could I measure the movement of a body, that is, measure how long the movement lasted and how long the body took to move between two points, unless I measured the time in which it moved?

If this is so, what means do I use to measure time? Do we measure longer periods of time by means of shorter ones, as we measure yards by means of feet? This is how we measure the duration of a long syllable, for we compare it with a short one and conclude that it is twice as long. We use the same method when we measure the length of a poem by the lengths of the lines, the lengths of the lines by the lengths of the feet, the lengths of the feet by the lengths of the syllables, and the lengths of the long syllables by the lengths of the short ones. We do not measure them by pages – that would give us a measurement in terms of space, not time – but by the pronunciation as they are read. This enables us to say, 'This is a long poem, because it consists of so many lines. The lines are long, because they each consist of so many feet. The feet are long, because they each contain so many syllables. This or that syllable is long, because it is the double of a short one.'

Even so, this is not an accurate means of measuring time, because it can happen that a short line spoken slowly may take longer to recite than a long one spoken hurriedly. The same applies to a whole poem, a foot, or even a single syllable.

It seems to me, then, that time is merely an extension, though of what it is an extension I do not know. I begin to wonder whether it is an extension of the mind itself.

Tell me, my God, I beseech you, what is it that I am measuring when I say either, by a rough computation, that one period of time is longer than another, or, with more precision, that it is twice as long? I know that I am measuring time. But I am not measuring the future, because it does not yet exist; nor the present, because it has no extent; nor the past, because it no longer exists. Am I measuring time which is in process of passing, but has not yet passed? This was the suggestion which I put forward before.

Be resolute, my soul. Onward with all your endeavour. *God is our defence*,[1] for *his we are, he it was that made us*.[2] Onward, where truth begins to dawn!

Suppose that we hear a noise emitted by some material body. The sound begins and we continue to hear it. It goes on until finally it ceases. Then there is silence. The sound has passed and is no longer sound. Before it began it was future and could not be measured, because it did not yet exist. Now that it has ceased it cannot be measured, because it no longer exists. It could only be measured while it lasted, because then it existed and could be measured. But even then it was not static, because it was transient, moving continually towards the point when it would no longer exist. Was it all the more measurable because of this fact? While it was transient it was gaining some extent in time by which it could be measured, but not in present time, for the present has no extent.

Let us assume, then, that it could be measured at this stage. Now let us imagine another noise. The sound begins and goes on continuously and evenly without variation. If we are to measure it, we must do so while it lasts, because once the sound has ceased it will be a thing of the past, and if it no longer exists it cannot be measured. So let us try to measure it and give an accurate estimate of its duration. But the noise is still to be heard, and it can only be measured from the point when the sound begins to its final point, when it ceases. In fact, what we measure is the interval between a beginning and an end. For this reason a sound which has not yet come to an end cannot be measured in such a way as to enable us to say how long or short it is, or to say that it is equal in duration to any other noise, or to make any statement of comparison such as that it is half as long or twice as long as another. But when it comes to an end it will no longer exist. How, then, shall we be able to measure it?

Nevertheless we do measure time. We cannot measure it if it is not yet in being, or if it is no longer in being, or if it has no duration, or if it has no beginning and no end. Therefore we measure neither the future nor the past nor the present nor time that is passing. Yet we do measure time.

Take the line *Deus Creator omnium*, which consists of eight syllables,

[1] Ps. 61: 9 (62: 8).   [2] Ps. 99: 3 (100: 3).

alternately short and long. The four short syllables, the first, third, fifth, and seventh, are single in quantity compared with the four long ones, that is, the second, fourth, sixth, and eighth. Each of the long syllables is a double quantity compared with each of the short ones. I can tell this because, by pronouncing them, I find it to be the case, in so far as I can rely upon the plain evidence of my own hearing. As far as my ear enables me to do so, I judge the length of a long syllable by comparing it with a short one, and my ear tells me that it is twice as long. But I hear the two syllables one after the other, and if the short one comes first and the long one second, how is my ear to retain the sound of the short one in order that I may compare the two for the purpose of measurement? I must do this if I am to find out that the long one is double the quantity of the short one, but how can I do it if the long sound does not begin until the short one has ceased? Nor can I even measure the long one while it is still present, because I cannot measure it until it is completed, and once it is completed it is no longer there to be measured.

What, then, is it that I measure? What has become of the short syllable, which I use as the standard of measurement? What has become of the long one, which I measure? The sound of both is finished and has been wafted away into the past. They no longer exist. All the same I measure them and, in so far as I can trust my practised ear, I say confidently that one is a single and the other a double quantity – and by quantity, of course, I mean their duration in time. I can only do this because they are both completed and are now things of the past. So it cannot be the syllables themselves that I measure, since they no longer exist. I must be measuring something which remains fixed in my memory.

It is in my own mind, then, that I measure time. I must not allow my mind to insist that time is something objective. I must not let it thwart me because of all the different notions and impressions that are lodged in it. I say that I measure time in my mind. For everything which happens leaves an impression on it, and this impression remains after the thing itself has ceased to be. It is the impression that I measure, since it is still present, not the thing itself, which makes the impression as it passes and then moves into the past. When I measure time it is this impression that I measure. Either, then, this is what time is, or else I do not measure time at all.

When we measure silences and say that a given period of silence has lasted as long as a given period of sound, we measure the sound mentally, as though we could actually hear it, and this enables us to estimate the duration of the periods of silence. Even without opening our mouths or speaking at all we can go over poems and verses and speech of any sort in our minds, and we can do the same with measurable movement of any kind. We can estimate that one poem takes proportionately more, or less, time than another, just as if we were reciting them both aloud. If a man wishes to utter a prolonged sound and decides beforehand how long he wants it to be, he allows this space of time to elapse in silence, commits it to memory, and then begins to utter the sound. It sounds until it reaches the limit set for it, or rather, I should not use the present tense and say that it sounds, but the past and the future, saying that it both has sounded and will sound. For as much of it as has been completed at any given moment has sounded, and the rest will sound. In this way the process continues to the end. All the while the man's attentive mind, which is present, is relegating the future to the past. The past increases in proportion as the future diminishes, until the future is entirely absorbed and the whole becomes past.

28

But how can the future be diminished or absorbed when it does not yet exist? And how can the past increase when it no longer exists? It can only be that the mind, which regulates this process, performs three functions, those of expectation, attention, and memory. The future, which it expects, passes through the present, to which it attends, into the past, which it remembers. No one would deny that the future does not yet exist or that the past no longer exists. Yet in the mind there is both expectation of the future and remembrance of the past. Again, no one would deny that the present has no duration, since it exists only for the instant of its passage. Yet the mind's attention persists, and through it that which is to be passes towards the state in which it is to be no more. So it is not future time that is long, but a long future is a long expectation of the future; and past time is not long, because it does not exist, but a long past is a long remembrance of the past.

Suppose that I am going to recite a psalm that I know. Before I begin, my faculty of expectation is engaged by the whole of it. But once I have begun, as much of the psalm as I have removed from the province of expectation and relegated to the past now engages my memory, and the scope of the action which I am performing is divided between the two faculties of memory and expectation, the one looking back to the part which I have already recited, the other looking forward to the part which I have still to recite. But my faculty of attention is present all the while, and through it passes what was the future in the process of becoming the past. As the process continues, the province of memory is extended in proportion as that of expectation is reduced, until the whole of my expectation is absorbed. This happens when I have finished my recitation and it has all passed into the province of memory.

What is true of the whole psalm is also true of all its parts and of each syllable. It is true of any longer action in which I may be engaged and of which the recitation of the psalm may only be a small part. It is true of a man's whole life, of which all his actions are parts. It is true of the whole history of mankind, of which each man's life is a part.

29

But *to win your favour is dearer than life itself*.[1] I see now that my life has been wasted in distractions, but *your right hand has supported me*[2] in the person of Christ my Lord, the Son of man, who is the Mediator between you, who are one, and men, who are many. He has upheld me in many ways and through many trials, in order that through him *I may win the mastery, as he has won the mastery over me*;[3] in order that I may be rid of my old temptations and devote myself only to God's single purpose, *forgetting what I have left behind*.[3] I look forward, not to what lies ahead of me in this life and will surely pass away, but to my eternal goal. I am intent upon this one purpose, not distracted by other aims, and *with this goal in view I press on, eager for the prize, God's heavenly summons*.[3] Then I shall *listen to the sound of your praises*[4] and *gaze at your beauty*[5] ever present, never future, never past.

But now *my years are but sighs*.[6] You, O Lord, are my only solace.

[1] Ps. 62: 4 (63: 3).   [2] Ps. 17: 36 (18: 35).   [3] Philipp. 3: 12–14.
[4] Ps. 25: 7 (26: 7).   [5] Ps. 26: 4 (27: 4).   [6] Ps. 30: 11 (31: 10).

You, my Father, are eternal. But I am divided between time gone by and time to come, and its course is a mystery to me. My thoughts, the intimate life of my soul, are torn this way and that in the havoc of change. And so it will be until I am purified and melted by the fire of your love and fused into one with you.

30

Then I shall be cast and set firm in the mould of your truth. I shall no longer suffer the questions of men who, for their punishment, are sick of a disease which makes them thirst for more than they can drink, so that they ask 'What was God doing before he made heaven and earth?' or 'How did it occur to God to create something, when he had never created anything before?'

Grant them, O Lord, to think well what they say and to recognize that 'never' has no meaning when there is no time. If a man is said never to have made anything, it can only mean that he made nothing at any time. Let them see, then, that there cannot possibly be time without creation. Let them have done with this nonsense. Let them instead *be intent on what lies before them*.[1] Let them understand that before all time began you are the eternal Creator of all time, and that no time and no created thing is co-eternal with you, even if any created thing is outside time.

31

O Lord my God, how deep are your mysteries! How far from your safe haven have I been cast away by the consequences of my sins! Heal my eyes and let me rejoice in your light. If there were a mind endowed with such great power of knowing and foreknowing that all the past and all the future were known to it as clearly as I know a familiar psalm, that mind would be wonderful beyond belief. We should hold back from it in awe at the thought that nothing in all the history of the past and nothing in all the ages yet to come was hidden from it. It would know all this as surely as, when I sing the psalm, I know what I have already sung and what I have still to sing, how far I am from the beginning and how far from the end. But it is unthinkable that you, Creator of the universe, Creator of souls and bodies,

[1] Philipp. 3: 13.

should know all the past and all the future merely in this way. Your knowledge is far more wonderful, far more mysterious than this. It is not like the knowledge of a man who sings words well known to him or listens to another singing a familiar psalm. While he does this, his feelings vary and his senses are divided, because he is partly anticipating words still to come and partly remembering words already sung. It is far otherwise with you, for you are eternally without change, the truly eternal Creator of minds. In the Beginning you knew heaven and earth, and there was no change in your knowledge. In just the same way, in the Beginning you created heaven and earth, and there was no change in your action. Some understand this and some do not: let all alike praise you. You are supreme above all, yet your dwelling is in the humble of heart. For *you comfort the burdened*,[1] and none fall who lift their eyes to your high place.

[1] Ps. 145: 8 (146: 8).

BOOK XII

1

THE message of your Holy Scriptures has set my heart throbbing, O Lord, and with the meagre powers that are mine in this life I struggle hard to understand it. The poverty of our human intellect generally produces an abundance of words, for more talk is spent in search than in discovery. It takes longer to ask than to obtain, and the hand that knocks toils harder than the one that receives. But we have your promise and who shall annul it? *Who can be our adversary, if God is on our side?*[1] *Ask, and the gift will come; seek, and you shall find; knock, and the door shall be opened to you. Everyone that asks, will receive; that seeks, will find; that knocks, will have the door opened to him.*[2] These are your promises, and who need fear to be deceived when Truth promises?

2

Humbly my tongue confesses to you in the height of your majesty that it was you who made heaven and earth, the heaven I see and the earth I tread, from which, too, came this earthly body that I bear. It was you who made them. But where, O Lord, is the Heaven of Heavens, of which we hear in the words of the psalm: *To the Lord belongs the Heaven of Heavens, the earth he gives to the children of men?*[3] Where is that other heaven which we cannot see and compared with which all that we see is merely earth?

Beauty of form has been added to the whole of this material creation, even in its lowest parts, though not uniformly throughout, since it is not itself one whole throughout. Its lowest part is this earth on which we live, but compared with the Heaven of Heavens even the heaven above our world is merely earth. So it is reasonable to refer to both these great bodies, the earth and the vault above it, as earth, when they are compared with that mysterious heaven which belongs to the Lord and not to the children of men.

[1] Rom. 8: 31.   [2] Matt. 7: 7, 8.   [3] Ps. 113: 16 (115: 16).

3

Undoubtedly the reason why we are told that this earth was 'invisible and without form',[1] a kind of deep abyss over which there was no light, is that it had no form whatsoever; and the reason why you commanded it to be written that 'darkness reigned over the deep'[1] could only be that there was total absence of light. For if there had been light, where else would it have been but high above, shedding brilliance over all? But since as yet there was no light, what else was the presence of darkness but the absence of light? Darkness, then, reigned over all, because there was no light above, just as silence reigns where there is no sound. For what else is the presence of silence but the absence of sound?

Was it not you, O Lord, who taught my soul these truths which it now confesses to you? Was it not you, O Lord, who taught me that before you fashioned that formless matter into various forms, there was nothing – no colour, no shape, no body, no spirit? Yet there was not complete and utter nothingness: there was this formless matter entirely without feature.

4

How, then, could it be described in such a way that even dull minds could grasp it, except by means of some familiar word? And of all that goes to make up this world what can be found nearer to utter formlessness than 'earth' and 'the deep'? Since they are the lowest in the scale of created things, they have beauty of form in a lower degree than the other, higher things, which are radiant in their splendour. Why, then, should I not assume that the words 'earth, invisible and without form' are meant to convey to men, in a way that they can understand, that formless matter which you created without beauty in order to make from it this beautiful world?

5

Granted that this is the meaning of those words, when we consider what conclusions we can reach about this formless matter, we tell

---

[1] See Gen. 1: 2. '*Earth was still an empty waste, and darkness hung over the deep*' (Knox).

ourselves that it cannot be some abstract conception, such as the mind can grasp, like life or justice, because it is the substance of which bodies have been made; nor can it be anything that the senses can perceive, because there is nothing to be seen or felt in what is invisible and formless. We may reason about it in this way, but we must be content to know without knowing, or should I say, to be ignorant and yet to know?

6

As for myself, O Lord, if I am to tell you all that you have given me to understand about this formless matter, and if I am to set it down in this book, I must confess that when I first heard it mentioned, I did not understand what it meant, nor did those who told me of it. I used to picture it to myself in countless different forms, which means that I did not really picture it at all, because my mind simply conjured up hideous and horrible shapes. They were perversions of the natural order, but shapes nevertheless. I took 'formless' to mean, not something entirely without form, but some shape so monstrous and grotesque that if I were to see it, my senses would recoil and my human frailty quail before it. But what I imagined was not truly formless, that is, it was not something bereft of form of any sort. It was formless only by comparison with other more graceful forms. Yet reason told me that if I wished to conceive of something that was formless in the true sense of the word, I should have to picture something deprived of any trace of form whatsoever, and this I was unable to do. For I could sooner believe that what had no form at all simply did not exist than imagine matter in an intermediate stage between form and non-existence, some formless thing that was next to being nothing at all.

So I gave up trying to find a solution in my imagination, which produced a whole series of pictures of ready-made shapes, shuffling them and rearranging them at will. Instead I turned my attention to material things and looked more closely into the question of their mutability, that is, the means by which they cease to be what they have been and begin to be what they have not been. I suspected that this transition from one form to another might take place by means of an intermediate stage in which they were deprived of all form but were not altogether deprived of existence.

However, I was not satisfied with a mere theory: I wanted to be sure. But if I were to tell of all the problems to which this gave rise and which you unravelled for me, and if I were to set the whole story down in these confessions, which of my readers would have the patience to follow it through to the end? Yet this will not deter my heart from giving you honour and singing your praises for things which it cannot express in words.

Mutability, which belongs to all things that are subject to change, comprehends all the forms which those things take when changes occur in them. But what is it? Is it soul or body? Is it some particular kind of soul or body? If it did not sound nonsensical, I should say that it was nothing and yet something, or that it was and yet was not. Whatever it is, it must have been there first, able to be the vehicle for all the composite forms which we can see in the world.

7

If it was to be there first, in order to be the vehicle for all these visible, composite forms, what can have been its own origin? It can only have derived its being from you, for all things have their origin in you, whatever the degree of their being, although the less they are like you, the farther they are from you – and here I am not speaking in terms of space. This means, then, that you, O Lord, whose being does not alter as times change but is ever and always one and the same, the very same, *holy, holy, holy, Lord God Almighty*,[1] made something in the Beginning, which is of yourself, in your Wisdom, which is born of your own substance, and you created this thing out of nothing.

You created heaven and earth but you did not make them of your own substance. If you had done so, they would have been equal to your only-begotten Son, and therefore to yourself, and justice could in no way admit that what was not of your own substance should be equal to you. But besides yourself, O God, who are Trinity in Unity, Unity in Trinity, there was nothing from which you could make heaven and earth. Therefore you must have created them from nothing, the one great, the other small. For there is nothing that you cannot do. You are good and all that you make must be good, both

[1] Apoc. (Rev.) 4: 8.

the great Heaven of Heavens and this little earth. You were, and besides you nothing was. From nothing, then, you created heaven and earth, distinct from one another; the one close to yourself, the other close to being nothing; the one surpassed only by yourself, the other little more than nothing.

8

The one was the Heaven of Heavens, which belongs to you, O Lord. The other was the earth, which you gave to the children of men, the world which they could see and touch. But it was not yet like the world which we now see and touch. It was invisible and without form. It was a great chasm, over which there was no light. In other words, darkness reigned over its depths, which means that the darkness above it was denser even than the darkness in the depths of the sea. For even in its deepest parts the ocean which we can now see has its own kind of light, discernible to fish and the living creatures that crawl upon the sea-bed. But in those days the whole world was little more than nothing, because it was still entirely formless. Yet by now it was something to which form could be added.

For you, O Lord, made the world from formless matter, which you created out of nothing. This matter was itself almost nothing, but from it you made all the mighty things which are so wonderful to us. The sky above us, this great work of wonder, you made on the second day, after you had created light on the first. You made it as a firmament to divide the waters from the waters.[1] You said 'Let it be made',[1] and it was made. This firmament you called heaven, which means, not the Heaven of Heavens, but the heaven above our earth and sea. On the third day you made the earth and the sea by giving visible form to that formless matter which you had created before the first day. You had made a heaven, too, before the first day, because we are told that 'in the Beginning you made heaven and earth'. But this was the heaven of our heaven. And the earth which you had made before the first day was that formless matter. This must be so, because we are told that it was 'invisible and without form, and darkness reigned over the deep'. It was from this invisible and formless earth, this utter formlessness, this next-to-nothing, that you were to make

[1] See Gen. 1: 6. *'God said, too, Let a solid vault arise amid the waters, to keep these waters apart from those'* (Knox).

all the things of which our changing world consists – though it is not right to speak of consistency in this world, because its susceptibility to change is obvious from the fact that we are aware of time and can measure its passage. For time is constituted by the changes which take place in things as a result of variations and alterations in their form, and the matter of all these things is that invisible earth of which we have spoken.

9

This is why the Holy Spirit, who inspired your servant Moses to write, says nothing about times or days when he tells us that you created heaven and earth 'in the Beginning'. For clearly the Heaven of Heavens, which you created 'in the Beginning', that is, before the days began, is some kind of intellectual creature. Although it is in no way co-eternal with you, the Trinity, nevertheless it partakes in your eternity. Through the rapture and joy of its contemplation of God it has power to resist the propensity to change, and by clinging to you unfailingly ever since its creation it transcends every vicissitude of the whirl of time.

Neither is the creation of that formless matter, the invisible, unformed earth, reckoned among the days of creation. For where there is no form and no order, nothing is dissolved, nothing renewed; and without this process of succession there can be no days or any changes denoting periods of time.

10

Let me listen to Truth, the Light of my heart, and not to the voices which I heard in the days of my darkness. I deserted truth for worldly things and the night closed over me, but even then, even in my darkness, I continued to love you, O Truth. I wandered away, but I remembered you. I heard your voice at my back, calling me to return, though I was scarcely able to hear it in the uproar raised by men who would not live at peace with you. Now I return from the heat of the fray, panting to reach your fountain. Let none keep me from it. There I shall drink and its waters shall give me life. Let me not be my own life, for when I lived of myself I lived evilly: I was death to myself. But in you I live again. Speak to me; breathe the words of truth to me. I have faith in your Books, but their message is hard indeed to fathom.

11

In my heart, O Lord, I have heard your voice telling me loud and clear that you are eternal and that *to you alone immortality belongs*.[1] For in you there is no change, either of form or motion. Your will does not alter as times change, for a will which varies is not immortal. In your presence this is clear to me. I pray that it may become ever more clear and that in the light of this truth I may persevere wisely to the end beneath the shelter of your wings.

In my heart, O Lord, I have also heard your voice telling me loud and clear that it was you who made all natures and substances that are not what you are, yet are. All derives from you, except what has no being at all. The movement of a will away from you, the supreme Being, towards some inferior being does not derive from you. Such movement is wicked and sinful, but no man's sin can harm you or disturb the order of your rule, either at its summit or at its base. In your presence this is clear to me. I pray that it may become ever more clear and that in the light of this truth I may persevere wisely to the end beneath the shelter of your wings.

In my heart, O Lord, I have also heard your voice telling me loud and clear that not even the Heaven of Heavens, your creature, is co-eternal with you. Though it delights in you alone and enjoys your savour in untiring purity, at no time and in no way does it shed its mutability. But being always in your presence and clinging to you with all its love, it has no future to anticipate and no past to remember, and thus it persists without change and does not diverge into past and future time. How happy must this creature be, if such it is, constantly intent upon your beatitude, forever possessed by you, forever bathed in your light! I can think of no description better suited to the Heaven of Heavens, which *belongs to the Lord*[2] than to call it your dwelling which forever contemplates the blessedness of God, never forsaking it for lesser things, a pure mind at one and undivided in the sure and settled peace of the holy spirits, the dwellers in your heavenly city far above our earthly heaven.

In this there is a lesson for the soul, which travels far upon its

[1] i Tim. 6: 16.   [2] Ps. 113: 16 (115: 16).

earthly pilgrimage. If *it thirsts for you*; if *morning and evening its diet is of tears*; if *daily it must listen to the taunt, Where is your God now?*[1] if it now *makes one request of you, and one alone, to dwell in your house its whole life long*[2] – and what is its life but you? What are your days but your eternity? What else but eternity are your years, which *can never fail, because you are unchanging?*[3] – if this is what it asks, let it learn, as far as it is able, how far above all time you are in your eternity, by reflecting that the Heaven of Heavens, which is your dwelling and travels upon no worldly pilgrimage, although it is not co-eternal with you, nevertheless is free from all vicissitudes of time because it clings to you unfailingly and without cease. In your presence this is clear to me. I pray that it may become ever more clear and that in the light of this truth I may persevere wisely to the end beneath the shelter of your wings.

As for the changes which occur in the things of this world, the last and lowest parts of your creation, it is clear that they take place in formless matter of some kind. And if all form were removed and swept away, so that nothing remained but this formless fundamental, through which things are altered and changed from one form to another, none but a dreamer, at the mercy of his wild imaginings, would claim that it could then show evidence of changes of time. It would be utterly impossible for it to do so, because without change of movement there is no time, and there can be no change where there is no form.

12

I have given thought to these things, my God, to the limit of the power you give me and in so far as you both prompt me to knock and also open your door to my knocking. I find that you made two things from which time is absent, though neither is co-eternal with you. Time is absent from the one because it is so formed that without any lapse in its contemplation of you, without any interim of change, mutable but without mutation, it is constant in its enjoyment of your eternity and absolute immutability; and from the other because it was so utterly formless that it could not relinquish one form and adopt another, either one of motion or one of rest, which would have made it subject to time. But you did not leave it formless. You made these

[1] Ps. 41: 3, 4, (42: 2, 3).   [2] Ps. 26: 4 (27: 4).   [3] Ps. 101: 28 (102: 27).

two things, heaven and earth, in the Beginning before the days began. But 'the earth was invisible and without form, and darkness reigned over the deep'. This sentence, so worded as to be intelligible in some degree to people who are unable to conceive of utter absence of form that is nevertheless not merely nothing at all, describes the formlessness from which you made the firmament above our world, the visible earth to which you gave order, water in all its beauty, and whatever else goes to make up this world and was made, as we are told, on the different days of the creation. All these were made after the days began, because their nature is such that they display the changes of time effected by the regular processes of change in movement and form.

13

This then, my God, is how I interpret your Scripture when I read the words: 'In the Beginning God made heaven and earth. The earth was invisible and without form, and darkness reigned over the deep.' Scripture does not say on which day you made them, and I understand the reason for this to be that 'heaven' here means the Heaven of Heavens – that is, the intellectual heaven, where the intellect is privileged to know all at once, not in part only, not as if it were *looking at a confused reflection in a mirror*,[1] but as a whole, clearly, *face to face*;[1] not first one thing and then another but, as I have said, all at once, quite apart from the ebb and flow of time – and 'earth' means the invisible, formless earth, also unaffected by the ebb and flow of time which always marks the change from this to that, since where there is no form there can be no this and no that. These, then, are the heaven and earth that are meant, as I understand it, when the Scripture says 'In the Beginning God made heaven and earth' without mention of day – heaven, that is, the Heaven of Heavens which was given form from the very beginning, and earth, that is, earth invisible and without order, which was utterly formless. In fact the Scripture explains in the very next sentence what earth is meant by this. And since it says that on the second day the firmament was made and that it was called heaven, it gives us to understand which heaven was meant by the first sentence, which makes no mention of days.

[1] I Cor. 13: 12.

14

How wonderful are your Scriptures! How profound! We see their surface and it attracts us like children. And yet, O my God, their depth is stupendous. We shudder to peer deep into them, for they inspire in us both the awe of reverence and the thrill of love.

How hateful to me are the enemies of your Scripture! How I wish that you would slay them with your two-edged sword, so that there should be none to oppose your word! Gladly would I have them die to themselves and live to you.

But there are others, not opponents of the book of Genesis but acclaimers of it, who say, 'This is not what the Spirit of God, who wrote these words through Moses his servant, meant us to understand by them. He did not mean them to be understood as you explain them. He meant them to be taken in another way, the way that we say is right.'

My answer to them is this and I make it before you as our Judge, for you are both my God and theirs.

15

This is the case I put to them.

Within me I hear the loud voice of Truth telling me that since the Creator is truly eternal, his substance is utterly unchanged in time and his will is not something separate from his substance. This they will surely not deny. It follows that he does not will first one thing and then another, but that he wills all that he wills simultaneously, in one act, and eternally. He does not repeat his act of will over and over again or will different things at different times, and he neither starts to will what he did not will previously nor ceases to will what he willed before. A will which acts in this way is mutable, and nothing that is mutable is eternal. But our God is eternal.

Again, I am told by that inner voice that expectation of things to come changes to direct perception when they are present, and direct perception changes to memory when they are gone. My opponents will not deny this. Yet any intellectual activity which varies in this way is mutable, and nothing that is mutable is eternal. But our God is eternal.

By linking these two truths and consolidating them I find, first, that my God, the eternal God, did not create the world by any new act of his will; and, second, that his knowledge does not admit of anything that is transitory.

What do my opponents reply to this? Will they deny that it is true? 'We do not,' they say. Will they then deny that every nature that has form and all matter which is susceptible of form can only derive its being from him who is the sovereign Good because he is the sovereign Being? 'We do not deny this either,' they say. Then do they deny that there is a sublime creature which is bound to the true God, the truly eternal God, by so pure a love that, though it is not co-eternal with him, it never parts from him and never falls away to become subject to the fluctuation and succession of time, but remains serene in the sure contemplation of God alone? It does this, O God, because it loves you as much as you command, and therefore you reveal yourself to it. Such a creature has need of nothing else, and therefore neither deviates from you nor turns towards itself. This creature is God's dwelling. It is not a material house of earth or even of some heavenly matter. It is spiritual, partaking in your eternity because it is forever without blemish. *You have set it there unaging for ever, given it a law which cannot be altered.*[1] Yet it is not co-eternal with you, because it is not without a beginning: it was made.

This is not to say that time was created before it, because *wisdom is first of all created things.*[2] 'Wisdom' here does not mean the Wisdom who is co-eternal and equal with you who are our God, with you who are his Father, the Wisdom through whom all was created, the Beginning in whom you made heaven and earth. It means created wisdom, that intellectual nature which is light because it contemplates the Light. This too we call wisdom, although it is created wisdom. But there is as great a difference between the Wisdom which creates and wisdom which is created as between the Light which enlightens and light which receives its brilliance by reflection, or between the Justice which brings justification and justice which results from it. Even we have been called your justice, for your servant Paul says that Christ came into the world *that in him we might be turned into the holiness of God,*[3] that is, into your justice. There was, then, a created wisdom which was created before all else. It was the rational, intellectual mind of God's pure city, *our mother, the heavenly Jerusalem, a city of freedom,*[1] which *lasts eternally in heaven.*[2] Can this be any other than the Heaven of Heavens which *belongs to the Lord,*[3] the heaven which resounds with your praises? We find no time before it, because it precedes even the creation of time, having been created before all else. But before it is the eternity of its Creator, by whom it was made and from whom it derived, not the beginning of its time, since as yet there was no time, but the beginning of its being.

So, though it derives from you, our God, it is something quite other than yourself. It is not God, who is in himself. And we find that not only is there no time before it, but no time in it, because it is fitted *to behold your face continually*[4] and is never turned away from it. This means that it undergoes no change. Yet mutability is inherent in it, and it would grow dark and cold unless, by clinging to you with all the strength of its love, it drew warmth and light from you like a noon that never wanes.

O house of light and beauty! *How well I love the house where the Lord dwells, the shrine of his glory!*[5] It was he who made you and it is he who possesses you. In my pilgrimage let me sigh for you, and I pray to him who made you that he should possess me too in you, for I also was made by him. I have been *wayward, like a lost sheep,*[6] but I hope to be carried back to you on the shoulders of my Shepherd, who built you for himself.

What do my opponents say to this? Although they disagree with me, they believe that Moses was a devout servant of God and that the Holy Spirit speaks in his books. Do they agree that this house of God, though not co-eternal with him, nevertheless in its own way *lasts eternally in heaven,*[7] where we search in vain for changes of time? We shall not find them there, because the house of God, which *knows no other content but clinging to him*[8] for ever, rises above every extension and every fugitive span of time.

'We agree to this,' they say. Then, of all that my heart cried out to my God, when inwardly *it listened to the sound of his praises,*[9] what do they claim is false? Do they say that I was wrong to say that there was

---

[1] Gal. 4: 26. [2] II Cor. 5:1. [3] Ps. 113: 16 (115: 16).
[4] Matt. 18:10. [5] Ps. 25: 8 (26: 8). [6] Ps. 118: 176 (119: 176).
[7] II Cor. 5: 1. [8] Ps. 72: 28 (73: 28). [9] Ps. 25: 7 (26: 7).

formless matter, in which there was no order because there was no form? But where there was no order there could be no successive movement of time. Yet this next-to-nothing, in so far as it was not utterly nil, must have had its being from him from whom everything that in any degree is derives its being. 'This also we do not deny', they say.

16

In your presence, my God, I wish to reason a little with those who admit all that your Truth tells me inwardly in my mind. As for those who deny these truths, let them snarl and deafen themselves as much as they like. I shall try to persuade them to be silent and to open a way to their hearts for your word. But if they refuse, if they repulse me, I beseech you, my God, *do not leave my cry unanswered*.[1] Whisper words of truth in my heart, for you alone speak truth, and I will leave these unbelievers outside to fan the earth with their breath, stirring up the dust into their own eyes, while I withdraw to my secret cell and sing you hymns of love, groaning with grief that I cannot express as I journey on my pilgrimage. Yet I shall remember the heavenly Jerusalem and my heart shall be lifted up towards that holy place, Jerusalem my country, Jerusalem my mother. And I shall remember you her Ruler, you who give her light, you her Father, her Guardian, and her Spouse, you who are her pure, her deep Delight, you who are her constant Joy, you who are at once all that is good beyond the power of words to describe, because you alone are Goodness itself, the sovereign Good, the true Good. I shall not turn aside until I come to that abode of peace, Jerusalem my beloved mother, where *my spiritual harvest*[2] is laid, the fountainhead of all that I know for certain on this earth. My God, my Mercy, I shall not turn aside until you gather all that I am into that holy place of peace, rescuing me from this world where I am dismembered and deformed, and giving me new form and new strength for eternity.

But there are others who do not say that all these truths are false. They honour your sacred Scripture, which you gave to us through your holy servant Moses, and just as I do, they look on it as the highest authority that we must follow. But they disagree with me on some points, and it is to them that I now address myself. You are my God

[1] Ps. 27: 1 (28: 1).   [2] Rom. 8: 23.

and theirs: be the judge between my confessions and the objections which they make.

17

'We do not quarrel with anything you say,' they tell me, 'except your interpretation of the words "In the Beginning God made heaven and earth". When Moses wrote them by the revelation of the Holy Spirit, he did not have in mind the two beings which you describe. By "heaven" he did not mean that spiritual or intellectual creature which forever contemplates God face to face; and by "earth" he did not mean matter without form.'

'What, then, did he mean?' I ask.

'We can explain what Moses had in mind and what he meant to convey by those words.'

'What is your explanation?'

'The words "heaven and earth" are a brief and comprehensive preliminary phrase used by Moses to mean the whole of the visible world. Afterwards he went on to detail, one by one, in the enumeration of the days, all the things which it pleased the Holy Spirit to make known in this way. The people for whom he wrote were so primitive and earth-bound that he thought it unsuitable to tell them of any but the visible works of God.'

Having said this they agree that the earth which was invisible and without form and the deep over which darkness reigned – that is, the substance from which, as we are subsequently told, all the visible things with which we are familiar were made and set in order during the six days – may without inconsistency be taken to mean the formless matter of which I have spoken.

Others may maintain that the phrase 'heaven and earth' was used in the first sentence of Genesis to signify the same formless and confused matter, because it was from it that our visible world, with all the phenomena which it so evidently contains and which we often enough refer to in the aggregate as 'heaven and earth', was created and perfected.

Others again may say that the phrase 'heaven and earth' not inappropriately signifies nature, whether visible or invisible, and therefore these two words cover the whole of creation, that is, all that God made in his Wisdom or, in other words, in the Beginning. Yet it was all made, not from God's own substance, but from nothing. (This I do not dispute, for created things are not the same as God. In all of them there is the principle of mutability, whether they remain steadfast like the eternal house of God, or undergo change like man's soul and body.) Therefore, the argument goes on, the common matter of all things, whether visible or invisible, is what is meant by those two words. It was still formless but had the potentiality of form. From it heaven and earth were to be made, in other words the invisible and the visible creation, to each of which form has now been added. This matter is referred to both as 'earth, invisible and without form' and as 'darkness over the deep', with the distinction that 'earth, invisible and without form' means corporeal matter before it was defined by form and 'darkness over the deep' spiritual matter before a limit was fixed to what we might call its unconstrained fluidity and before the light of wisdom banished its darkness.

Still another theory might be that when we read the verse 'In the Beginning God made heaven and earth', we are not meant to understand by the words 'heaven and earth' two natures, invisible and visible, already perfected and endowed with form, but a rudimentary beginning of things, matter still formless but capable of receiving form and serving the purpose of creation. These names were used to describe it, because there already existed in it, though confusedly and still without distinction of quality or form, the two creatures which, now that each has been set in its proper order, we call heaven and earth, the one spiritual, the other corporeal.

18

I listen to all these arguments and give them thought, but I will not engage in *wordy disputes, such as can only unsettle the minds of those who are listening.*[1] The law is intended for edification, and *it is an excellent thing, where it is applied legitimately,*[2] because *its end is charity, based on purity of heart, on a good conscience and a sincere faith.*[3] Christ our Master well knows which are the two commandments on which, he said, *all the law and the prophets depend.*[4] O my God, Light of my eyes in darkness, since I believe in these commandments and confess them to be true with all my heart, how can it harm me that it should be possible

[1] II Tim. 2: 14. [2] I Tim. 1: 8. [3] I Tim. 1: 5. [4] Matt. 22: 40.

to interpret these words in several ways, all of which may yet be true? How can it harm me if I understand the writer's meaning in a different sense from that in which another understands it? All of us who read his words do our best to discover and understand what he had in mind, and since we believe that he wrote the truth, we are not so rash as to suppose that he wrote anything which we know or think to be false. Provided, therefore, that each of us tries as best he can to understand in the Holy Scriptures what the writer meant by them, what harm is there if a reader believes what you, the Light of all truthful minds, show him to be the true meaning? It may not even be the meaning which the writer had in mind, and yet he too saw in them a true meaning, different though it may have been from this.

19

For the great truth, O Lord, is that you made heaven and earth. It is true that the Beginning is your Wisdom, in which you made all things. It is also true that this visible world is divided into two great parts, heaven and earth, and these two words comprise in brief all natures that have been created and put into the world. It is true that anything which is mutable implies for us some formless principle by which it receives form or is changed or converted into another form. It is true that time has no effect upon a being which adheres so closely to the eternally immutable that, though it is itself mutable, it undergoes no change. It is true that formlessness, which is almost nothingness, cannot be a vehicle for the passage of time. It is true that the matter of which something is made can, by an extension of meaning, be given the name of the thing which is made from it, and in this way the name 'heaven and earth' might be applied to that formless matter from which heaven and earth were made. It is true that of all things which have form none is closer to formlessness than earth and the deep. It is true that you, who are the origin of all things, made not only what has been created and given form but also any matter which can serve the purpose of creation or is capable of receiving form. It is true that whatever is formed from the formless principle was first formless and was then given form.

There is no doubt of these truths in the minds of those whom you have gifted with insight to understand such matters and who firmly believe that Moses, your servant, spoke in the spirit of truth. But from these truths each of us chooses one or another to explain the phrase 'In the Beginning God made heaven and earth'.

One man says that it means that in his Word co-eternal with himself God made the two creations, the one an intellectual or spiritual being, the other a being perceptible through the bodily senses, or in other words, corporeal.

Another says that it means that in his Word co-eternal with himself God made the whole mass of this corporeal world, together with all the natures which it contains and which are visible and familiar to us.

Another says that it means that in his Word co-eternal with himself God made formless matter from which both his spiritual and his corporeal creation were to be formed.

Another says that it means that in his Word co-eternal with himself God made the formless matter of his corporeal creation and that in it, though still in confusion, were the heaven and earth which we now see distinct from one another and endowed with form in the mass of the universe around us.

Another says that it means that at the very beginning of the act of creation God made formless matter in which heaven and earth were contained without distinction, and that from this matter they were formed as they now appear to us, together with everything that is in them.

21

The same applies to our interpretation of the words that follow. Of all the truths which I have listed each of us chooses one or another to explain the meaning of the phrase: 'The earth was invisible and without form, and darkness reigned over the deep.'

One man says that this means that the corporeal thing which God made was still only the matter of corporeal things, and that it was without form, order, or light.

Another says that it means that the whole of what we call heaven and earth was still matter without form or light, and that from it the corporeal heaven and the corporeal earth were to be made together with everything in them that we can perceive by our bodily senses.

Another says that it means that the whole of what we call heaven and earth was still the matter, without form or light, from which both heaven – that is, the heaven which we can only understand in our minds and which is elsewhere called the Heaven of Heavens – and earth – that is, all corporeal nature including the corporeal heaven above our earth – were to be made. In other words the whole of creation, invisible and visible alike, was to be made from it.

Another says that when the Scripture speaks of heaven and earth it does not mean the sheer formlessness of which we have spoken. This formlessness already existed and is what is meant by 'earth invisible and without form' and 'darkness over the deep'. From it, as Scripture tells us in the first sentence, God made heaven and earth, that is, the spiritual and the corporeal creation.

Another says that the words 'The earth was invisible and without form, and darkness reigned over the deep' mean that the formlessness already existed and that it was the matter from which the first verse of Genesis tells us that God made heaven and earth, that is, the whole corporeal mass of the world divided into its two main parts, the upper and the lower, together with all the creatures in them which are known and familiar to us.

22

As for these last two opinions, one might object that if those who hold them will not agree that the words 'heaven and earth' are used to mean formless matter, there must have been something which God had not made himself, but from which he made heaven and earth. There is nothing in Scripture to say that he made any such matter, unless we infer it from the words 'heaven and earth', or even 'earth' alone, as they are used in the verse 'In the Beginning God made heaven and earth'. In the next verse, which says 'The earth was invisible and without form', although it suited the writer to give this name to the formless matter, we can only understand it to mean what the first verse tells us that God made when it says that he 'made heaven and earth'.

If we put forward this objection, those who hold either of the two opinions which I set down at the end of the last chapter will reply,

'We do not deny that this matter was made by God, from whom all good proceeds. For, as we agree that what is created and given form is a higher good, we agree equally that what is made capable of serving the purpose of creation and of being used as the vehicle of form is a lesser good, but a good nevertheless. All the same we point out that Scripture does not say that God made this formless matter any more than it says that he made a great many other things, the cherubim and seraphim, for example, and all the other separate orders mentioned by Saint Paul, the *thrones and dominions, princedoms and powers*.[1] Yet it is clear that God made all of these.

'Again, if the verse "God made heaven and earth" includes everything, what are we to say of the waters over which "the Spirit of God moved"?[2] If we understand the word "earth" to comprise the waters also, how can we take the same word to apply to formless matter, when we see that the waters are so beautiful?

'Moreover, if we suppose "earth" to mean formless matter, why is it written that from this same formless principle the firmament was made and was called heaven, whereas it is not written that the waters were made? They are not still formless and invisible, for we can see them and admire their beauty as they flow.

'Again, if the waters were given their beauty when God said *Let the waters below the vault collect in one place*[3] – that is, if we take it that the gathering of the waters was the process by which they were endowed with form – what can we say of the waters which are above the firmament? If they were without form, they would not have been worthy of the place of honour that was given to them, and yet Scripture does not record any words spoken by God by which he gave them form.

'Therefore, even if Genesis does not record that God made a particular thing, neither true faith nor strict reasoning leave us in any doubt that he made it, and it would be preposterous to maintain that the waters above the firmament must be co-eternal with God simply because, though they are mentioned in Genesis, we can find no statement as to when they were made. Why, then, since Truth is our Teacher, should we not also take it that the formless matter, which this text of Scripture calls "earth, invisible and without form" and

---

[1] Col. 1: 16.   [2] See Gen. 1: 2 *'Already, over its waters, stirred the breath of God'* (Knox).   [3] Gen. 1: 9.

"darkness over the deep", was created by God out of nothing and is therefore not co-eternal with him, even though Genesis omits to mention when it was made?'

23

I listen to these arguments and take stock of them to the best of my power, feeble though it is, my God, as I confess to you, who know it without my telling. And I realize that when a message is delivered to us in words, truthful though the messenger may be, two sorts of disagreement may arise. We may disagree either as to the truth of the message itself or as to the messenger's meaning. It is one thing to inquire which is the true history of the creation, another to ask what Moses, who was so good a servant to the family of your faithful, meant those who read or heard his words to understand by them.

As for the first sort of disagreement, I wish to have no dealing with any who think things which in reality are false; and as for the second, I wish to have none with any who think that Moses wrote what was not true. But I pray that in you, O Lord, I may dwell in harmony and joy with those who feed upon your truth in the fullness of charity. May they and I together approach the words of your Book, and in them may we seek your meaning as we were meant to understand it by your servant, through whose pen you delivered those words to us.

24

But the truths which those words contain appear to different inquirers in a different light, and of all the meanings that they can bear which of us can lay his finger upon one and say that it is what Moses had in mind and what he meant us to understand by his words? Can he say this with as much confidence as he would say that what Moses wrote is the truth, whether he had that particular meaning in mind or another? O my God, I am your servant and have vowed to you a sacrifice of confession, which I make to you in this book. I pray that in your mercy I may *pay my vows to you*,[1] and I declare with all confidence that you created all things, invisible and visible alike, in your immutable Word. But can I declare with equal confidence that this and none other was the meaning which Moses had in mind when

[1] Ps. 21: 26 (22: 25).

he wrote: 'In the Beginning God made heaven and earth'? I cannot believe that this was what he was thinking when he wrote those words with as much certainty as I know in your truth that what he wrote is true. It is possible that when he said 'in the beginning', he was thinking of the first beginning of creation, and by 'heaven and earth' he may here have meant us to understand, not any nature already formed and perfected, whether spiritual or corporeal, but both of these in a rudimentary state and still without form. I see that either meaning could be the true one, whichever of the two he may have meant. But it is not so clear to me which of them he in fact had in mind. Nevertheless, whether this great man had one of these two meanings in mind when he wrote those words, or was thinking of some other meaning which I have not set down here, I am quite sure that he saw the truth and expressed it accordingly.

25

Let no one irritate me further by saying, 'Moses did not mean what you say. He meant what I say.' If anyone were to ask me 'How do you know that Moses meant his words to be taken in the way that you explain them?' it would be my duty to listen to the question with composure, and in answer I should give the explanation which I have already given, perhaps rather more fully if the questioner were slow to understand. But when a man says 'Moses did not mean what you say, but what I say', and yet does not deny that both his interpretation and mine are consistent with the truth, then, O Life of the poor, O my God, in whose bosom there is no contradiction, I beg you to water my heart with the rain of forbearance, so that I may bear with such people in patience. They speak as they do, not because they are men of God or because they have seen in the heart of Moses, your servant, that their explanation is the right one, but simply because they are proud. They have no knowledge of the thoughts in his mind, but they are in love with their own opinions, not because they are true, but because they are their own. If this were not so, they would have equal respect for the opinions of others, provided that they were consistent with the truth, just as I respect their opinions when they do not depart from the truth, not because the opinions are theirs, but because they are within the truth. And in fact for the very reason that they are true, these opinions are not their own property. If, on the other hand, they love them because they are true, they are both theirs and mine, for they are the common property of all lovers of the truth. But I will not tolerate their contention that Moses meant, not what I say he meant, but only what they say. It appals me, because even if their explanation is the right one, the arbitrary assurance with which they insist upon it springs from presumption, not from knowledge. It is the child of arrogance, not of true vision.

We must dread your judgements, O Lord, because your truth is not mine alone nor does it belong to this man or that. It belongs to us all, because we all hear your call to share it and you give us dire warning not to think it ours alone, for fear that we may be deprived of it. If any man claims as his own what you give to all to enjoy and tries to keep for himself what belongs to all, he is driven to take refuge in his own resources instead of in what is common to all. For he who utters falsehood utters what is his alone.[1]

O good Judge, O God, O Truth, listen as I lay before you the answer that I shall give to any man who contradicts me in this fashion. I speak before you and before my brothers in the faith, who *apply the law legitimately,*[2] that is, to the end of charity. Listen, if it so please you, and hear what I shall say to him.

Speaking peaceably, as between brothers, I shall say, 'If we both see that what you say is true and also that what I say is true, what enables us to recognize this truth? I do not see it in you, nor do you see it in me, but we both see it in the immutable Truth which is above our minds. Therefore, since there is no dispute between us about the light which shines from the Lord our God, why do we argue about the thoughts of a fellow man, which we cannot see as clearly as we see the immutable Truth? Even if Moses were to appear to us and say "This is what I meant", we should not see his thoughts but would simply believe his word. Let us not, therefore, *go beyond what is laid down for us, one man slighting another out of partiality for someone else.*[3] *Let us love the Lord our God with our whole heart and our whole soul and our whole mind, and our neighbour as ourselves.*[4] Whatever Moses meant in his books, unless we believe that he meant it to be understood in the spirit of these two precepts of charity, we are *treating God as a liar,*[5] for

[1] See John 8: 44. [2] 1 Tim. 1: 8. [3] 1 Cor. 4: 6. [4] Matt. 22: 37, 39.
[5] 1 John 5: 10.

we attribute to his servant thoughts at variance with his teaching.

'When so many meanings, all of them acceptable as true, can be extracted from the words that Moses wrote, do you not see how foolish it is to make a bold assertion that one in particular is the one he had in mind? Do you not see how foolish it is to enter into mischievous arguments which are an offence against that very charity for the sake of which he wrote every one of the words that we are trying to explain?'

26

O my God, whose high majesty is the measure of my lowliness, my God, Repose of my labour, since you who hear my confessions and forgive me my sins command me to love my neighbour as myself, I cannot believe that Moses, who served you so faithfully, received a lesser gift from you than I should have wished with all my heart to receive for myself, if I had been born when he was born and you had placed me in his position so that mine should have been the heart and tongue which were to serve you in giving to the world those writings which, so long after they were written, were still to benefit all nations and were to prevail as a paramount authority over every doctrine inspired by falsehood and pride. For we are all made from the same clay[1] and man is nothing unless you remember him,[2] and if I had been Moses and you had made it my task to write the book of Genesis, I should have wished you to give me such skill in writing and such power in framing words, that not even those who as yet cannot understand how God creates should reject my words as beyond their comprehension, and those who can should find expressed in the few words of your servant whatever true conclusions they had reached by their own reasoning; and if, in the light of truth, another man saw a different meaning in those words, it should not be impossible to understand this meaning too in those same words.

27

The account left by Moses, whom you chose to pass it on to us, is like a spring which is all the more copious because it flows in a confined space. Its waters are carried by a maze of channels over a wider area

[1] See Rom. 9: 21.   [2] See Ps. 8: 5 (8: 4).

than could be reached by any single stream drawing its water from the same source and flowing through many different places. In the same way, from the words of Moses, uttered in all brevity but destined to serve a host of preachers, there gush clear streams of truth from which each of us, though in more prolix and roundabout phrases, may derive a true explanation of the creation as best he is able, some choosing one and some another interpretation.

Some people, when they read or hear what Moses wrote, imagine God as a kind of man or as a vast bodily substance endowed with power, who by some new and sudden decision created heaven and earth. They were two great bodies, an upper and a lower, apart from God as though they were in some separate place, and in them everything was to be contained. When these people hear that God said 'Let such and such be made', and accordingly it was made, they think of speech with a beginning and an end, heard for a while and then done with. They think that once the words had been pronounced, whatever was ordered to come into existence immediately did so. Any other thoughts which occur to them are limited in the same way by their attachment to the familiar material world around them.

These people are still like children. But the very simplicity of the language of Scripture sustains them in their weakness as a mother cradles an infant in her lap. On it is built the faith that is their salvation, the faith by which they believe, surely and certainly, that God made all the natures which they can see and hear and touch in the world about them in all their wonderful variety. But if any man despises the words of Scripture as language fit for simpletons and, in the stupidity of pride, climbs out of the nest where he was reared, woe betide him, for he shall meet his fall. Have pity on such callow fledgelings, O Lord, for those who pass by on the road may tread them underfoot. Send your angel to put them back in the nest, so that they may live and learn to fly.

28

But there are others for whom the words of Scripture are no longer a nest but a leafy orchard, where they see the hidden fruit. They fly about it in joy, breaking into song as they gaze at the fruit and feed upon it. For when they read or hear these words, they see that you endure, constant and unchanging, supreme above all past or future time, and yet there is no temporal creature that was not of your making. They see that because your will is identical with your being, it underwent no change when by it you created all things, nor was it a newly emerged will which had not existed before. They see that you made the world, not by creating it from your own substance in your own likeness, which is the form of all things, but by creating from nothing formless matter utterly unlike yourself. By resort to your unity this matter was to receive form in your likeness, each created thing in its allotted degree. All things were thus to be good, whether they remain close to you or, at different degrees of distance from you in time and place, undergo, or themselves cause, all the wonderful variations which take place in the world.

All this they see, and as far as the meagre powers they have in this life enable them to do so, they rejoice in the light of your truth. Some of them, reading the words 'In the Beginning God made heaven and earth', understand 'Beginning' to mean Wisdom, who also speaks to us.[1] Others, reading the same words, take 'Beginning' to mean the commencement of creation, and therefore they understand the sentence as 'In the first place God made heaven and earth'.

Of those who understand 'Beginning' to mean Wisdom, some think that 'heaven and earth' is another name for matter which could be used for the creation of heaven and earth. Others think that the words refer to two natures, already distinct and endowed with form. Others again think that 'heaven' means a spiritual nature, endowed with form, whereas 'earth' means the formless nature of corporeal matter.

There are differences of opinion too among those who take 'heaven and earth' to mean the as yet formless matter from which heaven and earth were to be formed. Some think that it means matter from which both creations, that which we can only reach through the mind and that which we can perceive through the senses, were to be perfected. Others think that it means matter from which only this corporeal world, of which we are aware through our senses, was to be produced, containing in its vast folds all such natures as are readily perceptible to us.

There is also disagreement among those who think that 'heaven and earth' in this context means heaven and earth already formed and

[1] See John 8: 25.

disposed in due order. Some think that the words refer to the invisible and the visible creation, others that they refer to the visible creation alone, in which we see both the heaven above our earth, resplendent with light, and the earth, shrouded in darkness, together with all that they contain.

29

Anyone who takes the words 'in the Beginning' to be another way of saying 'in the first place' can only understand 'heaven and earth' in this context as the matter of heaven and earth, that is, the matter of the whole of creation, both spiritual and corporeal. For if he maintains that at this stage the universe already had form, we might well ask him what God made afterwards, if this was what he made first. He will not find anything still remaining to be created once the creation of the universe was complete, and he lays himself open to the awkward question 'How can the universe be said to have been made first, if nothing was made after it?'

If, on the other hand, he says that God first created matter without form and then gave it form, this is not an unreasonable theory provided that he is able to see the distinction between priority in eternity, in time, in choice, and in origin. By priority in eternity we mean that which is God's, because he pre-exists all things; in time, the priority of the blossom, for instance, in relation to the fruit; in choice, the priority of the fruit, which we should choose before the blossom; and in origin, the priority of sound, for example, before song.

Though the second and third of these examples are easy enough to understand, the first and last are extremely difficult. For it is only rarely and with great difficulty that a man can discern your eternity, O Lord, creating things that are subject to change yet never suffering change itself and thereby being prior to them all. It also requires acute mental perception to see, without great effort, how sound precedes song. For song is ordered sound, and although a thing may very well exist without order, order cannot be given to a thing which does not exist. In the same way matter precedes what is made from it, though neither in the sense that it makes anything, because its role is passive rather than active, nor in the sense that it precedes it in time. We do not first emit formless sounds, which do not constitute song, and then adapt them and fashion them in the form of song as we do with wood when we make a box, or with silver when we make a bowl. Materials such as wood or metal do of course precede in time the forms of the things which are made from them. But this is not the case with song. For when a song is sung, the sound that is heard is the song itself: it is not first heard as a formless noise, which is afterwards formed into a song. For a sound is no sooner uttered than it dies away, and nothing remains of it for a singer to take up and compose into a song. Therefore the song is inseparable from the sound, which is its material. In order to become a song the sound receives form. This is what I meant when I said that the material, which is sound, precedes the form, which is song. It does not precede it in the sense that it has power to make it, because it is not the sound, but the singer, who makes the song. The sound is simply the material which the singer's voice makes available to his mind in order that he may make a song from it. Nor is it earlier in time, for the sound is emitted at the same time as the song. It does not take precedence in the sense that we should choose it before song, because song, being not merely sound but sound with beauty added, is preferable to sound. But it does have priority in origin, because it is not the song that receives form in order to be a sound, but vice versa.

I hope that those who are able to follow my argument will see from this example that the matter of things was made first and was called heaven and earth because heaven and earth were made from it. But this does not mean that it was made first in terms of time, because there is time only where there is form, whereas this matter was formless and we are only aware of it in time together with its form. However, we can only speak of it as if it were first in order of time, although it is last in order of value, since that which has form is obviously better than that which has none; and it must also be preceded by the eternity of the Creator – otherwise how could he create it from nothing in order that something might be made from it?

30

For all the differences between them, there is truth in each of these opinions. May this truth give birth to harmony, and may the Lord our God have pity on us so that we may *apply the law legitimately*,[1]

[1] 1 Tim. 1: 8.

that is, to the end prescribed in the commandment, which is charity undefiled. This same precept of charity obliges me, if I am asked which of these opinions was held by Moses your servant, to admit that I do not know. If I did not confess this to you, O Lord, these words that I write would not be my confessions. But I do know that all these opinions are consistent with the truth, except those child-like beliefs of which I have already said as much as I thought fit to say. Nevertheless, those who hold such beliefs are children of good promise: they are not deterred from accepting the message of your Book, which reveals its mysteries in language simple enough for them to grasp and tells so much in so few words. As for the rest of us, who all, as I admit, see true meanings in those words and explain them accordingly, let us love one another, and if our thirst is not for vanity but for the truth, let us likewise love you, our God, who are the Source from which it flows. Let us also honour Moses your servant, who delivered your Scriptures to us and was filled with your Spirit, by believing that when he wrote those words, by your inspiration his thoughts were directed to whichever meaning sheds the fullest light of truth and enables us to reap the greatest profit.

31

For this reason, although I hear people say 'Moses meant this' or 'Moses meant that', I think it more truly religious to say 'Why should he not have had both meanings in mind, if both are true? And if others see in the same words a third, or a fourth, or any number of true meanings, why should we not believe that Moses saw them all? There is only one God, who caused Moses to write the Holy Scriptures in the way best suited to the minds of great numbers of men who would all see truths in them, though not the same truths in each case.'

For my part I declare resolutely and with all my heart that if I were called upon to write a book which was to be vested with the highest authority, I should prefer to write it in such a way that a reader could find re-echoed in my words whatever truths he was able to apprehend. I would rather write in this way than impose a single true meaning so explicitly that it would exclude all others, even though they contained no falsehood that could give me offence. And if this is what I would choose for myself, I will not be so rash, my God, as to

suppose that so great a man as Moses deserved a lesser gift from you.
As he wrote those words, he was aware of all that they implied. He
was conscious of every truth that we can deduce from them and of
others besides that we cannot, or cannot yet, find in them but are
nevertheless there to be found.

32

Finally, O Lord, since you are God and not flesh and blood, even if
men have seen less in those words than there is to be seen, is it possible
that anything should be concealed from your gracious Spirit, who
shall *lead me on till I find sure ground under my feet*?[1] Could anything
that you were to reveal by those words to readers in later times have
been hidden from your Holy Spirit, even though the man through
whom they were spoken may have had in mind only one of many
true meanings? And if he had only one meaning in mind, let us admit
that it must transcend all others. O Lord, make clear to us this meaning or any other true meaning that it may please you to reveal, so that
whether you disclose to us the one which your servant Moses had in
mind or any other which can be extracted from the same words, we
shall feed from your hand and not be deluded by error.

O Lord my God, how much I have written on so few words!
What endurance I should need and how much time, if I were to
comment upon the whole of your Scriptures at such length! Let me,
then, continue to lay before you my thoughts upon the Scriptures,
but more briefly; and in so doing let me be content to give one
explanation only, the one which I see by your inspiration to be true
and certain and good, even though many may occur to me in places
where more than one is possible. Let me lay this confession before you
in the firm belief that if the explanation I give accords with the meaning which Moses had in mind, I shall have done what is right and
best. This is what I must try my utmost to do. But if I fail, let me at
least say what your Truth wills to reveal to me by the words of
Scripture, just as he revealed what he willed to Moses.

[1] Ps. 142: 10 (143: 10).

BOOK XIII

1

I CALL upon you, O God, my Mercy, who made me and did not forget me when I forgot you. I call you to come into my soul, for by inspiring it to long for you you prepare it to receive you. Now, as I call upon you, do not desert me, for you came to my aid even before I called upon you. In all sorts of ways, over and over again, when I was far from you, you coaxed me to listen to your voice, to turn my back on you no more, and to call upon you for aid when, all the time, you were calling to me yourself. You blotted out all my evil deeds, in order not to repay me with the punishment I deserved for the work of my hands, which had led me away from you; and even before I did them, you took into account all the good deeds by which I should deserve well of you, in order to recompense yourself for the work of your hands which made me. For before I was, you were: I was nothing, that you should give me being. Yet now I am; and this is because out of your goodness you provided for all that you have made me and all from which you have made me. You had no need of me, nor am I a creature good in such a way as to be helpful to you, my Lord and my God. It is not as though you could grow tired by working and I could serve you by preventing your fatigue, nor would your power be any the less if my service were lacking. I cannot serve you as a peasant tills the land, for your works bear fruit even if I fail to serve you with my husbandry. I can only serve you and worship you so that good may come to me from you, and but for you no good could come to me, for I should not even exist to receive it.

2

It is from the abundance of your goodness that your creation subsists, for you do not withhold existence from good which neither benefits you nor is of your own substance and therefore equal

311

to you, but exists simply because it can derive its being from you.

Could the heaven and the earth which you made in the Beginning make any claim on you by their own deserts? Had the spiritual and the corporeal natures, which you made in your Wisdom, deserved anything of you? All things were still in their primal, formless state, whether they were of the spiritual or the corporeal order. They were prone to fall away from you into confusion utterly alien from yourself, though the spiritual nature, even in its formless state, was better than if it had been a body with form added, and the corporeal, formless as it was, was better than if it had been altogether nothing. What claim had they to be sustained in existence by your Wisdom? And they would have remained in that formless state, sustained in it by your Word, unless by that same Word they had been recalled to your Unity and had been given form and all things had been made very good[1] by you, the one supreme Good. What had they deserved of you that they should exist even in a formless state? They would not have had even this measure of existence unless they had it from you.

What had corporeal matter deserved of you that it should exist even as a being invisible and without form, since it would not have existed even in that state except by reason of the fact that you created it? It did not exist before you created it, and therefore it could not earn any right to exist.

Had the spiritual creation, in its incipient state, deserved of you even the fluidity and darkness which was all that it then was? It was like the depths of the ocean and it would have remained in that state, estranged from your likeness, unless that same Word had turned it towards its Creator and made it light by casting his own brightness upon it, not in equal degree with yourself, but allowing it to take form in your likeness. For, just as, to a corporeal being, to be is not the same as to be beautiful, in the same way, to a created spirit, to live is not the same as to live wisely. If this were not so, the one could not be ugly and the other would be immutably wise. The good of the spirit is to *cling to you*[2] for ever, so that it may not, by turning away from you, lose the light which it gained by turning towards you and relapse into that existence which resembles the dark depths of the sea.

In our souls we too are a spiritual creation. *Once we were all dark-*

[1] See Gen. 1: 31. [2] Ps. 72: 28 (73: 28).

ness[1] in this life, because we were turned away from you, our Light, and in the remnants if our darkness we labour on until, in your only-begotten Son, we become your justice[2] and are made as the everlasting hills,[3] high in holiness. For, then, we were deep in sin, like a fathomless ocean:[3] we were not your justice[2] but ourselves under sentence of your judgements.[3]

3

At the beginning of creation you said *Let there be light; and the light began.*[4] I think these words are properly to be understood to refer to the spiritual creation, because it was already life of a certain kind, able to be given light by you. But just as, previously, it could make no claim on you, by its own deserts, to be the kind of life which could receive your light, so, now that it existed, it could not claim to receive this gift by its own merits. In its formless state it would not have been pleasing to you unless it became light. And it became light, not simply by existing, but by fixing its gaze upon you and clinging to you, the Light which shone upon it. In this way it owes to your grace, and to your grace alone, both the gift of its very existence and the gift of a life that is lived in happiness. For, by undergoing a change which bettered it, it was turned towards that which cannot change, either for better or for worse, that is, towards you. Only you can never change, because you alone are absolute simplicity, for whom to live is the same as to live in blessed happiness, since you are your own beatitude.

4

Since, then, your good is in yourself, what would have been lacking to that good, if the creature which you made had not even existed or had remained in its formless state? You created, not because you had need, but out of the abundance of your own goodness. You moulded your creation and gave it form, but not because you would find your own happiness increased by it. To you, who are perfect, its imperfection is displeasing, and you perfect it so that it may please you. But it is not as though you were imperfect and could only reach perfection yourself through the perfection of your creatures.

[1] Eph. 5: 8.   [2] See II Cor. 5: 21.   [3] See Ps. 35: 7 (36: 6).   [4] Gen. 1: 3.

Your good Spirit moved over the waters. But he was not upheld by them as though he rested upon them, for when he is said to rest upon a man, it is he who gives that man rest in himself. It was your incorruptible and immutable will, which is sufficient in itself and to itself, that moved over the life which you had created. To that life living and living in happiness are not one and the same, because it lives even in its state of fluidity and darkness. To gain happiness it must still be turned from that state towards God, its Creator. It must live ever closer to the Fountain of life. In his light it must see the light; in him it must be given perfection, splendour, and bliss.

5

When I read that your Spirit moved over the waters, I catch a faint glimpse of the Trinity which you are, my God. For it was you, the Father, who created heaven and earth in the Beginning of our Wisdom – which is your Wisdom, born of you, equal to you, and co-eternal with you – that is, in your Son. I have had much to say of the Heaven of Heavens, of the earth invisible and without form, and of the deep, showing how its darkness was in keeping with the spiritual creation, which, in its formlessness, had no cohesion or stability. Such it would have remained unless, by being turned to God, from whom it already drew such life as it had, it had received beauty as well as life by the reflection of his glory. In this way the Heaven of Heavens came into being, that is, the heaven of the heaven which was later created between the waters above and the waters below. When I spoke of these things, I took the word 'God', who made them, to mean the Father and the 'Beginning', in which he made them, to mean the Son. But, believing that my God is a Trinity, I searched for this truth in the sacred words of his Scripture and found it where it says that your Spirit moved over the waters. Here, then, is the Trinity, my God, Father, Son, and Holy Ghost, the Creator of all creation.

6

But, O Light from whom we learn the truth, tell me, I beseech you through Charity our mother, what reason was there why your Scripture did not mention your Spirit until after it had told of heaven and earth, invisible and without form, and the darkness over the deep? I lift my heart to you for fear that it may play me false. Banish its darkness and tell me, I beseech you, why this was.

Was it because it was necessary that we should first learn of your Spirit by being told that he 'moved over' something? This could not be said unless something had previously been mentioned over which your Spirit could be understood to move. It was neither over the Father nor over the Son that he moved, and he could not properly be said to 'move over' if he moved over nothing. For this reason, if it was appropriate that the Holy Spirit should be named as moving over something, it was first necessary to tell us what it was over which he moved. The question therefore arises why it was necessary that this should be the only way in which the Holy Spirit was to be revealed to us.

7

To understand this we must listen to your Apostle Paul, and those who can must try to grasp what he means when he writes that *the love of God has been poured.out in our hearts by the Holy Spirit, whom we have received*.[1] In other passages, where he tells us about spiritual gifts, we find him pointing out the way of charity, which is *better than any other*,[2] and *falling on his knees*[3] before you on our behalf, so that we may *be enabled to measure the love of Christ*,[3] which, he says, surpasses all else. This is the meaning of the words 'the Holy Spirit moved over the waters'. They mean that he surpassed all else, from the very beginning.

To whom am I to speak of this? How shall I find words to explain how the weight of concupiscence drags us down into the sheer depths and how the love of God raises us up through your Spirit, who moved over the waters? To whom am I to speak? How can I explain what this means? The depths to which we sink, and from which we are raised, are not places in space. We can well speak of them in this way by analogy, but how different they are in reality! They are our passions, our loves, the unclean leanings of our own spirits, which drag us downward in our love of the world and its cares; but in our love of that life where all care is banished, the holiness of your Spirit raises us aloft, so that we may lift up our hearts to you, to the place

---

[1] Rom. 5: 5.   [2] 1 Cor. 12: 31.   [3] Eph. 3: 14, 19.

where your Spirit moved over the waters; and when we have *ventured our lives on the flood*[1] of sin, which cannot bear them up, we may come to that peace which is high above all.

8

The angels fell; man's soul fell; and their fall shows us what a deep chasm of darkness would still have engulfed the whole spiritual creation if you had not said at the beginning '*Let there be light*'; *and the light began.*[2] The darkness would have closed over your heavenly city, unless every obedient mind in it had adhered to you and remained at rest in your Spirit, who moves over all the changing world, himself immutable. If you had not created light, even the Heaven of Heavens, left to itself, would have been a dark abyss. *But now, in the Lord, it is all daylight.*[3]

When spirits fall, their darkness is revealed, for they are stripped of the garment of your light. By the misery and restlessness which they then suffer you make clear to us how noble a being is your rational creation, for nothing less than yourself suffices to give it rest and happiness. This means that it cannot find them in itself. For you, our God, will *shine on the darkness about us.*[4] From you proceeds our garment of light, and *our dusk shall be noonday.*[5]

Give yourself to me, my God; restore yourself to me. I show you my love, but if it is too little, give me strength to love you more. I cannot measure its shortcomings and learn how much more I need to love you in order that my life may hasten to your embrace and never turn away from you until it is hidden in the sanctuary of your presence.[6] All that I know is this, that unless you are with me, and not only beside me but in my very self, for me there is nothing but evil, and whatever riches I have, unless they are my God, they are only poverty.

9

Did not the Father and the Son also move over the waters? If we think of this as movement in space, as a body moves, we cannot say that even the Holy Spirit moved in this sense. But if we think of it as

---

[1] Ps. 123: 5. [2] Gen. 1: 3. [3] Eph. 5: 8. [4] Ps. 17: 29 (18: 28).
[5] Is. 58: 10. [6] See Ps. 30: 21 (31: 20).

Divinity, changeless and supreme, moving over all that is mutable, then the Father, the Son, and the Holy Ghost moved over the waters. Why, then, does Genesis here speak only of your Holy Spirit? Why is it only in his case that he is mentioned as if he were in a particular place, which of course is not a place at all? We are also told of him alone that he is *your free gift*.[1] It is in your Gift that we find our rest. It is in him that we enjoy you. The place where we find rest is the rightful one for us. To it we are raised by love. To it your Spirit lifts us up, lowly creatures as we are, *from the gate of death*.[2] It is in goodness of will that we find our peace.

A body inclines by its own weight towards the place that is fitting for it. Weight does not always tend towards the lowest place, but the one which suits it best, for though a stone falls, flame rises. Each thing acts according to its weight, finding its right level. If oil is poured into water, it rises to the surface, but if water is poured on to oil, it sinks below the oil. This happens because each acts according to its weight, finding its right level. When things are displaced, they are always on the move until they come to rest where they are meant to be. In my case, love is the weight by which I act. To whatever place I go, I am drawn to it by love. By your Gift, the Holy Ghost, we are set aflame and borne aloft, and the fire within us carries us upward. *Our hearts are set on an upward journey*,[3] as we sing the *song of ascents*.[4] It is your fire, your good fire, that sets us aflame and carries us upward. For our journey leads us upward to the peace of the heavenly Jerusalem; it was a *welcome sound when I heard them saying, We will go into the Lord's house*.[5] There, if our will is good, you will find room for us, so that we shall wish for nothing else but to remain in your house for ever.

10

How happy must that creature be, the Heaven of Heavens, which has known no other state than this! And yet it would have been other than it is, if your Gift, who moves over all that changes, had not raised it up in the very moment of its creation, before any time had elapsed, when you summoned it to yourself with the words 'Let there be light' and it became light. In our case there is an interval of time,

[1] Acts 8: 20.   [2] Ps. 9: 15 (9: 13).   [3] Ps. 83: 6 (84: 5).
[4] Ps. 119-33 (120-34).   [5] Ps. 121: 1 (122: 1).

for we were darkness and one day we shall be made light. But of the Heaven of Heavens we are only told what it would have been if it had not been made light. Genesis speaks of it as though it was first in a state of fluidity and darkness, and the reason for this is to enable us to understand clearly what caused it to be otherwise, in other words, how it was made light itself by being turned towards the Light that never fails. Let all who are able understand this truth. They must ask you for the gift of understanding and not appeal to me as if it were I who *enlightened every soul born into the world.*[1]

11

Who can understand the omnipotent Trinity? We all speak of it, though we may not speak of it as it truly is, for rarely does a soul know what it is saying when it speaks of the Trinity. Men wrangle and dispute about it, but it is a vision that is given to none unless they are at peace.

There are three things, all found in man himself, which I should like men to consider. They are far different from the Trinity, but I suggest them as a subject for mental exercise by which we can test ourselves and realize how great this difference is. The three things are existence, knowledge, and will, for I can say that I am, I know, and I will. I am a being which knows and wills; I know both that I am and that I will; and I will both to be and to know. In these three – being, knowledge, and will – there is one inseparable life, one life, one mind, one essence; and therefore, although they are distinct from one another, the distinction does not separate them. This must be plain to anyone who has the ability to understand it. In fact he need not look beyond himself. Let him examine himself closely, take stock, and tell me what he finds.

But when he has found a common principle in these three and has told me what he finds, he must not think that he has discovered that which is above them all and is unchangeable, that which immutably is, immutably knows, and immutably wills. For none of us can easily conceive whether God is a Trinity because all these three – immutable being, immutable knowledge, and immutable will – are together in him; whether all three are together in each person of the Trinity, so

[1] John 1: 9.

that each is threefold; or whether both these suppositions are true and in some wonderful way, in which the simple and the multiple are one, though God is infinite he is yet an end to himself and in himself, so that the Trinity is in itself, and is known to itself, and suffices to itself, the supreme Being, one alone immutably, in the vastness of its unity. This is a mystery that none can explain, and which of us would presume to assert that he can?

12

Beyond this let my faith speak for me. Let it say to its Lord: Holy, holy, holy, Lord, my God, it is in your name that we are baptized, Father, Son, and Holy Ghost, and it is in your name that we baptize, Father, Son, and Holy Ghost, because amongst us too, in Christ his Son, God has made a heaven and earth, the members of his Church, spiritual and carnal. This earth was given form, the form of doctrine, but before it received this gift it was invisible and without form. We were veiled in the darkness of ignorance. For *you have chastened man to punish his sins*[1] and *the wisdom of your decrees is deep as the abyss.*[2] But because your Spirit moved over the waters, your mercy did not abandon us in our misery. You said: *Let there be light.*[3] *Repent; for the kingdom of heaven is at hand.*[4] You told us to repent. You commanded light to be made. In our sad mood we thought of you; in the land of Jordan we remembered you, O Lord.[5] We remembered you in Christ, in the mountain[5] high as yourself, who humbled himself for us. We realized how hateful our darkness was. We turned to you, and light was made. And so it is that *once we were all darkness,* but *now, in the Lord, we are all daylight.*[6]

13

But as yet we are light *with faith*[7] only, not *with a clear view.*[7] For *our salvation is founded upon the hope of something. Hope would not be hope at all if its object were in view.*[8] Deep still calls to deep, but now the call is made *amid the roar of the floods you send.*[9] Even Paul, who says *I had to approach you as men with natural, not with spiritual thoughts,*[10] tells us that *he does not claim to have the mastery already but forgetting what he has*

[1] Ps. 38: 12 (39: 11).   [2] Ps. 35: 7 (36: 6).   [3] Gen. 1: 3.   [4] Matt. 3: 2.
[5] See Ps. 41: 7 (42: 6).   [6] Eph. 5: 8.
[7] II Cor. 5: 7.   [8] Rom. 8: 24.   [9] Ps. 41: 8 (42: 7).   [10] I Cor. 3: 1.

left behind and intent on what lies before him,[1] *he goes sighing and heavy-hearted.*[2] *His soul thirsts for the living God, as a deer for running water,* and asks *Shall I never again make my pilgrimage into God's presence?*[3] He longs for the shelter of that home which heaven will give him.[4] He calls upon those who are sunk deeper than himself in the abyss and tells them *You must not fall in with the manners of this world; there must be an inward change, a remaking of your minds.*[5] *Do not be content to think childish thoughts; keep the innocence of children, with the thoughts of grown men.*[6] *Senseless Galatians, who is it that has cast a spell on you?*[7]

But now it is not Paul's voice that speaks these words. It is your voice that calls to us, for you have sent your Spirit from on high, through Christ, who ascended into heaven and opened the floodgates of his bounty, so that *the flowing waters might enrich your city.*[8]

It is for Christ that the friend of the Bridegroom longs.[9] Already he has laid *his spiritual harvest*[10] in Christ's keeping, but still, *he groans in his heart, waiting for that adoption which is the ransoming of our bodies from their slavery.*[10] He longs for Christ, for he is a member of the Church, the Bride of Christ. His love for Christ is great, for he is the Bridegroom's friend, and his great love is for Christ, not for himself; for it is not in his own voice but *amid the roar of the floods you send*[11] that he calls upon those who are sunk deeper than himself in the abyss, and this is because, in his great love of Christ, he fears for them. He knows that *the serpent beguiled Eve with his cunning*[12] and he fears that, in the same way, *their minds may be corrupted and lose that innocence which is theirs in Christ,*[12] our Bridegroom, your only-begotten Son. How bright a light of beauty will shine before our eyes *when we see Christ as he is*[13] and gone are those *tears, which are still my diet, morning and evening,* as daily I listen to the taunt: *Where is your God now?*[14]

14

I, too, ask 'Where are you, my God?' and the answer I find is this. For a while I draw a breath of your fragrance when my soul melts

---

[1] Philipp. 3: 13. [2] II Cor. 5: 4. [3] Ps. 41: 3, 4 (42: 2, 3). [4] II Cor. 5: 2.
[5] Rom. 12: 2. [6] I Cor. 14: 20. [7] Gal. 3: 1. [8] Ps. 45: 5 (46: 4).
[9] See John 3: 29. The friend of the Bridegroom is Paul.
[10] Rom. 8: 23. [11] Ps. 41: 8 (42: 7). [12] II Cor. 11: 3. [13] I John 3: 2.
[14] Ps. 41: 4 (42: 3).

within me and I cry out in joy, confessing your glory, like a man exultant at a feast.[1] But my soul is still sad because it falls back again and becomes an abyss, or rather, it realizes that it is still a deep abyss. My faith, the lantern which you have lighted to guide my feet in the dark, speaks to my soul and asks *Are you still downcast? Will you never be at peace? Wait for God's help.*[2] *No lamp like his word to guide your feet.*[3] Have hope, and persevere until the night passes, the night that is the mother of sinners. Persevere until the Lord's anger passes. *His displeasure was our birthright*[4] and *once we too were all darkness.*[5] We bear the remnants of our darkness in our bodies, which are *dead things in virtue of our guilt,*[6] until the day breaks and the shadows are lifted.[7] *Wait for God's help.*[2] *Early in the morning I shall present myself before him and watch.*[8] For ever I shall confess to him. *Early in the morning I shall present myself before him.*[8] *I shall see my champion and my God,*[9] *who will give life to our perishable bodies too, for the sake of his Spirit who dwells in us,*[10] because in his mercy he moved over the dark waters of our souls. This is the pledge which has been given to us in our pilgrimage on earth, so that we may now be light. Yet *our salvation is founded upon the hope of something.*[11] It is by hope that we are *born to the light, born to the day, not to the night and its darkness*[12] which we once were. In the uncertainty which still restricts our human knowledge you alone can distinguish between us and those who are still darkness, for it is you who *scrutinize our hearts*[13] and *call the light day and the darkness night.*[14] Who but you can tell us apart? And yet, *whatever powers we have, did they not come to us by gift*[15] from you? We are all vessels made from the same clay, *some for noble and others for ignoble use.*[16]

15

And who but you, our God, made for us the firmament, that is, our heavenly shield, the authority of your divine Scriptures? For we are told that *the sky shall be folded up like a scroll*[17] and that, now, it is spread out like a canopy of skins above us.[18] The authority of your divine

---

[1] See Ps. 41: 5 (42: 4).   [2] Ps. 41: 6 (42: 5).   [3] Ps. 118: 105 (119: 105).
[4] Eph. 2: 3.   [5] Eph. 5: 8.   [6] Rom. 8: 10.   [7] See Cant. 2: 17.
[8] Ps. 5: 4 (5: 3).   [9] Ps. 41: 6 (42: 5).   [10] Rom. 8: 11.   [11] Rom. 8: 24.
[12] 1 Thess. 5: 5.   [13] 1 Thess. 2: 4.   [14] Gen. 1: 5.   [15] 1 Cor. 4: 7.
[16] Rom. 9: 21.   [17] Apoc. (Rev.) 6: 14.   [18] See Ps. 103: 2 (104: 2).

Scriptures is all the more sublime because the mortal men through whom you gave them to us have now met the death which is man's lot. You know, O Lord, how you clothed men with skins when by sin they became mortal. In the same way you have spread out the heavens like a canopy of skins, and these heavens are your Book, your words in which no note of discord jars, set over us through the ministry of mortal men. Those men are dead, and by their death this solid shield, the authority of your words delivered to us through them, is raised on high to shelter all that lies beneath it. While they lived on earth, it was not raised so high nor spread so wide. You had not yet spread out the heavens like a canopy of skins; you had not yet heralded to all the corners of the world the fame that came with their death.

O Lord, *let us look up at those heavens of yours, the work of your hands.*[1] Clear away from our eyes the cloud with which you have covered your firmament. There in the heavens, in your Book, we read *your unchallengeable decrees,* which *make the simple learned.*[2] My God, let nothing mar the praises which rise to you from the *lips of children and of infants at the breast.*[3] For I know no other book so destructive of pride, so potent a weapon to crush your enemies and all who are on their guard against you, refusing to be reconciled with you and trying to justify the wrong that they do. O Lord, I know no written words so pure as these, none that have induced me so firmly to make my confession to you, none that have so eased for me the task of bowing my neck to your yoke or so gently persuaded me to worship you for your sake and not for mine. Let me understand them, good Father. Grant me this gift, for I submit myself to them and it was for those who submit themselves that you made this solid shield.

Above this firmament of your Scripture I believe that there are other waters, immortal and kept safe from earthly corruption. They are the peoples of your city, your angels, on high above the firmament. Let them glorify your name and sing your praises, for they have no need to look up to this firmament of ours or read its text to know your word. For ever they gaze upon your face and there, without the aid of syllables inscribed in time, they read what your eternal will decrees. They read your will: they choose it to be theirs: they cherish

---

[1] Ps. 8: 4. By 'hands' Augustine understands the writers of the Scriptures.
[2] Ps. 18: 8 (19: 7).   [3] Ps. 8: 3.

it. They read it without cease and what they read never passes away. For it is your own unchanging purpose that they read, choosing to make it their own and cherishing it for themselves. The book they read shall not be closed. For them the scroll shall not be furled. For you yourself are their book and you for ever are. You allotted them their place above this firmament of ours, this firmament which you established to protect the weakness of your peoples here below, so that they might look up to it and know this work of your mercy which proclaims you in time, you who are the Maker of time.

For, *O Lord, your mercy is high as heaven and your faithfulness reaches to the clouds.*[1] The clouds pass, but the heavens remain. Those who preach your word pass on from this life to the next, but your Scripture is outstretched over the peoples of this world to the end of time. *Though heaven and earth should pass away, your words will stand.*[2] The scroll shall be folded and the mortal things over which it was spread shall fade away, as grass withers with all its beauty; *but your Word stands for ever.*[3] Now we see your Word, not as he is, but dimly, through the clouds, *like a confused reflection in the mirror*[4] of the firmament, for though we are the beloved of your Son, *what we shall be hereafter has not been made known as yet.*[5] Wearing the tissue of our flesh he turned his eyes to us. He spoke words of love and inflamed our hearts, and now *we hasten after the fragrance of his perfumes.*[6] But, *when he comes we shall be like him; we shall see him, then, as he is.*[5] It will be ours to see him as he is, O Lord, but that time is not yet.

16

Just as you are perfect being, so you alone have perfect knowledge; for your being, your knowledge, and your will are immutable. Your being knows and wills unchangeably; your knowledge is and wills unchangeably; and your will is and knows unchangeably. In your eyes it does not seem right that a mutable being, illumined by your immutable light, should know that light as the light knows itself. And therefore *for you my soul thirsts like a land parched with drought,*[7] for just as it cannot give light to itself, neither can it quench its own thirst. *In you is the source of all life; your brightness breaks on our eyes like dawn.*[8]

[1] Ps. 35: 6 (36: 5).　[2] Matt. 24: 35.　[3] Is. 40: 8.　[4] 1 Cor. 13: 12.
[5] 1 John 3: 2.　[6] Cant. 1: 3.　[7] Ps. 142: 6 (143: 6).　[8] Ps. 35: 10 (36: 9).

17

Who gathered the bitter sea of humanity into one society? All men are united by one purpose, temporal happiness on earth, and all that they do is aimed at this goal, although in the endless variety of their struggles to attain it they pitch and toss like the waves of the sea. None but you, O Lord, gathered them together, you who ordained that the waters should *collect in one place to make dry land appear,*[1] land dry and parched with thirst for you. For *yours is the ocean; who but you created it? what other power fashioned the dry land?*[2] By the 'sea' is meant all the waters, gathered into one, not the bitter brine of man's ill will. For you keep even the wicked desires of men's souls within bounds. You set limits beyond which the waters may not flow, so that their waves break upon themselves, and in this way you form them into a sea, subject to the order of your rule, which is over all things.

But there are souls that thirst for you, souls which in your eyes are set apart from the great main of the sea for a different purpose. These you water with the sweet streams that flow from your hidden spring, so that the earth too may bear its fruit. You are the Lord its God and it bears its fruit at your command. When we love our neighbour by giving him help for his bodily needs, our souls bear fruit in works of mercy proper to their kind, for they have seed in them according to their species. We are weak, and therefore pity leads us to give help to the needy, aiding them as we should wish to be aided ourselves if we were in like distress. This we do, not only when it can be done with the ease with which grass runs to seed, but also by giving help and protection with all our strength. Then we are like a great tree bearing fruit, for we do good to a neighbour, if he is the victim of wrong, by rescuing him from the clutches of his assailant and providing him with the firm support of true justice, just as a tree affords the protection of its shade.

18

In this way, O Lord, you create happiness and give it to us to ease our lives. In this same way, I pray, *may faithfulness grow up out of the earth and redress look down from heaven.*[3] *Let there be luminaries in the vault of the sky.*[4] *Let us share our bread with the hungry, give the poor and the*

[1] Gen. 1: 9. [2] Ps. 94: 5 (95: 5). [3] Ps. 84: 12 (85: 11). [4] Gen. 1: 14.

vagrant a welcome to our houses, meet the naked, clothe him, and from our own flesh and blood turn not away.[1] These good deeds are the fruits that spring from the earth. Look on them and say, 'It is good that this is so.' Let our light shine out in the world and from this humble crop of good deeds let us pass on to that more sublime harvest, the joy of contemplation, so that we may come to possess the Word of Life and shine in the world like stars set in the firmament of your Scripture. For it is in the Scriptures that you speak to us, teaching us to distinguish between the things that only our minds can know and those that the flesh can perceive, between souls that are wedded to the spirit and those that cling to worldly things, just as we know the difference between day and night. It is no longer as it was before the firmament was made, when you alone, in the secrecy of your judgement, distinguished night from day. Now those who have the gift of your Spirit are set like stars in that same firmament, for your grace has been made manifest to all the world. You have given them a place apart, where they shine out over the world. They too are *measures of time to mark out the day and the year.*[2] For the old order has passed and all is made new.[3] *Our salvation is closer to us now than when we first learned to believe. The night is far on its course; day draws near.*[4] *Your bounty it is that crowns the year,*[5] for you *send labourers out for the harvesting,*[6] so that they may reap what others laboured to sow[7] and also sow new fields whose harvest shall be reaped at the end of time.

In this way you grant the prayers of those who plead for your gifts. You crown the years of the just with blessings, but *you are unchanging, your years can never fail,*[8] and in them you prepare a granary for the years that pass. In your eternal wisdom you bestow your heavenly blessings upon the earth in due season. To some through your Spirit you give the power *to speak with wisdom,*[9] and this power is like the greater light which you made,[10] for it shines like the sun at dawn for those who know the joy of the light of lucid truth. Others you teach *to speak with knowledge, with the same Spirit for their rule,*[9] and this gift is like the lesser light. *One, through the same Spirit, is given faith; another, through the same Spirit, powers of healing; one can perform miracles, one can prophesy, another can test the spirit of the prophets; one*

[1] Is. 58: 7. [2] Gen. 1: 14. [3] See II Cor. 5: 17. [4] Rom. 13: 11, 12.
[5] Ps. 64: 12 (65: 11). [6] Matt. 9: 38. [7] See John 4: 38.
[8] Ps. 101: 28 (102: 27). [9] I Cor. 12: 8–12. [10] See Gen. 1: 16.

can speak in different tongues;[1] and all these gifts are like stars. But *all this is the work of one and the same Spirit, who distributes his gifts as he will to each severally*[1] and causes these stars to appear, shining brightly for our benefit.

But knowledge, embracing all mysteries which change – for as the moon varies with the seasons, so do they – and the other gifts, which I have compared to stars, differ from that pure light of wisdom which gladdens the day as dusk differs from dawn. Yet they are needed for such as those whom Paul, your far-sighted servant, *had to approach as men with natural, not with spiritual thoughts,*[2] though *there is a wisdom which he makes known among those who are fully grounded.*[3] Man with his natural gifts alone is like a mere infant in Christ's nursery. He must be fed on milk until he is strong enough to eat solid food, and until his sight is fortified to face the sun, if he is not to be left in a night of utter darkness, he must be content with the light of the moon and the stars.

In your great wisdom you, who are our God, speak to us of these things in your Book, the firmament made by you. And you do this so that in the wonder of contemplation we may see all things clearly, though we are still subject to signs and seasons, days and years.

19

But before we can see clearly the Lord says to us: *Wash yourselves clean, spare me the sight of your busy wickedness, of your wrong-doing take farewell,*[4] so that the dry land may appear. *Learn how to do good, protecting the orphan, giving the widow redress,*[4] so that the earth may produce grass for pasture and trees that bear fruit. *Then come back, says the Lord, and make trial of me,*[4] so that there may be lights in the firmament of heaven to shine out over the world.

The rich man asks the good Master what he is to do to win eternal life. Let him listen to the good Master, of whom he thinks as a man and no more, although it is because the Master is God that he is good. Let him listen to the good Master who tells him that if he wants to win eternal life, he must keep the commandments; he must rid himself of the bitterness of spite and mischief; he must not kill, or commit adultery, or steal, or tell lies against another. If he does this, the dry land will appear and the harvest it bears will be the honour which a

[1] 1 Cor. 12: 8–12. [2] 1 Cor. 3: 1. [3] 1 Cor. 2: 6. [4] Is. 1: 16–18.

child owes to his parents and the love which a man owes to his neighbour. All this, says the rich man, I have done. How, then, do all these thorns grow, if the earth is fruitful? Go and root out the thick brambles of selfish greed. Sell what you have. Win a full harvest by giving to the poor, and the treasure you have shall be in heaven. Follow the Lord, if you have a mind to be perfect.[1] Be in the company of those among whom God speaks his wisdom, God who knows which gifts to give to the day and which to the night, so that you too may know and for you there may be lights in the firmament of heaven. But this cannot be, unless you set your heart on heaven; and *where your treasure-house is, there your heart is too*,[2] as you have heard from the good Master. But the rich man is dismayed. He is barren earth, and *the briers grow up and smother*[3] the Master's word.

But you, *who are a chosen race*,[4] weaklings in the ways of the world, you who have *forsaken all that was yours and followed*[5] the Lord, you must go where he leads and *abash the strong*.[6] Go where he leads, you *the welcome messengers*.[7] Be lights shining in the firmament, so that *the skies may proclaim his glory*.[8] Divide the light of those who are perfect, but are not yet as the angels, from the darkness of those who are infants in God's nursery but are not without hope. Shine over all the earth and let the day, radiant in the sunlight, utter the word of wisdom to the day: let the night, gleaming in the light of the moon, impart the word of knowledge to the night. The moon and the stars shine by night, but the night does not darken them, for it is they that give it light in so far as it is able to receive it. It is as though, when God said '*Let there be luminaries in the vault of the sky*',[9] all at once a sound came from heaven, like that of a strong wind blowing, and then appeared to them what seemed to be tongues of fire, which parted and came to rest on each of them,[10] and they became lights in the firmament of heaven, possessed of the word of life. Go, then, for you are fires burning with holiness and glory. Spread throughout the world. For *you are the light of the world*;[11] you are not *put away under a bushel measure*,[11] for Christ to whom you have been loyal has been raised to heaven and he has raised you too on high. Spread throughout the world; let all men know the light.

[1] See Matt. 19: 17–21.   [2] Matt. 6: 21.   [3] Matt. 13: 7.   [4] 1 Pet. 2: 9.
[5] Luke 18: 28.   [6] 1 Cor. 1: 27.   [7] Is. 52: 7.   [8] Ps. 18: 2 (19: 1).
[9] Gen. 1: 14.   [10] Acts 2: 2, 3.   [11] Matt. 5: 14, 15.

Let the sea too conceive and give birth to your works. *Let the waters produce moving things that have life in them.*[1] For *by separating worth from dross* you become *true spokesmen*[2] of God, who bade the waters produce, not the living soul which the earth was to bear, but *moving things that have life in them and winged things that fly above the earth.*[1]

By the work of your saints, O God, your sacraments have moved amidst the flood of the world's temptations to bathe its peoples in the waters of your baptism and imprint your name upon them. Sometimes, too, great miracles have been worked, and these are like the *huge sea-beasts.*[3] The words of your messengers have soared like winged things above the earth beneath the firmament of your Book, for this was the authority given to them and beneath it they were to take wing wherever their journey lay. There is *no word, no accent of theirs that does not make itself heard, till their utterance fills every land, till their message reaches the ends of the world.*[4] And this is because you, O Lord, have blessed their work and multiplied it.

Can it be that what I say is untrue or that I am confusing the corporeal works which are accomplished in the sea, beneath the firmament, with the clear understanding of these mysteries, which belongs to the firmament of heaven? Do I fail to make this distinction? There are truths that are fixed and defined and are not enlarged by further evolution. Such are the lights of wisdom and knowledge. But the workings of these same truths in the material order are numerous and varied. They multiply and grow, one giving birth to another, and this happens because you, O God, bless their reproduction. For you compensate for the ease with which our mortal senses tire by providing that a single truth may be illustrated and represented to our minds in many ways by bodily means. These are the moving creatures, the signs and sacraments, that the waters brought forth. But they gave them birth in your Word. The peoples of the world were estranged from your eternal truth, and it was to meet their own need that they produced these signs. But they did so in your gospel, for though the waters themselves cast up these creatures, it was at the bidding of your Word that they were ushered into the world to cure its bitterness and sickness.

[1] Gen. 1: 20. [2] Jer. 15: 19. [3] Gen. 1: 21. [4] Ps. 18: 4, 5 (19: 3, 4).

All things are beautiful, because you are their Maker; but you, who made them all, are more beautiful than they, far more so than words can tell. If Adam had not fallen away from you, the seed that flowed from him would not have been this bitter sea, the human race, forever chafing for knowledge in the profound depths of its ignorance, buffeted by the storms of its pride, and never at rest from its surge and swell. There would have been no need for your saints to work in the midst of this great sea, performing wonders of a palpable, material kind and administering your sacraments in word and deed. For I understand 'moving creatures' and 'winged things' to mean the work they do. But even though men are primed and initiated by these signs and submit to the outward rites of your sacraments, they would not progress beyond them unless their souls had spiritual life of another order and looked forward beyond the word of initiation to the fulfilment that follows after.

21

It is not the deep sea but the dry land segregated from the bitter waters that, at the bidding of your Word, produces, not moving creatures that have life and winged things, but the living soul. This is because the earth no longer needs baptism as it did when it was covered by the waters and as the heathen need it still; for ever since you ordained that we should enter heaven through baptism there has been no other way to come into the Kingdom. The living soul no longer looks for great miracles since it is not such as *must see signs and miracles happen or it will not believe.*[1] The dry land, which has faith, has now been set apart from the waters of the sea, which are bitter because they do not believe. The gift of *talking with a strange tongue is a sign given to unbelievers, not to the faithful,*[2] and therefore the earth, which you have *poised upon the floods,*[3] no longer has need of the winged things which the waters brought forth at your word. Send your messengers to carry your word to the earth, for though we speak of their work, it is you who work in them so that their work may bring life to souls.

It is the earth that produces the living soul, because it is to meet the needs of the earth that your messengers carry on this life-giving work in it, just as it was to meet the needs of the sea that the moving

[1] John 4: 48. [2] I Cor. 14: 22. [3] Ps. 135: 6 (136: 6).

creatures which have life and the winged things which fly beneath the firmament of heaven were produced to work among the waters. The earth now has no need of these creatures, although, *at the banquet which you have spread*[1] and which you have shown to those who believe, it eats the Fish[2] that was raised from the deep, for the Fish was raised up to be the food of the dry earth. The winged things, too, first issued from the sea, but their brood is multiplied upon the earth. For it was because of man's lack of faith that the evangelists first began to preach, but the faithful too are stimulated by their teaching and the blessings they receive through them are daily multiplied. But the living soul takes its first beginnings from the earth, for only those who already have faith can profit by detaching themselves from earthly loves[3] so that the soul which lived in death when it lived in luxury[4] may live in you instead. For those pleasures kill, but you, O Lord, are the joy that gives life to a pure heart.

Let your servants, therefore, do their work upon this earth. They need not work as they would among the waters that are faithless, to whom they preach your word and proclaim you by means of miracles and signs and mystic words. Only mysteries and portents, of which they stand in awe, can draw the attention of the faithless, for ignorance is the mother of amazement and when the sons of Adam forget you, when they hide away from your sight[5] and become a deep sea, this is the door that opens the way to faith. But upon the earth let your servants work as they would upon dry land that stands high above the swirling waters of the sea. Let them be a pattern to the faithful by living among them and rousing them to imitation. In this way the words 'Seek God, and your soul shall have life',[6] are not mere sounds that strike men's ears. They are a call to action, so that the earth may produce a living soul. *Do not fall in with the manners of this world*,[7] but keep yourselves intact from it. The soul lives when it avoids the things which it is death to seek. Keep yourselves intact from the savage monster pride, from the sloth and the sensual pleasures of lust, and from *quibbling knowledge that is knowledge only in name*,[8] so that the beasts may be tamed, the herds be broken in, and the

---

[1] Ps. 22: 5 (23: 5).

[2] i.e. Ἰχθύς, a fish, the acrostic formed from the Greek words Ἰησοῦς Χριστὸς Θεοῦ Υἱὸς Σωτήρ 'Jesus Christ, Son of God, Saviour'.

[3] i.e. as dry land is raised above the sea. [4] See 1 Tim. 5: 6. [5] See Gen. 3: 8.

[6] See Ps. 68: 33 (69: 32). [7] Rom. 12: 2. [8] 1 Tim. 6: 20.

serpents be made to lose their sting. For these creatures are symbols of the impulses of the soul. But the arrogance of pride, the pleasures of lust, and the poison of vain curiosity are the impulses of a soul that is dead, not one so dead that it lacks all impulse, but one that is dead because it has forsaken the fountain of life and is swept along by the fleeting things of this world, lending itself to their ways.

But your Word, O God, is the fountain of eternal life. It does not pass away. This is why you forbid us to forsake it, telling us not to lend ourselves to the ways of this world, so that in the fountain of life the earth may produce a living soul, a soul which at your bidding, made known through your evangelists, keeps itself intact by imitating those who follow the example of Christ your Son. This is the meaning of the words 'Each according to its kind',[1] for a man will not imitate any but his friend. Be as I am, says Paul, for I am no different from yourselves.[2]

If the living soul does this, the beasts within it will be good. They will be gentle and tame. For you have told us: *Do all you do in lowly fashion; you shall win the love*[3] of all men. The cattle too, will be good, for if they eat, they will gain nothing, and if they abstain, they will lose nothing.[4] And the serpents will be good. Their sting will not be poisonous and harmful. They will be cunning only to be on their guard. They will pry into the secrets of the temporal world only as far as need be, to enable us to catch a glimpse of eternity *as it is known through your creatures.*[5] For these creatures are the servants of reason when they are allowed to live and be good and are kept from the path that leads to death.

22

First, then, O Lord our God, our Creator, we must learn to keep our love of worldly things in check, for the evil life we lived amongst them was leading us to death. We must live good lives so that the living soul may come to life in us. We must obey in full the message which you gave to us through your apostle when you said: *Do not fall in with the manners of this world.*[6] Only when we have done all this will the next part of your message come true for us. For the next words you spoke were *There must be an inward change, a remaking of*

---

[1] See Gen. 1: 21.   [2] See Gal. 4: 12.   [3] Ecclus. 3: 19.   [4] See 1 Cor. 8: 8.
[5] Rom. 1: 20.   [6] Rom. 12: 2.

your minds.[1] When you said this, you did not add 'according to your kind' as though you meant us to imitate others who had already led the way or to live by the example of someone better than ourselves. For when you created men, you did not say 'Let man be made according to his kind' but *Let us make man wearing our own image and likeness.*[2] You spoke in this way because you meant us to see for ourselves what your will is.

This was why your servant Paul, who begot children in the Gospel,[3] said *There must be an inward change, a remaking of your minds, so that you can satisfy yourselves what is God's will, the good thing, the desirable thing, the perfect thing.*[1] He did not wish the children whom he had begotten to be for ever infants whom he would have to feed on milk[4] and cherish like a nursing mother.[5]

Again, you do not say 'Let man be made' but *Let us make man.*[2] You do not say 'Let us make him according to his kind' but *Wearing our own image and likeness.*[2] The reason for this is that when he has remade his mind and can see and understand your truth, he has no need of other men to teach him to imitate his kind. You show him and he sees for himself *what is your will, the good thing, the desirable thing, the perfect thing.*[1] Now that he is able to do so you teach him to see the Trinity of Unity or the Unity of Trinity. It is because you are the Trinity that you speak in the plural when you say *Let us make man;*[2] yet in the next verse, which says *God made man,*[6] the singular is used; and the phrase: *Wearing our own image and likeness,*[6] in which the plural is used, is followed by the words *in his own image,*[2] where you speak in the singular. This is how, when we learn to know God, we become new men in the image of our Creator.[7] We gain *spiritual gifts* and *can scrutinize everything* – everything, that is, which it is right for us to judge – *without being subject, ourselves, to any other man's scrutiny.*[8]

23

It is man's power to judge all things that is symbolized by his rule over *the fishes in the sea, and all that flies through the air, and the cattle, and the whole earth and all the creeping things that move on earth.*[2] He rules

---

[1] Rom. 12: 2.   [2] Gen. 1: 26.   [3] See 1 Cor. 4: 15.   [4] See 1 Cor. 3: 2.
[5] See 1 Thess. 2: 7.   [6] Gen. 1: 27.   [7] See Col. 3: 10.
[8] 1 Cor. 2: 15.

them by his intelligence, which enables him *to take in the thoughts of God's Spirit*.[1] If this were not so, man, despite the place of honour that is his, would have no understanding. He would be *matched with the brute beasts and no better than they*.[2]

You are our God and *we are your design, pledged to good actions*.[3] So it is that your Church, by reason of the grace which you have given it, has the power of spiritual judgement, which is given both to those who have spiritual charge of others and to those who are in their spiritual care. For you created man male and female,[4] but in your spiritual grace they are as one. Your grace no more discriminates between them according to their sex than it draws distinction between Jew and Greek or slave and freeman.[5] Those who have the gifts of your Spirit, then, have the power of spiritual judgement, whether they are in authority over others or are subject to authority. They do not pass judgement upon spiritual truths, which are like lights shining in the firmament, for it is not right for a man to call such sublime authority in question, or upon your Book, even if there are passages in it which may not be clear; for we submit our intelligence to it and do not doubt that even those parts of it which are hidden from our ken are right and true. Even though he has spiritual gifts and has *been refitted for closer knowledge, so that the image of God who created him is his pattern*,[6] a man must obey the law, not pass judgement on it.[7] Nor does such a man judge between those who are spiritual and those who are worldly-minded. You are the God of all and they are known in your sight, but to us they have not yet been revealed by the things that they do and we cannot *know them by their fruit*.[8] Nevertheless, you know them, O Lord. You separated them and called them in secret before the firmament was made. Furthermore no man, even though he has the gifts of the Spirit, can pass judgement on the peoples of this world who still struggle on without your grace. *How can he claim jurisdiction over those who are without*,[9] when he does not know which of them will come into the sweet domain of your grace and which remain for ever in the bitter exile where you are not loved?

Man, therefore, whom you created in your own image, has not received power over the lights of heaven, nor over heaven itself,

[1] I Cor. 2: 14.　[2] Ps. 48: 13 (42: 19).　[3] Eph. 2: 10.　[4] See Gen. 1: 27.
[5] See Gal. 3: 28.　[6] Col. 3: 10.　[7] See James 4: 11.　[8] Matt. 7: 20.
[9] I Cor. 5: 12.

which is hidden from him, nor over day and night, which you made before heaven was created, nor over the waters which were gathered together, that is, the sea. He has been given rule over *the fishes in the sea, and all that flies through the air, and the cattle, and the whole earth, and all the creeping things that move on earth.*[1] He judges them, approving what he finds to be right and blaming what he finds to be wrong. He exercises his power through the ceremonies of the sacraments by which those whom your mercy has sought out from the many waters of the sea are admitted to your grace; through the sacrament of the Eucharist, when the Fish which was raised from the depths is held out to us and is received as food by the faithful earth; and by means of signs and the words that he speaks, which are subject to the authority of your Book like birds on the wing beneath the firmament. He can explain and illustrate your teaching; he can argue and discuss; he can praise you and invoke your aid; and the words that break from his lips bear a meaning to which the people may respond and cry 'Amen'. If the words he utters have to be spoken aloud so that the ear can hear, this is because the world is a deep sea and the flesh is blind: men cannot see thoughts and therefore the truth must be dinned in their ears. It is in this sense that, although there is *abundance of flying things on earth,*[2] they have their origin in the sea.

The man who has spiritual gifts also judges the faithful, approving what he finds to be right and blaming what he finds to be wrong in their deeds and their morals. He judges them by their almsgiving, which is like the earth bearing fruit, and by their passions, which, in the living soul, are tamed into submission by the practice of chastity, by fasting, and by the soul's regard for its duty to God when it reflects upon the sensations of which it is conscious through the body. For he judges only those things which he also has power to correct.

24

You bless men, O Lord, and bid them to *increase and multiply and fill the earth.*[3] What are we to understand by this? What mystery do these words contain? You must have intended us to attach a special meaning to them, for you did not give the same blessing to the light which you called day, or to the firmament of heaven, or to the heavenly lights, or to the stars or the earth or the sea.

[1] Gen. 1: 26.   [2] Gen. 1: 22.   [3] Gen. 1: 28.

If you had not given this blessing to the fish and the whales, commanding them to *increase and multiply and fill the waters of the sea*,[1] and to the birds as well, that there should be *abundance of flying things on earth*,[1] I would say that you, our God, who created us in your own image, had willed that it should be a special gift bestowed on man. If I found that the same blessing had been given to trees and plants and the beasts of the earth, I might say that it properly belonged to all species which are reproduced from their own kind. But neither plants and trees nor beasts and reptiles were told to increase and multiply, yet all of these preserve and increase their species by reproduction in the same way as fish and birds and men.

What, then, am I to say, my Light, my Truth? Am I to say that there is no significance in this and that these words of yours have no special meaning? It is unthinkable, O Father of piety, that a servant of your Word should say such a thing. If I do not understand what you mean by these words, let my betters put them to better use – that is, those whose intelligence is greater than mine according to the degree of understanding which you give to each. But let my confession, too, find favour in your sight, O Lord, for I confess that I do not believe that you used these words except for a special purpose, and I shall not hesitate to give the explanation which occurs to me as I read them. My explanation is consistent with the truth and I see nothing to prevent me from interpreting the words of your Scriptures in this figurative sense.

I know that a truth which the mind understands in one way only can be materially expressed by many different means, and I also know that there are many different ways in which the mind can understand an idea that is outwardly expressed in one way. Take the single concept of the love of God and our neighbour. How many different symbols are used to give it outward expression! How many different languages have words for it and, in each of them, how many different forms of speech there are by which it can be conveyed! The creatures of the sea increase and multiply in this way. On the other hand, consider the verse 'In the Beginning God made heaven and earth'. Scripture presents this truth to us in one way only, and there is only one way in which the words can be shaped by the tongue. But it may be understood in several different ways without falsification or error, because various interpretations, all of which are true in themselves,

[1] Gen. 1: 22.

may be put upon it. The offspring of men increase and multiply in this way.

We may conclude, then, that if we think of nature not allegorically but literally, the command to increase and multiply applies to all species which are reproduced from seed. If, on the other hand, we take these words in a figurative sense – and this, I think is more likely to be the way in which we are meant to take them, since it cannot be a mere accident that Scripture mentions this blessing as a gift bestowed only on the offspring of marine creatures and of men – if, as I say, we take the words in a figurative sense, we do of course find the process of multiplication at work in many other creatures as well. We find it in spiritual and corporeal creatures, figuratively described as 'heaven and earth'; in good and wicked souls, described as 'light and darkness'; in the sacred writers who deliver God's law to us, described as *a vault by which God would separate the waters which were beneath it from the waters above it*;[1] in the community of peoples who are bitter because they have no faith, described as 'the sea'; in the zeal of pious souls, described as 'the dry land'; in works of mercy which help our neighbour in this life, described as *grasses that seeded and trees that bore fruit*;[2] in spiritual gifts disclosed to us for our profit, described as *luminaries in the vault of the sky*;[3] and in passions curbed by restraint, described as 'the living soul'. As I said, in all these we find the process of multiplication at work. In all of them we find fertility and increase. But it is only in the case of signs outwardly given that we find increase and multiplication in the sense that a single truth can be expressed by several different means; and it is only in the case of concepts apprehended by the mind that we find increase and multiplication in the sense that a single expression can be interpreted in several different ways.

I therefore understand the reproduction and multiplication of marine creatures to refer to physical signs and manifestations, of which we have need because the flesh which envelops us is like a deep sea; and I take the reproduction of human kind to refer to the thoughts which our minds conceive, because reason is fertile and productive. I am convinced that this is what was meant, O Lord, when you commanded man and the creatures of the sea to increase and multiply. I believe that by this blessing you granted us the faculty

[1] Gen. 1: 7.   [2] Gen. 1: 12.   [3] Gen. 1: 14.

and the power both to give expression in many different ways to things which we understand in one way only and to understand in many different ways what we find written obscurely in one way. This explains how the fish and the whales *fill the waters of the sea*,[1] because mankind, which is represented by the sea, is impressed only by signs of various kinds; and it explains how the offspring of men *fill the earth*,[2] because the dry land appears when men are eager to learn and reason prevails.

25

Let us now go on, O Lord my God, to explain the meaning which the next verse of your Scripture holds for me. I shall speak without fear, for if you inspire me to give the meaning which you have willed me to see in these words, what I say will be the truth. If any other than you were to inspire me, I do not believe that my words would be true, for you are the Truth, whereas every man is a liar,[3] and for this reason *he who utters falsehood is only uttering what is natural to him*,[4] what is his alone. If, then, I am to speak the truth, let me utter not what is mine, but what is yours.

We read that you have given us for our food *all the herbs that seed on earth, and all the trees, that carry in them the seeds of their own life.*[5] And it was not only to us that you gave this food. You gave it also to *all the beasts on the earth, all that flies in the air, all that creeps along the ground.*[6] But you did not give it to the fish and the great sea-beasts.

We have seen that these fruits of the earth represent, in allegory, the works of mercy which the fertile earth produces to help us in the needs of this life. An example of such fertile earth was the devout Onesiphorus, to whose household you granted mercy, because he had often given comfort and help to Paul and was not *ashamed of a prisoner's acquaintance.*[7] Others who did the same for Paul and bore fruit in this way were the brethren who came from Macedonia to bring him what he needed.[8] But how distressed he was by some trees, which did not yield the fruit which they owed him! *At my first trial,* he says, *no one stood by me. I was deserted by everybody. May it be forgiven them.*[9] For we owe these fruits to those who minister spiritual doctrine

[1] Gen. 1: 22.   [2] Gen. 1: 28.   [3] See Rom. 3: 4.   [4] John 8: 44.
[5] Gen. 1: 29.   [6] Gen. 1: 30.   [7] II Tim. 1: 16.   [8] See II Cor. 11: 9.
[9] II Tim. 4: 16.

to us through their understanding of divine mysteries. We owe these fruits to them as men and also in recognition of 'the living soul', for they hold themselves up before us as examples for our imitation in every matter where our passions need to be mastered. We owe them these fruits as 'winged things' as well, because the blessings which come to us through them are multiplied on earth; for *their message reaches the ends of the world.*[1]

26

This food nourishes only those who take joy in it, and there is no joy in it for those whose *own hungry bellies are the god they worship.*[2] Furthermore, in those who do these works of mercy the fruit is not the service or the gift that they bring, but the spirit in which they give it. Paul was the servant of God, not of *his own hungry belly,*[3] and it is plain to me what it was that delighted him when others gave him gifts. I see this clearly and it gives me great joy for his sake. He had received from the Philippians the gifts which they had sent to him by Epaphroditus, and I understand why it was that he was so content to receive them. It was the joy that he felt on receiving their gifts that gave him nourishment, for he spoke the truth when he wrote *It has been a great happiness to me in the Lord that your remembrance of me should have blossomed out afresh. You had never forgotten me.*[4] It was only that they had found it irksome to remember his needs, for they had in fact been enfeebled by a long period of listlessness. It was as though they had withered and no longer bore the fruit of good works. Paul's joy, therefore, was for them, because they had yielded another crop, not for himself simply because they had provided for his needs. So he goes on to say: *I am not thinking of my own want; I have learned by now to be content with my circumstances as they are. I know what it is to be brought low, and what it is to have abundant means; I have been apprenticed to everything, having my fill and going hungry, living in plenty and living in want; nothing is beyond my powers, thanks to the strength God gives me.*[4]

What, then, was the secret of this great man's joy? What was it that delighted and nourished this man who had been *refitted for closer knowledge, so that the image of God who created him was his pattern,*[5] this 'living soul' who had learnt so well how to master his passions, this

[1] Ps. 18: 5 (19: 4).   [2] Philipp. 3: 19.   [3] Rom. 16: 18.   [4] Philipp. 4: 10–13.
[5] Col. 3: 10.

'winged thing' who gave voice to hidden truths? To such as him this food is due. What, then, was the nourishment that it gave him?

His nourishment was joy. For if we read his next words, in which he wrote that *it was kindness in the Philippians to share his hardships*,[1] we see that his joy, his spiritual nourishment, was in the fact that they had done a good deed. It was not joy at the relief of need, such as caused David to cry out *In time of trouble, you have brought me relief*.[2] For Paul himself tells us that *he knew what it was to be brought low, and what it was to have abundant means, thanks to the strength God gave him*.[3] *You remember as well as I do*, he tells the Philippians, *that when I left Macedonia in those early days of gospel preaching, yours was the only church whose sympathy with me meant alms given and received. Not once, but twice, when I was at Thessalonica, you contributed to my needs*.[1] He now rejoices that they have returned to these good works. He is glad because they have borne fruit once more, like a field restored to fertility.

When he says: *You contributed to my needs*, he does not mean that he is glad that his needs have been met. We know this because he goes on to say: *It is not that I set store by your alms; I set store by the rich increase that stands to your credit*.[1] My God, you have taught me to distinguish between a gift and its fruit. The gift is the thing itself, a necessity of life given by one man to another. It may be money, food, drink, clothing, shelter, or help. But the fruit is the good will, the right will, of the giver. For our good Master did not only say: *He who gives a prophet welcome*, but: *He who gives a prophet the welcome due to a prophet*.[4] He did not only say: *He who gives a just man welcome*, but: *He who gives a just man the welcome due to a just man*. If they welcomed them in this way, the one would *receive the reward given to prophets* and the other *the reward given to just men*. Our Master did not only say: *If a man gives so much as a draught of cold water to one of the least of these here*, but also: *Because he is a disciple of mine*. And it was only after saying this that he added: *I promise you, he shall not miss his reward*.[4] The gift consists in welcoming the prophet or the just man or in offering the cup of cold water to the disciple, but the fruit consists in doing this just because the one for whom it is done is a prophet or a just man or a disciple. It was with fruit such as this that

---

[1] Philipp. 4: 14-17. [2] Ps. 4: 2 (4: 1). [3] Philipp. 4: 12.
[4] Matt. 10: 41, 42.

the widow fed Elias, for she knew that he was a man of God and this was why she fed him. But when the raven brought him food, he fed only upon the gift, and it was not the inner, spiritual, man that this food nourished, but only the outer man, his body, which might also have died for want of it.

27

I speak in your presence, O Lord, and therefore I shall say what is true.

If they are to be won over and admitted to the faith, ignorant men and unbelievers need sacraments of initiation and miraculous portents. These, I believe, are figuratively represented by the fish and the sea-beasts. Such men may furnish your children with bodily comforts or help them in some necessity of this life. But since they neither know why they are required to do this nor understand the true purpose for which it is done, they do not truly feed your children, nor do your children truly receive food from them. This is because they do not act with a right and holy will, and your children do not find true joy in their gifts, for they do not yet see the fruit in the givers. It is only where it finds this true joy that the soul is nourished. This is why the fish and the sea-beasts do not feed upon the food which the earth produces only after it has been separated and set apart from the bitter waters of the sea.

28

And you saw all that you had made, O God, and found it very good.[1] We, too, see all these things and know that they are very good. In the case of each of your works you first commanded them to be made, and when they had been made you looked at each in turn and saw that it was good. I have counted and found that Scripture tells us seven times that you saw that what you had made was good, and when you looked for the eighth time and saw the whole of your creation, we are told that you found it not only good but very good, for you saw all at once as one whole. Each separate work was good, but when they were all seen as one, they were not merely good: they were very good.

The same can be said of every material thing which has beauty.

[1] Gen. 1: 31.

For a thing which consists of several parts, each beautiful in itself, is far more beautiful than the individual parts which, properly combined and arranged, compose the whole, even though each part, taken separately, is itself a thing of beauty.

29

I read the Scripture carefully to discover whether it was seven or eight times that you saw that your works were good, when they pleased you. But, realizing that your vision is outside time, I wondered how I should understand the statement that there were a number of times when you looked at what you had made. I turned to you, O Lord, and said, 'Surely these words of Scripture must be true, for you can tell no lie and you, who are the Truth, spoke them. Why, then, do you tell me that your vision is not subject to time, and yet here your Scripture tells me that day by day you looked at what you had made and saw that it was good? I counted and found how often you had done so.'

You answered me, for you are my God and your voice can speak aloud in the voice of my spirit, piercing your servant's deafness. 'Man, O man', your voice rang out, 'What my Scripture says, I say. But the Scripture speaks in time, whereas time does not affect my Word, which stands for ever, equal with me in eternity. The things which you see by my Spirit, I see, just as I speak the words which you speak by my Spirit. But while you see those things in time, it is not in time that I see them. And while you speak those words in time, it is not in time that I speak them.'

30

I heard your answer, O Lord my God. It was a drop of your truth, sweet as honey on the tongue. It helped me to understand why it is that some men, who have no liking for the things which you have created, say that you made many of them only because you were compelled to do so by necessity – the structure of the heavens, for example, and the orderly arrangement of the stars. They say that you did not make them from material which you had yourself created, but that they had already been made elsewhere from other materials, and that you merely assembled them and pieced them together and welded them into one. They claim that you did this after you had defeated your enemies and from them constructed the walls of the world, so that once they were held down by these ramparts they would be powerless to rise against you again. Besides this they say that there are other things which you did not make or even piece together – all flesh, for instance, all the most minute of living creatures, and everything that is rooted in the earth. These things, they assert, were generated and formed in the lower regions of the world by a mind hostile to you, another nature alien from yourself, not created by you but opposed to you. These are madmen's claims, for those who make them do not see your works by your Spirit, nor do they recognize you in them.

31

But when men see your works by your Spirit, it is you who see through their eyes. When they see that your works are good, it is you who see that they are good. When it is because of you that things please us, it is you who please us in them; and when it is by your Spirit that they please us, they please you in us. *For who else can know a man's thoughts, except the man's own spirit that is within him? So no one else can know God's thoughts, but the Spirit of God. And what we have received is no spirit of worldly wisdom; it is the Spirit that comes from God, to make us understand God's gifts to us.*[1]

This raises a question in my mind. For since it is undoubtedly true that none but the Spirit of God can know God's thoughts, how can we understand the gifts that he has given us? The answer to this question is, of course, that even when we know things by God's Spirit, none but his Spirit truly knows them. For if it is right that those who speak by the Spirit of God should be told: *It is not you who speak*,[2] it is equally right to say to those who know by the Spirit of God 'It is not you who know', and it is no less right to say to those who see by the Spirit of God 'It is not you who see'. If, therefore, by the Spirit of God, men see that a thing is good, it is God, not they, who sees that it is good.

It is one thing, then, for a man to think that what is good is evil, which is the belief of the madmen whom I have just mentioned. It is another thing for a man to see that what is good is good. There are

[1] 1 Cor. 2: 11, 12.   [2] Matt. 10: 20.

many, in fact, who find your creation pleasing because it is good, but what they find pleasing in it is not you. They choose to look for happiness, not in you, but in what you have created. It is yet another thing for a man to see that something is good, when all the time it is God who sees through his eyes that the thing is good, that is, when God is loved in the thing that he has made. But God would not be loved if it were not for the Spirit which he has given us, for *the love of God has been poured out in our hearts by the Holy Spirit, whom we have received*,[1] and it is by the Holy Spirit that we see that whatever exists is good, no matter what may be the degree of its existence. For the Holy Spirit comes from God, who does not exist in degree but is absolute being.

32

Thanks be to you, O Lord, for all that we see!

We see heaven and earth, which may be either the upper and the lower parts of the material world or the spiritual and material creations. For their adornment, whether they constitute the whole of the material world or the entire creation, spiritual and material alike, we see the light that was created and separated from the darkness. We see the firmament of heaven, by which we may understand either the uppermost part of the material world, which divides the spiritual waters above from the material waters below, or simply the space of air through which the birds take flight. For this space also is called the heavens, and it divides the waters which rise in the form of vapour and descend again on calm nights, distilled in the form of dew, from those which are heavier and flow upon the earth. We see the waters gathered together, so that the surface of the sea is like a great plain, and the dry land, first rising bare from the waters and then with form added so that it might become visible and order might be given to it and it should become the mother of plants and trees. We see the lights shining from above, the sun furnishing its light to the day and the moon and the stars giving comfort to the night, and all of them marking the passage of time. All about us we see how the sea and the rivers and the lakes teem with fish and the great creatures that live in the water, and with birds as well, for it is the evaporation of moisture which makes the air dense enough to support them in flight. We see

[1] Rom. 5: 5.

the face of the earth graced by the animals that live upon it. And finally we see man, made in your image and likeness, ruling over all the irrational animals for the very reason that he was made in your image and resembles you, that is, because he has the power of reason and understanding. And just as in man's soul there are two forces, one which is dominant because it deliberates and one which obeys because it is subject to such guidance, in the same way, in the physical sense, woman has been made for man. In her mind and her rational intelligence she has a nature the equal of man's, but in sex she is physically subject to him in the same way as our natural impulses need to be subjected to the reasoning power of the mind, in order that the actions to which they lead may be inspired by the principles of good conduct.

All this we see. Taken singly, each thing is good; but collectively they are very good.

33

Your works proclaim your glory, and because of this we love you; and it is in our love for you that they proclaim your glory.

They have their beginning and their end in time, their rising and their setting, their progress and decline, their beauty and defect. So it is that they pass in due course through their morning and their evening, in part hidden from our sight, in part plainly to be seen. For you created them from nothing, not from your own substance or from some matter not created by yourself or already in existence, but from matter which you created at one and the same time as the things that you made from it, since there was no interval of time before you gave form to this formless matter. For the matter of heaven and earth is one thing, their form another. You created the matter from absolutely nothing and the form of the world from this formless matter. But you created both in one act, so that the form followed upon the matter with no interval of delay.

34

I have also considered what spiritual truths you intended to be expressed by the order in which the world was created and the order in which the creation is described. I have seen that while each single one of your works is good, collectively they are very good, and that heaven and earth, which represent the Head and the body of the Church, were predestined in your Word, that is, in your only-begotten Son, before all time began, when there was no morning and no evening.

But then you began to enact in time all that you had predestined in eternity, for it was your purpose to reveal what had been hidden and to introduce order where disorder reigned. For we were overwhelmed by our sins; we had fallen away from you into the depths of darkness, and your good Spirit was moving over us, ready to bring help when the time was due. You made just men of sinners and set them apart from the wicked; you established the authority of your Book between those above, who would be obedient to you, and those beneath, who would be made subject to them; and you gathered all the faithless together into one body, so that the earnest devotion of the faithful might be clearly seen and they might bear you fruit in works of mercy, by distributing their worldly wealth to the poor in order to acquire heavenly riches for themselves. Next you set special lights to burn in the firmament. These were your saints, who are possessed of the word that gives life. In them there shines the sublime authority that is conferred upon them by their spiritual gifts. After this, from corporeal matter, you produced sacraments, miracles that men could see, and voices to carry your message according to the firmament of your Book. These were meant for the initiation of unbelievers and also for the blessing of the faithful. Next you formed the living soul of the faithful, the soul that lives because it has learnt to control its passions by unremitting continence. Then you took man's mind, which is subject to none but you and needs to imitate no human authority, and renewed it in your own image and likeness. You made rational action subject to the rule of the intellect, as woman is subject to man. And since your ministers are needed for the perfection of the faithful in this life, you willed that the faithful, by providing them with what they need for temporal use, should do good works that would bear fruit in the future life.

All these works of yours we see. We see that together they are very good, because it is you who see them in us and it was you who gave us the Spirit by which we see them and love you in them.

35

O Lord God, grant us peace, for all that we have is your gift. Grant us the peace of repose, the peace of the Sabbath, the peace which has no evening. For this worldly order in all its beauty will pass away. All these things that are very good will come to an end when the limit of their existence is reached. They have been allotted their morning and their evening.

36

But the seventh day is without evening and the sun shall not set upon it, for you have sanctified it and willed that it shall last for ever. Although your eternal repose was unbroken by the act of creation, nevertheless, after all your works were done and you had seen that they were very good, you rested on the seventh day. And in your Book we read this as a presage that when our work in this life is done, we too shall rest in you in the Sabbath of eternal life, though our works are very good only because you have given us the grace to perform them.

37

In that eternal Sabbath you will rest in us, just as now you work in us. The rest that we shall enjoy will be yours, just as the work that we now do is your work done through us. But you, O Lord, are eternally at work and eternally at rest. It is not in time that you see or in time that you move or in time that you rest: yet you make what we see in time; you make time itself and the repose which comes when time ceases.

38

We see the things which you have made, because they exist. But they only exist because you see them. Outside ourselves we see that they exist, and in our inner selves we see that they are good. But when you saw that it was right that they should be made, in the same act you saw them made.

It was only after a lapse of time that we were impelled to do good, that is, after our hearts had received the inspiration of the Holy Spirit. Before then our impulse was to do wrong, because we had deserted you. But you, who are the one God, the good God, have never ceased to do good. By the gift of your grace some of the works that we do are good, but they are not everlasting. After them we hope that we shall find rest, when you admit us to the great holiness of your presence. But you are Goodness itself and need no good besides yourself. You are for ever at rest, because you are your own repose.

What man can teach another to understand this truth? What angel can teach it to an angel? What angel can teach it to a man? We must ask it of you, seek it in you; we must knock at your door. Only then shall we receive what we ask and find what we seek; only then will the door be opened to us.

PENGUIN CLASSICS

www.penguinclassics.com

- Details about every Penguin Classic

- Advanced information about forthcoming titles

- Hundreds of author biographies

- FREE resources including critical essays on the books and their historical background, reader's and teacher's guides.

- Links to other web resources for the Classics

- Discussion area

- Online review copy ordering for academics

- Competitions with prizes, and challenging Classics trivia quizzes

PENGUIN CLASSICS ONLINE